A Study of India's Textile Exports and Environmental Regulations

K.S. Kavi Kumar
Editor

A Study of India's Textile Exports and Environmental Regulations

Springer

Editor
K.S. Kavi Kumar
Madras School of Economics
Chennai
India

ISBN 978-981-10-6294-0 ISBN 978-981-10-6295-7 (eBook)
https://doi.org/10.1007/978-981-10-6295-7

Library of Congress Control Number: 2017949157

Printed on acid-free paper

This Springer imprint is published by Springer Nature
The registered company is Springer Nature Singapore Pte Ltd.
The registered company address is: 152 Beach Road, #21-01/04 Gateway East, Singapore 189721, Singapore

Preface

This study was undertaken by the Centre of Excellence in Environmental Economics at Madras School of Economics with financial support from the Ministry of Environment and Forests, Government of India.

The study was initiated and largely coordinated by Dr. K.S. Kavi Kumar. The project team included Dr. Zareena Begum and Dr. Sukanya Das. In the initial stages of the project, Dr. S. Dinda, Dr. E. Kannan, and Dr. S. Subash have provided crucial inputs. Dr. G. Badri Narayanan of Purdue University, USA, served as consultant towards the end of the project term. Research assistance was provided by Ms. Prachi Pandey, Mr. Kalaiselvan, Mr. S. Raju, and Dr. A. Balasubramanian at different stages of the work. Ms. Saraswathi and Ms. Geetha provided secretarial help.

The book was written jointly by Dr. K.S. Kavi Kumar, Dr. Zareena Begum, Dr. Sukanya Das, Dr. Elumalai Kannan, and Dr. G. Badri Narayanan. While the analysis presented in the core chapters pertains to the year 2012, the data and discussion was subsequently updated to the year 2014–2015.

The research team would like to gratefully acknowledge the support and inputs received from Mr. R.S. Ahlawat, Senior Economic Adviser, Ms. Gur Pyari, Addl. Economic Adviser, and Mr. Anushman Mohanty, Deputy Economic Adviser during the course of the project. The research team would like to place on record their sincere thanks to the Chairman, Director, and staff of MSE for their help during the project.

The research team would like to gratefully acknowledge the comments made by the participants of various workshops where the project findings were shared and in particular would like to thank Prof. Paul P. Appasamy, Prof. V.R. Muraleedharan, Dr. M. Madhusoothanan, Dr. Kurian Joseph, Mr. S. Karthikeyan, Dr. L. Venkatachalam, Dr. Prakash Nelliyat, and Shri Anushman Mohanty. The research team gratefully acknowledges the useful comments given by Prof. Ramprasad Sengupta and the officials of Departments of Industrial Policy and Promotion and Department of Commerce of the MoEF&CC.

Chennai, India K.S. Kavi Kumar
June 2017

Contents

Editor and Contributors

About the Editor

K.S. Kavi Kumar is Professor, Madras School of Economics (MSE), Chennai, India. He coordinated activities of the Centre of Excellence in environmental economics, supported by the Ministry of Environment and Forests, Government of India, at the MSE during 2007–2015. He is also a Member, Expert Committee of Climate Change, Government of India; and a Member, State Environment Appraisal Committee, Tamil Nadu. Prof. Kumar is an M.Tech. from Indian Institute of Technology (IIT) Kharagpur and obtained his Ph.D. in development economics from Indira Gandhi Institute of Developmental Research (IGIDR), Mumbai, India. His areas of research interest are economics of environment, economics of climate change, and development economics.

Contributors

Zareena Begum Madras School of Economics, Chennai, India

Sukanya Das Department of Policy Studies, TERI University, New Delhi, India

Elumalai Kannan Centre for the Study of Regional Development, School of Social Sciences, Jawaharlal Nehru University, New Delhi, India

K.S. Kavi Kumar Madras School of Economics, Chennai, India

G. Badri Narayanan School of Environmental and Forestry Sciences, University of Washington, Seattle, WA, USA

List of Figures

List of Tables

Chapter 1
Introduction

K.S. Kavi Kumar

The Indian textile industry covers a wide range of activities—from production of raw materials like cotton, jute, silk and wool to providing high value-added products such as fabrics, furnishings and garments. It also uses a wide range of raw fibres including natural fibres like cotton, jute, silk and wool to man-made fibres like polyester, viscose, acrylic and multiple blends of such fibres. As a sector, it provides direct employment to over 35 million people and contributes to 4% of the country's gross domestic product. The Indian textile industry is the second largest after agriculture in providing employment. Indian textile industry has the potential to increase its share in the world trade from current level of 5 to 20% by 2024–2025 with a 20% cumulative annual growth rate in exports and could reach US$ 300 billion exports in textile and apparel by 2024–2025. The Ministry of Commerce, Government of India, has identified agricultural commodities, processed food, leather and leather products, and textile garments and clothing as major commodities for export promotion based on India's comparative advantage in these commodities. Yet, at the same time, there are concerns regarding the pollution (especially water pollution) that the textile processing causes and the potential trade implications it could have.

Driven by growing consumer awareness, a number of voluntary initiatives such as Worldwide Responsible Apparel Production (WRAP) and Apparel Industry Initiative (AIP) are attempting to instil social and environmental standards in textile and clothing sectors. It is in this 'buyer-driven global commodity chain' that India has to position itself. Like every product, clothes and other textiles products affect the environment to varying degrees throughout their life cycles, through use of chemicals, solvents and huge quantities of water. Studies have shown that some of the chemicals used in textile industry are carcinogenic and others may trigger allergic reactions. Some flame retardants that are used in certain textiles contain

K.S. Kavi Kumar (✉)
Madras School of Economics, Chennai, India
e-mail: kavikumar@gmail.com

K.S.K. Kumar (ed.), *A Study of India's Textile Exports and Environmental Regulations*, https://doi.org/10.1007/978-981-10-6295-7_1

organic bromine compounds that are persistent (i.e. break down very slowly in the environment). Textile industry is known to use restricted chemicals such as azo dyes and formaldehyde. Natural resources such as water constitute an important input for the textile industry. Thus, manufacturing of all variants of textiles has an impact on the environment. Heavy use of natural resources such as water leads to resource depletion and the release of effluents and emissions contributes to the degradation of the environment. To remain competitive, Indian textile industry should reduce operating costs and enhance environmental compliance. Government should not only strive to integrate environmental goals into the national textile policy but also in the plans and programmes. Textile sector cannot have independent growth strategies that are bereft of environmental concerns arising at various points of value chain because environmental costs are proving to be a drag on its own long-term growth and development.

Against this backdrop, this chapter attempts to discuss the following:

- Structure and performance of Indian textile sector
- An overview of the environmental concerns with regard to textile sector
- An overview of the domestic and global policy environment with regard to textile sector.

1.1 Structure and Performance of Indian Textile Sector

The textile industry in India is dominated by small-scale players across the entire value chain. Figure 1.1 provides an overview of the value chain of the industry from raw material to the garment manufacture. In terms of the raw materials, India has abundant supply—of both cotton acreage and polyester yarn. The textile industry in India accounts for about 20% of the world's spindle capacity and has the second largest spindleage in the world. The country also boasts the highest loomage in the world and has about 61.6% of global weaving capacity. The weaving and knitting segment, however, is highly fragmented with several small-scale operators. It is one of the most labour-intensive operations in the entire value chain. The processing units are also largely decentralised with several units employing hand processing. The garment manufacturing, though fares well on technology front, is again dominated by small-scale fabricators. Based on calculations from different data sources, Table 1.1 shows that unorganised and SSI textile sector employs 90% and contributes 41% to gross value of output.

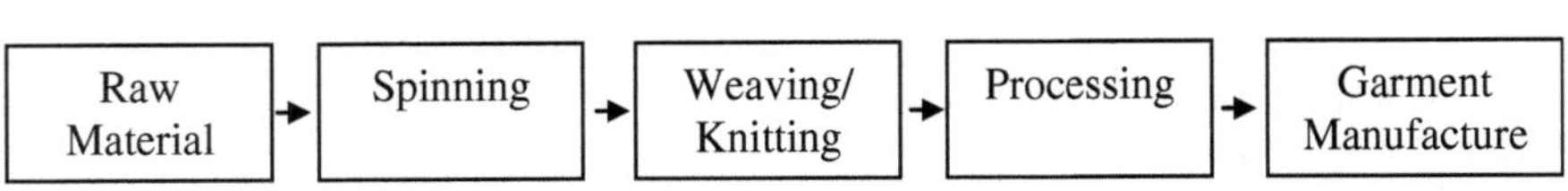

Fig. 1.1 Textile industry—value chain

Table 1.1 Unorganised and organised sectors in Indian textiles and apparel: 2005–2006

Parameter	Organised sector	Unorganised sector	Registered SSI	Unregistered SSI
Employment (millions)	1.9 (11%)	12.4 (70%)	0.5 (3%)	3.0 (17%)
Value added (Rs. billion)	297.8 (58%)	215.7 (42%)	NA	NA
Output (Rs. billion)	1563.9 (59%)	430.5 (16%)	96.4 (4%)	578.4 (22%)

Source Own calculations from ASI (http://mospi.nic.in/asi_table2_2005_06.htm), Ministry of Micro, Small and Medium Enterprises (Third All India Census, 2001–2002 http://www.dcmsme.gov.in/publications/books/fcensus.htm) and NSSO

Table 1.2 provides an overview of the performance of Indian textile industry over the past one-and-half decades. There has been impressive growth both in infrastructure and the output from the industry. Both raw cotton and man-made fibre processing have almost doubled during the decade. With the exception of composite mills, all the installed capacities have increased from 26 to 36% over the period. In terms of production, the spun yarn increased by about 46% while fabrics registered a 66% increase. In both spun yarn and fabrics, the non-cotton segment registered significantly higher increase in production compared to cotton and blended production.

Indian textile industry enjoys advantages on account of ample availability of a variety of raw materials at relatively low costs, availability of skilled labour and low labour costs, significantly large and growing domestic demand and continued support from the government. The government support comes in the form of encouraging institutes, such as National Institute of Fashion Technology and Apparel Training and Design Centre, and also several engineering colleges that offer courses in textile engineering. While the Technology Upgradation Fund Scheme (TUFS) provides support for adopting state-of-the-art technology, the national textile corporation continues to provide help for the revival of the sick mills. Estimates show that in case of open-ended yarn and ring yarn, cost of production in India is lower than its competitors such as South Korea, China and Brazil. However, in case of textured yarn and the fabrics, the cost competitiveness of India is not very obvious.

1.2 Environmental Issues: Indian Textile Sector

The textile industry is not a single entity but encompasses a range of industrial units which use a variety of natural and synthetic fibres to produce various fabrics. As per the data available at the Textile Commissioner's office, while the organised mills produce almost entire yarn in the country, the small-scale industries contribute about 85% of the total cloth production. Textile units contribute both water and air pollution, and some of the significant pollution problems in Indian context include:

Table 1.2 Structure and production of Indian textile industry—1998–1999 to 2012–2013

Item	1998–1999	1999–2000	2000–2001	2000–2002	2002–2003	2003–2004	2004–2005
Number of mills	2652	2771	2842	2906	3021	2922	2950
Spinning units	2371	2486	2561	2625	2745	2699	2727
Composite mills	281	285	281	281	276	223	223
Installed spindles (million)	35.59	37.08	37.91	38.33	39.03	37.03	37.47
Spun yarn (million kg)	2808	3049	3160	3101	3081	3052	3223
Fabrics (million sq.m.)	35,543	38,874	40,233	42,034	41,973	42,383	45,378
Raw cotton (lakh bales)	165	156	140	158	136	179	243
Man-made fibre filament (1000 tons)	850	889	919.72	962.17	1100.3	1118.0	1108.9

Item	2005–2006	2006–2007	2007–2008	2008–2009	2009–2010	2010–2011	2011–2012	2012–2013[a]
Number of mills	2953	3044	2995	3084	3090	3264	3270	3275
Spinning units	2743	2844	2816	2900	2606	3090	3097	3102
Composite mills	210	200	176	177	177	183	196	199
Installed spindles (million)	37.51	39.5	39.07	41.3	41.27	47.58	48.26	48.66
Spun yarn (million kg)	3458	3813	4003	3912	4193	4713	4359	1949
Fabrics (million sq.m.)	49,577	53,389	56,025	54,966	60,333	62,559	61,364	26,554
Raw cotton (lakh bales)	241	280	307	290	305	339	347	334
Man-made fibre filament (1000 tons)	1179.3	1370.5	1509.3	1418	1523	1550	1462	605

Source Office of the Textile Commissioner, Ministry of Textiles, GoI; http://texmin.nic.in
[a]2012–2013 (Apr–Aug) (Prov)

- Liquid wastes from textile mills arise mainly from wet-finishing treatments, where large volume of water and chemicals are used in textile baths. If the bath is discharged directly to the surroundings, it becomes a major source of pollutants. Most dyes and chemicals used are synthetic and are not readily biodegradable. For instance, effluents from textile mills around Erode district in Tamil Nadu contribute significantly towards contamination of Bhavani River. Similar pollution problems are also reported in other places such as Pali–Jodhpur–Balotra in Rajasthan and Jaitpur in Gujarat.
- High BOD and COD and suspended solids in the effluents from textile units adversely influence water bodies. For instance, the effluents from textile units in Punjab and Tamil Nadu are reported to have resulted in significant agricultural and biodiversity loss, besides affecting human welfare.
- Ground water pollution is also reported in Tamil Nadu, Punjab and Uttar Pradesh caused among other things by the effluents from the textile units.

Conventional regulatory instruments for pollution control from small units may have limited success as such units face significant capital and other resource constraints to comply with the norms. As in the case of leather industry, common effluent treatment plants provide scope for cost-effective pollution control. However, the interaction of investment in pollution control with the trade competitiveness needs careful analysis. In Tiruppur alone around 20 common effluent treatment plants,[1] involving a financial outlay of Rs. 750 crores, are nearing completion. However, with slump in textile exports, the dyers are finding it difficult to repay even the interest rates of this massive pollution control investment. Hence, it is imperative that while on the one hand the environmental issues associated with the dyeing and bleaching units of textile industry are addressed immediately and systematically, favourable policy measures should also be in place to retain India's export competitiveness in this crucial sector.

Another environment-trade linkage in textile sector is with regard to the indigenous availability of raw material and its quality. For instance, in India, about 30% of large exporters import over 60% of their grey cloth requirements, as the grey cloth produced in the country is of poor quality. Poor quality grey cloth demands greater use of chemicals while processing and thus increases the pollution load. Focus on improvement of quality of raw material could not only minimise pollution but also reduce Indian textile industry's dependence on external sources.

While textile sector may not be one of the largest emitters of greenhouse gases in the country, it provides scope for cheaper emission reductions. Such options could have twin benefits of reducing greenhouse gas emissions and also improving the local environmental quality. Since investment opportunities from developed countries to developing countries in cleaner technologies exist, careful attention could be paid to tap such potential in Indian context.

[1]The common effluent treatment plants (CETPs) mentioned here and elsewhere in the report refer to treatment plants with recovery and reuse of water having potential in zero liquid discharge.

1.2.1 Textile Industry and Resource Utilisation

Another environmental issue of concern with regard to textile industry is the resource exploitation. In case of wet processes—bleaching and dyeing—there is significant utilisation of water. For instance, in Tiruppur—one of the major textile export hubs in India—the number of wet processing units increased rapidly. In 1981, there were only 26 bleaching and dyeing units in Tiruppur. But the number had increased to 324 in 1991 and 702 in 2001. The majority of the units are small in size and function as job workers for the hosiery industry. Out of the 702 wet processing units, 125 are located in Tiruppur municipality and the remaining 577 are spread out in the peripheral villages. Most of the units are located on both sides of the Noyyal River which is convenient to discharge the effluent. Low investment, bright future of colouring in clothing industry, good profit margins and prior experience in textile processing are some of the factors which encouraged the entrepreneurs to select textile processing from other segments of the hosiery industry. The quantity of cloth processed by these units is around 15,000 tonnes per month. For processing, various chemicals such as soda ash, dyes and bleaching agents are used, and their consumption rate has increased over time in proportion to the quantum of cloth processed. Much of the chemicals and acids used for processing are not retained in the cloth but discharged as waste material, which ultimately leads to high pollution load in the effluents.

Since water is an unavoidable input for textile processing, corresponding to the growth in the volume of cloth processed, the quantity of water consumed by the processing units has also increased over time from 4.4 million litres per day (mld) in 1980 to 40.8 mld in 1990 and to 86 mld in 2000. Earlier, industries extracted their required water from the Noyyal River or their own wells. But from the early 1990s onwards due to water quality degradation in Tiruppur, substantial quantity of fresh water (91% of the total demand) is transported from peripheral villages through tankers. The continuous functioning of the 'water market' has adversely affected the ground water availability of the villages, and in many places, ground water tables have declined. Recently, industries are also getting water through the Tiruppur Area Development Project's water supply scheme to transport water from the Cauvery River.

The water requirement per kilogram of cloth processed has shown a declining trend from 226.5 litres per kg in 1980 to 144.8 litres per kg in 2000. Low availability of good quality water in the Tiruppur area, increase in the cost of water transportation and the technology improvements in processing are some of the reasons attributed to the reduction in water usage per kilogram of cloth processed. The average water requirement for dyeing 1 kilogram of cloth is 175 l in small- and medium-level units, but only 120 litres per kg in larger units. Processing technology is the major determinant factor in water requirement. Generally, smaller units exclusively depend on winches, while larger units depend on soft machines, which use less water for processing.

1.2.2 *Public and Private Initiatives for Environmental Management*

Government of India has been emphasising the importance of environment-related improvements in the textile sector. National Textile Policy (2000) gives thrust on setting up modern processing units meeting international environmental norms, providing support to the units in achieving environmental standards and developing eco-friendly dyes. TUFS provides subsidised capital credit, while other schemes ensure importing high-tech machines with zero or low duties. Further, eco-testing and quality-testing facilities have been created throughout the country with an investment of over Rs. 60 crores to facilitate eco-friendly textile processing.

Industries have also been striving to meet the national and international environmental requirements. Such requirements are of different types: some of them are product standards (e.g. market access restriction on Azo dyes since the mid-1990s by the EU); others are process standards (e.g. environmental regulations, ISO 14,000 and environmental process standards are required by many EU importers). While the product standards merely concern about the health/environmental implications of the end-products, the process standards are about the technologies, methods and processes involved in producing them. For meeting the product standards, the industries face challenges in terms of finding cost-effective eco-friendly alternatives. As for the process standards, they have to invest in abatement technologies. In either case, the industries incur enormous abatement costs, which might have some impact on their cost competitiveness, while making them more competitive in terms of quality and environmental standards globally.

1.3 Domestic and Global Policy Environment: Textile Sector

For long time, the textile industry in India was protected from domestic private and international competition so as to enable the growth of small-scale sectors and to maintain employment potential. In fact, the interests of the handloom sector shaped the textiles polices of India. As import substitution being development strategy, textile industry was not an exception to that till the 1980s. Relative high emphasis on growth of small-scale sectors has discriminated vertically integrated composite mill sector. Initial restrictions on loom capacity expansion (removed in 1984) and establishment of automatic loom (removed in 1977) had hugely affected new technology acquisition and investment. Discriminatory taxation policies on mill sector in relation to powerloom and handloom sectors have stifled growth of mill sector in the country.

Further, hank yarn obligation imposed in 1974 with the intention of making adequate supply of low priced yarn to the handloom sector. There are considerable amount of diversion of such low priced yarn to powerloom sector to take cost advantages with respect to cone yarn (World Bank 1999). As hank yarn fetches lower prices than cone yarn, spinning mills are forced to lose their profits. Further, to make available raw cotton and yarn to domestic industry, export of these items were banned often. In other words, earlier policies have aimed at exporting value-added yarn rather than raw cotton; exporting only surplus cotton after meeting the domestic requirements and keeping cotton prices low for domestic industry.

Meanwhile, the Textile Policy of 1985 had introduced sweeping reforms in the sector. Economic reforms of 1991 and WTO agreements have also brought down major restrictions on this sector. Imports of cotton-based and man-made textile products were liberalised. The participation of private traders in export of textile products restricted till 1995 was finally removed. Overall, opening of domestic economy and increasing international market opportunities led to relaxation of export restrictions and promote the growth of the industry.

Textile was one of contentious issues in WTO negotiations. The textile trade was regulated by Multi-Fibre Agreement (MFA) till the end of Uruguay Round. MFA was a bilateral agreement or unilateral actions that intended to limit the imports into importing countries through establishing import quotas. The quotas were against the principles of basic WTO rules particularly non-discrimination. Under the quota system, importing countries specified how much they are going to accept from individual exporting countries. However, on 1 January 1995, WTO Agreement on Textiles and Clothing (ATC) replaced the MFA and set out a process for ultimate removal of the quotas within a period of ten years. Consequently, on 1 January 2005, quotas came to an end, and the operation of ATC ceased to exist. Now, textile and clothing sectors were fully integrated into the WTO system. Any importer of textiles and clothing can no longer discriminate against any exporter. There were predictions that India would gain considerably from the removal of quota system through expansion its export destinations (Uchikawa 1999; Verma 2002; Balasubramanyam and Wei 2005). But, empirical evidence to support such contentions are scanty.

Notwithstanding, economic policies and trade reforms have brought significant changes in the textile and clothing sectors. However, from the point of view of maintaining and generating employment opportunities in the sector, government often intervenes through various policy measures including the trade policies. According to economic survey 2008–2009, textile sector has relatively a large number of tariff lines that are not bound by the *ad valorem* rates. As per the HS Code, 47 items at the four digit level and 523 items at the eight digit level have specific duties. The specific duties hide the actual tariff protection that a sector enjoys. In fact, the applied tariff rates for textile and clothing stood at 12.2 and 13.0%, respectively, during 2012–2013 (Fig. 1.2). But, the *ad valorem* equivalents (AVEs) of specific duties (including applied tariffs) provided the average protection of 16.2% for textiles and 25.7% for clothing (WTO 2011). Further, bound tariff rates are much higher than applied tariff rates indicating that there is scope for the government to increase the level of protection in the sector.

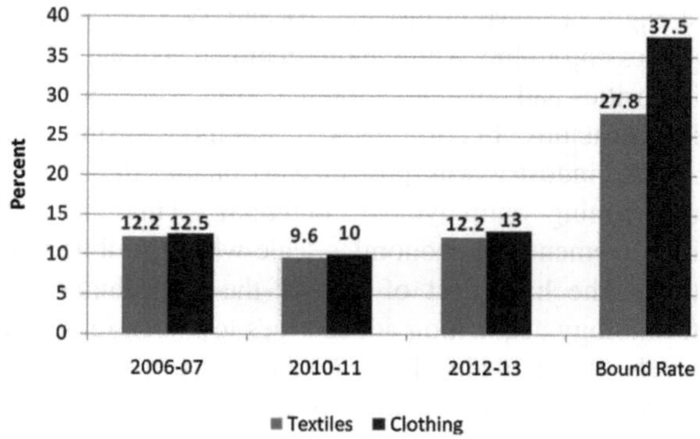

Fig. 1.2 Applied and bound tariff rates (color figure online)

At the global level, market distorting policies such as continuing US subsidy on cotton, despite a series of adverse rulings by WTO are having significant adverse implications for textile sector in India. As per a recent estimate by the Congressional Research Service, the US cotton subsidy averaged $5 billion during the period 1994–2008. While other countries, including China, EU and India do provide farm subsidies including that for cotton, their subsidies unlike that in the USA are well within WTO commitments. Despite being relatively inefficient producer, the cotton subsidies facilitate the USA to be the largest exporter of cotton accounting for 30–40% of the world exports of cotton. The artificially suppressed price of cotton on account of US subsidy deprives the producers of cotton and man-made fibres from getting remunerative prices for their products.

At the domestic level, cotton (carded and not carded) and cotton yarn exports are subject to export ban and/or restrictions in order to make them available for meeting the requirements of domestic industries. The export of cotton requires an export licence and export authorisation certificate from the Textile Commissioner of India or Directorate General of Foreign Trade (DGFT). This is made mandatory since April 2011. The exports against the registration certificate or export contract should be completed within 30 days from the date of issuance of the certificate. A failure to do so may debar the exporters concerned from further registration and may attract penal action. These stringent conditions are meant for discouraging cotton and yarn exports from India and support the growth of the domestic textile industry.

Since Indian textile industry is significantly cotton based and uses variety of fibres and yarn, Government of India has introduced various policy schemes during recent years. This was intended to foster a favourable environment for growth of the industry. Technology Mission on Cotton (TMC) introduced in February 2000 helped to augment cotton production and has made available raw materials at reasonable prices to the industry. Availability of raw materials domestically at competitive prices made the industry globally competitive. TMC comprises four mini-missions. The Mini-missions I and II were intended to increase the income of cotton growers and make available quality cotton to the industry. This was to be achieved through increasing the productivity of cotton, reducing the cost of cultivation and improving fibre attributes qualities like staple length, micronaire and strength. The Mini-missions III and IV were intended to achieve high quality in processing in line with the international standards through removing trash and other impurities and contamination in cotton. This was to be achieved through improving infrastructure of cotton markets and modernising ginning and processing factories.

The industry was protected to enable the growth of small scale sectors and maintaining employment potential. This had restricted new technological improvement and economies scale which inhibited growth of this industry for long time. The high cost of state-of-the-art technology and cost of capital to fund technology acquisition added woes to the entrepreneurs in upgrading technological levels. It was realised that textile industry should have access to timely and adequate capital at internationally comparable/reasonable interest rates to upgrade the technology level. Thus, TUFS was launched for textiles, jute and cotton ginning and pressing industries in 1999. TUFS helped to introduce state-of-the-art technology/machinery. The main focus of this scheme was the reimbursement of the 5% points on interest charged by the financial institutions on the project sanctioned for technological upgradation. For eligibility to get assistance, the technology levels are benchmarked in terms of specified machinery for each sector of the textile industry. Machinery with technology lower than that of the specified will not be eligible for funding under the scheme. Over the period 1999–2010, TUFS assistance was availed maximum by the spinning sector (39%); followed by composite mills (22%); cotton ginning and pressing (12%); processing of fibres, yarn, fabrics and garments (10%); weaving (8%); and garment manufacturing (6%).

Meanwhile, National Textile Policy 2000 promised to unshackle various impediments constraining the growth of this sector. Among others, it has achieved de-reserving garment sector from the small-scale industry sector, launching Technology Mission on Jute, expansion of Technology Upgradation Fund Scheme and strengthening of handloom sector. The National Textile Policy also aims to achieve textile and apparel exports of US$ 50 billion by 2010. However, the Handloom (Reservation of Articles for Production) Act 1985 continues to reserve about 11[2] items for exclusive production by the handloom industry. This should be reviewed to allow power loom and mills undertake production activities in which they may have comparative advantage.

Scheme for Integrated Textile Parks (SITP) was introduced in 2005 to integrate various sub-sectors of textile value chains and provide quality infrastructure for vertical integration of value chains. SITP provides facilities for spinning, sizing, weaving, processing, knitting, garmenting and embellishments. The main aim was to consolidate individual units in a cluster and provide world-class infrastructure facilities on public–private partnership (PPP) mode. This is expected to increase investment potential in this sector. In 2005, FDI in textiles and clothing was only

[2]These include (1) Saree, (2) Dhoti, (3) Towel, Gamcha and Angawastaram, (4) Lungi, (5) Khes, Bedsheet, Bedcover, Counterpane, Furnishing (including tapestry, upholstery), (6) Jamakkalam Durry or Durret, (7) Dress Material, (8) Barrack Blankets, Kambal or Kamblies, (9) Shawl, Loi, Muffler, Pankhi etc., (10) Woollen Tweed, (11) Chaddar, Mekhala/Phanek, subject to technical specification as contained in the Handloom (Reservation of Articles for Production) Act, 1985.

$78.99 million constituting 1.8% of total FDI in contrast to 8.3% ($5.4 billion) in China.

There were concerns on rupee appreciation and competitiveness of Indian exports. The rupee appreciated by 9.8% against US dollar between 3 April 2007 and 16 January 2008. To allay the concerns of exporters labour-intensive sectors including textiles, the Government of India announced several relief measures. These included enhancement by 3% of the Duty Entitlement Pass Book (DEPB) rates, interest subvention of 2% for pre-shipment and post-shipment credit to readymade garments and carpets, enhancement of rates of duty drawback from 10 to 40%, reduction of customs duty on textile machinery, reduction in customs duty on intermediates like polyester chips from 7.5 to 5% and on paraxylene from 2 to 0% (Government of India 2008).

As an important measure, the government has exempted all textile and textile machinery manufactured in India from textile committee cess on 24 May 2007. Cess was collected for financing textile committee. Further, during 2007, to give boost to man-made textile sector, Central Government has reduced customs duty to 5% from the existing levels on polyester filament yarn and polyester staple fibres, filament yarn and fibre made of acrylic, viscose, spun yarns of man-made staple fibres and filament yarns and polyester chips. Further, in 2008, basic customs duty was abolished to meet the growing needs of the garment industry. As part of economic stimulus package announced in December 2008 to tide over global financial meltdown, 4% optional excise duty on cotton textiles and also other textile products was abolished.

The Expert Committee to Ministry of Textile in its submission (2014), 'Vision, Strategy and Action Plan for Indian Textile and Apparel Sector' had outlined vision 2024–2025 for Indian textile sector. It acknowledges that after phasing out of export quotas in 2005 India's export performance has been below expectations and notes that other competing countries like Vietnam and Bangladesh have shown remarkable success in improving their exports. The Expert Committee outlines a target production of US$ 350 billion by 2024–2025 from the current level of about US$ 100 billion for the domestic sector; and export target of US$ 300 billion by the same year. The Expert Committee prescribes several structural reforms that would enable India to export only finished products and in the process maximise employment generation and value creation within the country. The Expert Committee envisages an investment requirement of about US$ 120 billion to fulfil the vision targets and anticipates creation of 35 million additional jobs in the textile sector.

1.3.1 Trade-Environment Inter-Linkages: Textile Sector

Of several trade and environment issues that arise from the simultaneous evolution of the trade and environmental regimes, special interest in the present context is with regard to the environmental requirements that several countries prescribe and the associated market access (see Sankar 2006 for further discussion). The Rio Declaration Principle 2 endorses that states have the sovereign right to exploit their resources pursuant to their own environmental and development own policies. Principle 11 states that environmental standards, management objectives and priorities should reflect the environmental and developmental context to which they apply. Standards applied by some countries may be inappropriate and that of unwarranted economic and social cost to other countries, in particular developing countries. Further, the TBT and SPS Agreements permit countries to prescribe higher standards under certain conditions. The diversity in environmental standards can be rationalised on the following grounds:

- Differences in trade-offs between income and environmental quality
- Differences in baseline emissions
- Differences in pollution absorption capacities

The concerns of the developed and developing countries are different in this context and their responses have also been divergent. The developed country's concerns include, (a) flight of industries due to pollution havens argument—i.e. due to lower environmental standards in developing countries some industries that have greater potential to pollute may shift to developing countries; (b) differential environmental standards may translate into 'race-to-the-bottom'—i.e. in order to prevent migration of industries to countries with lower environmental standards, the environmental standards in developed countries may also be lowered; (c) the differential environmental standards across countries may constitute 'unfair' trade and non-level-playing fields across countries and hence effect the competitiveness of firms in countries with higher environmental standards.

The developed country responses included, (a) eco-labelling of products, (b) specifying environmental requirements on products and processes with emphasis on life cycle assessment and (c) specification of anti-dumping measures.

The developing country concerns on the other hand include, (a) inappropriateness of higher environmental standards being imposed on developing countries with the potential of such measures being turned into non-tariff barriers to trade from developing countries to developed countries, and (b) non-realisation of the anticipated gains from export of resource-intensive and labour-intensive products.

Many developing countries including India possess comparative advantage in exports of natural resource-intensive and labour-intensive goods like textiles and garments, leather and leather products, and agricultural and fishery products. As most of the units engaged in these activities are in traditional/cottage and small-scale sectors, where the levels of technological sophistication are low and per unit environmental compliance costs are high, they face difficulties in complying with domestic environmental requirements. Now, these countries face the stringent environmental requirements like product-specific regulations, standards and eco-labelling, process and production methods and packaging prescribed by some developed countries, which would prevent or raise the cost of access to their goods in developed countries' markets and hence erode the anticipated gains from trade due to trade liberalisation.

Given this background of India's textile industry and the trade and environmental inter-linkages, the present study attempts to assess the needs and policy imperatives to achieve maximum gains from the Indian textile exports while complying with environmental requirements at home and abroad.

1.4 Overview of the Book

This book is structured as follows. After the discussion on trade and environment inter-linkages in the context of textile sector provided in this introduction chapter, the second chapter titled 'Global and Indian Supply Chain of Textiles' discusses in detail supply chains of textile industry in global and Indian contexts. In the global context, the situation of textile industry in India's competing countries from South Asia and China are discussed using the SWOT (strengths, weaknesses, opportunities and threats) framework especially in the post-MFA regime of world trade. Arguing that the textile supply chains compete on low cost, high quality, accurate delivery and flexibility in variety and volume, the discussion pertaining to Indian supply chain in the second chapter maintains that the new market in the post-MFA world will be won on the basis of capabilities across the supply chain. It is further argued that policy will need to facilitate the building of capabilities at the firm level and encourage adoption of flexible strategies that firms will need to periodically devise.

The third chapter titled 'India's Comparative Advantage in Export of Textile and Apparel Products' describes the comparative advantage of India's export of textile products using the measures such as revealed comparative advantage and revealed symmetric comparative advantage. These measures are estimated for India's textile exports using three and four digit level trade data. The results indicate the worrying feature of declining trend in recent years in India's comparative advantage in the export garments. Even at a disaggregate level, the declining trend in the comparative advantage is apparent in many products like women/girl dresses woven, women/girl suit woven, men/boys shirt woven and men/boy knit/crochet shirt.

The next three chapters explore the potential role played by the environmental regulations in India's export of textile products. Chapter 4 titled 'Global Environmental Requirements—Textile Industry' discusses in detail the basis for environmental concerns in the importing countries in the context of textile and other products and the environmental quality standards adopted by several developed countries including USA and EU. The chapter also discusses the measures undertaken by several developing countries exporting textile products to the developed countries to meet the growing environmental demands.

While it is relatively easy to perceive the impact of non-tariff measures on trade prospects, it is extremely difficult to systematically establish the presence of such measures and even more difficult to measure the impact of such measures on the trade and welfare. The literature has adopted at least three approaches to address this issue:

(a) to elicit the perceptions through primary survey of the exporters and use the survey data to quantify the impact of the environmental regulations and standards on trade;
(b) to use firm-level data from exporting countries along with appropriate proxies to measure the additional costs incurred by the exporters to meet the growing environmental demands in the importing countries to analyse the influence of environmental regulation on the exit decisions of the exporters and on the productivity improvements; and
(c) to use estimates of the compliance costs (to meet the environmental standards imposed by the importing country) obtained from critical review of the literature and incorporate them in large-scale computable general equilibrium models including trade component to analyse the welfare implications and trade prospects under various plausible future scenarios.

Chapters 5 and 6 provide discussion on influence of environmental regulations on textile trade assessed through approaches (a) and (c) mentioned above, respectively.[3] Chapter 5 titled 'Non-tariff Barriers in Textiles—Incidence and Perceptions' describes extent of non-tariff barriers/measures (including the environmental regulations) adopted by the importing countries as revealed by various secondary databases and recent surveys. Using the time-series data of textile sector, the chapter also analyses the impact of pollution abatement on India's textile trade. In an attempt to further understand the exporters' perception on the role of environmental regulations, a survey was undertaken by the study. Though the survey questionnaire was administered to a larger sample of over 150 firms, only sixty firms provided answers to at least 50% of the questions. The survey results largely provided information on the perceptions of the textile firms and relatively less insight on the exact quantification of the impact of environmental regulations on trade and productivity.

Chapter 6 titled 'Exploring Linkages between Pollution Abatement and Trade in Textile Industry' discusses in detail the cost of pollution abatement among textile firms and integrates such costs in a large-scale modelling framework. Using the GTAP model, the chapter further discusses the interplay between the costs incurred to meet the environmental regulations and the potential price premiums that the cleaner products would get in the international market to assess future trade prospects for India in the textile sector.

Finally, Chap. 7 titled 'Conclusions' provides summary of the findings along with discussion on strategies to enhance export of textile products. The chapter also presents a SWOT analysis of textile sector in India. The chapter ends with a brief discussion on emerging environmental challenges such as the need for reducing carbon footprint. The dynamics of environment and trade inter-linkages could get significantly affected in the context of these emerging environmental challenges and hence could require fresh assessment.

---

[3]A recent study by Chakraborty (2011) follows approach (b) mentioned above.

Chapter 2
Global and Indian Supply Chain of Textiles

Zareena Begum and Sukanya Das

This chapter focuses on global and Indian supply chain of the textile industries with a view to understand the trade linkages and environmental concerns. This chapter is organized as follows: the first section discusses the global supply chain of textile and clothing sector by analysing the UN Comtrade data. The second section discusses the comparative advantages of Asia's leading textile exporting countries and describes the features of textile sector in some of important export competitors of India. The last section discusses the key features of the Indian supply chain.

2.1 Global Supply Chain

Table 2.1 presents the major exporters of textiles in the world. China has emerged as the largest exporter of textiles in the world. China's exports of textiles increased from 7.6% in 1990 to 34.8% of total world export in 2013. However, the share of European Union has drastically declined from 51.6% in 1990 and to about 20% in 2013. The progressive phasing out of MFA seemed to have impacted the European Union's exports. This is also evident from the decline in exports of Germany, Italy, Belgium, France and the Netherlands during 1990–2013. The export share of the USA also appears to have declined during this period. However, two countries, viz., India and Turkey, have performed better by exploiting the free world market situation. While the world textile market share of India has increased from 2.5 to 6.2%, Turkey has improved its export share from 1.6 to 3.9%. The share of exports from Pakistan has almost remained constant throughout the study period.

Z. Begum (✉)
Madras School of Economics, Chennai, India

S. Das
Department of Policy Studies, TERI University, New Delhi, India

K.S.K. Kumar (ed.), *A Study of India's Textile Exports and Environmental Regulations*, https://doi.org/10.1007/978-981-10-6295-7_2

Table 2.1 Major exporters of textiles in the world (% share)

Country	1990	1995	2000	2005	2010	2013
European Union-25	51.6	36.5	31.2	31.1	25.0	23.6
China	7.6	7.9	9.2	17.7	28.1	34.8
USA	8.2	6.9	7.6	7.5	7.2	4.5
Germany	13.7	8.8	6.7	6.5	5.2	4.8
Italy	9.1	7.1	6.6	6.4	4.8	4.4
Hong Kong, China	7.8	7.9	7.4	5.9	4.1	3.5
Korea, Rep.	5.9	7.2	7.3	4.8	4.4	3.9
India	2.5	2.4	3.3	3.9	5.9	6.2
Belgium	6.3	4.6	3.7	3.3	2.7	2.0
Turkey	1.6	1.5	2.1	3.1	3.3	3.9
Japan	6.1	4.5	4.3	3.3	3.0	2.2
France	6.4	4.5	3.9	3.1	2.2	1.8
Pakistan	2.9	2.4	2.5	3.0	2.9	3.0
UK	4.8	2.9	2.4	2.1	1.6	1.4
The Netherlands	2.9	2.0	1.5	1.9	1.6	1.7

Source UN Comtrade

Interestingly, China is also the largest importer of textiles in the world. China's imports constitute about 11.1% of total world imports in 2010 (Table 2.2). By 2013, China's imports dropped to 6.7%. These are basically raw materials and intermediate products that China imports from various countries including India. These products are converted into value added finished products and then exported. USA is the second largest importer of textiles followed by Germany and Hong Kong. The import share of European Union constituted about 28.2% in 2010. The combined import share of the European Union and the USA was about 37.9% (including intra-EU trade) in 2010.

As far as clothing exports concerned, exports from China constituted about 38.5% of total world exports in 2013 (Table 2.3). China has improved its world market share tremendously over time. Similarly, clothing exports from Bangladesh increased considerably from 0.8% in 1990 to 5.1% in 2013. The market share of India remained almost constant around 3.5% throughout the period. However, the export share of European Union has almost halved between 1990 and 2010. Within European Union, most of the member countries have shown declining share of exports in the world market. Similarly, Korea has lost its market share considerably over time.

USA is the largest importer of clothing in the world constituting over a little less than 20% of the total imports (Table 2.4). The other major importers were Germany, UK, Japan and France. The imports of European Union as a whole constituted about 44.7% in 2010. However, its import share has remained constant

Table 2.2 Major importers of textile products in the world (% share)

Country	1990	1995	2000	2005	2010	2013
European Union	58.7	39.3	33.6	32.7	28.2	22.8
China	7.1	8.7	9.0	10.3	11.1	6.7
USA	7.2	6.6	9.5	10.3	9.7	8.4
Germany	13.1	8.3	5.9	6.0	5.5	4.2
Hong Kong, China	10.5	10.6	8.1	6.5	4.6	3.2
Italy	8.8	5.4	4.9	4.4	4.1	2.6
France	8.6	5.1	4.1	3.7	3.1	2.3
UK	7.8	5.0	4.3	3.7	2.9	2.3
Turkey	1.0	1.5	1.8	2.8	3.7	2.1
Japan	6.6	4.5	3.4	3.0	3.1	2.7
Mexico	0.7	1.2	3.8	3.1	2.4	1.9
Spain	2.5	2.0	2.1	2.3	1.8	1.3
Belgium	4.3	2.8	2.4	2.1	1.7	1.2
Korea, Rep.	3.4	3.2	2.4	2.0	2.3	1.6
Canada	2.5	2.1	2.6	2.1	1.8	1.4
The Netherlands	3.8	2.2	1.5	1.5	1.4	1.2

Source UN Comtrade

Table 2.3 Major exporters of clothing in the world (% share)

Country	1990	1995	2000	2005	2010	2013
European Union-25	53.3	34.5	26.8	27.9	26.9	25.7
China	12.4	15.3	18.3	26.4	36.7	38.5
Hong Kong, China	19.9	13.6	12.3	9.7	6.8	4.8
Italy	15.3	9.0	6.8	6.6	5.7	5.2
Germany	9.1	4.8	3.5	4.4	4.8	4.0
USA	3.3	4.2	4.4	1.8	1.3	1.3
Turkey	4.3	3.9	3.3	4.2	3.6	3.3
India	3.3	2.6	3.1	3.3	3.2	3.6
France	6.0	3.6	2.7	3.0	2.8	2.4
Indonesia	2.1	2.2	2.4	1.8	1.9	1.7
Korea, Rep.	10.2	3.2	2.6	0.9	0.5	0.5
Belgium	2.6	1.7	2.0	2.4	2.2	1.9
Bangladesh	0.8	1.3	2.1	2.5	–	5.1
UK	3.9	2.8	2.0	1.8	1.6	1.6
Thailand	3.6	3.2	1.9	1.5	1.2	0.9
The Netherlands	2.8	1.8	1.2	1.4	1.8	1.8

Source UN Comtrade

Table 2.4 Major importers of clothing in the world

Country	1990	1995	2000	2005	2010	2013
European Union	55.0	43.7	37.0	43.3	44.7	35.4
USA	26.0	24.8	32.1	27.0	23.3	18.9
Germany	19.2	14.7	9.3	8.9	9.3	7.4
UK	6.7	5.0	6.2	7.5	6.6	4.8
Japan	8.4	11.3	9.4	8.0	7.7	7.0
France	8.1	6.2	5.4	6.3	6.2	4.9
Hong Kong, China	6.7	7.6	7.7	6.5	4.7	3.4
Italy	2.5	2.8	2.9	4.3	4.7	3.3
Spain	1.6	1.6	1.8	3.4	4.0	3.1
Belgium	3.5	2.6	2.2	2.7	2.3	1.9
The Netherlands	4.6	3.0	2.3	2.2	2.6	2.7
Canada	2.3	1.6	1.8	2.1	2.4	2.1
Austria	2.3	1.9	1.3	1.5	1.5	1.3
Switzerland	3.3	2.3	1.5	1.6	1.5	1.2
Denmark	1.0	1.1	1.1	1.2	1.2	0.9
Sweden	2.4	1.3	1.0	1.0	1.1	0.9

Source UN Comtrade

during the recent years. Both European Union and the USA accounted for about 68% (including intra-EU trade) of total world imports during the study period.

To analyse the growth in export and import of textiles and clothing, the study period was divided into three sub-periods, viz., pre-ATC period (1990–1995), ATC period (1996–2004) and post-ATC period (2005–2010). The purpose of analysing growth rates during these periods was to gauge impact of removal of quota regime on exports and imports of textiles and clothing among the major exporting and importing countries. As expected, China has registered the highest growth rate of 11.8% in textiles during the post-ATC period when compared to other periods (Table 2.5). This indicates that the removal of quotas has immensely helped Chinese exporters to capture major textile markets in the world. India has also recorded positive and higher growth rate of 8.9% during the post-ATC period. However, growth in world textile exports during post-ATC period has not increased as compared to the pre-ATC period and it remained the same.

Similar pattern can also be observed for growth in exports of clothing across major exporters in the world (Table 2.6). During the post-ATC period, the highest growth in export of clothing was registered by China (9.6%) followed by the Netherlands (9.5%), Germany (6.5%) and India (5.3%). India's clothing export performance during post-ATC period seems to be low when compared to its performance in textile exports. In fact, growth in India's clothing exports declined to 5.3% in the post-ATC from 6.1% registered in the ATC period. Nevertheless,

Table 2.5 Growth in export of textile products (%)

Country	1990–1995	1996–2004	2005–2010	2010–2013
European Union-25	−0.3	0.2	−2.3	1.9
China	9.7	10.2	11.8	17.7
USA	2.7	3.1	0.0	7.0
Germany	−2.1	−1.5	−2.5	2.6
Italy	2.4	0.9	−4.0	1.9
Hong Kong, China	10.9	−1.2	−5.8	−2.6
Korea, Rep.	14.7	−1.9	0.3	4.8
India	9.5	4.7	8.9	21.4
Taiwan, China	11.5	−2.6	−2.3	
Belgium	1.2	−1.1	3.6	−2.7
Turkey	7.0	8.7	0.2	16.5
Japan	3.5	−0.9	−4.8	−1.74
France	−0.5	−1.3	0.6	−2.5
Pakistan	6.5	2.5	−3.7	9.1
UK	−2.3	−1.9	−1.2	4.6
The Netherlands	−3.1	−1.4	1.5	4.6
World	9.5	1.5	1.5	10.1

Source UN Comtrade

Table 2.6 Growth in export of clothing (%)

Country	1990–1995	1996–2004	2005–2010	2010–2013
European Union	2.5	2.1	3.9	5.4
China	24.9	10.0	9.6	16.9
Hong Kong, China	8.5	1.2	−3.7	−4.5
Italy	0.6	1.4	1.1	8.6
Germany	−2.3	3.4	6.5	3.2
USA	21.8	−4.2	−2.1	11.8
Turkey	9.0	6.0	0.7	9.9
India	9.7	6.1	5.3	22.5
France	0.8	3.1	3.6	4.8
Indonesia	19.3	4.2	4.7	6.2
Korea, Rep.	−8.1	−2.9	−10.3	14.2
Belgium	1.7	8.1	4.0	4.9
Bangladesh	23.5	11.9		25.8
UK	4.9	−1.1	1.8	17.1
Thailand	11.3	−1.5	−0.3	−2.3
The Netherlands	3.3	−1.5	9.5	10.8
World	18.3	4.9	4.0	14.1

Source UN Comtrade

growth in India's clothing exports was lower than growth in world exports. USA, Korea, Hong Kong and Thailand appear to have lost competitiveness in export of clothing products during the post-ATC period. These countries have registered negative growth rates during this period.

Growth in imports of textiles across major importing countries is presented in Table 2.7. Most of the importing countries have registered negative growth during pre-ATC and ATC period. This can be attributed to quota regime under which most of the developed countries restricted imports of textiles from developing countries. Turkey has recorded the highest growth in imports followed by Korea and Japan during the post-ATC period. China registered growth rate of 1.5% per annum. At global level, growth in textile imports was 1.7%.

Regarding growth in imports of clothing, it was the highest in Spain and the Netherlands each recording 7.5% followed by Canada (6.0%) and Italy (5.5%) during the post-ATC period (Table 2.8). Other countries which have registered high growth rates are Germany, Sweden and Austria. However, growth in world import of clothing had declined during the post-ATC period as compared to the previous periods.

Table 2.7 Growth in import of textile products

Country	1990–1994	1995–2004	2005–2010	2010–2013
European Union	−2.4	−0.4	−1.2	1.7
China	11.2	3.0	1.5	10.4
USA	9.5	6.8	−0.2	7.6
Germany	−3.4	−2.3	0.1	2.5
Hong Kong, China	9.3	−3.6	−5.9	−3.8
Italy	−4.1	−0.3	−0.9	0.1
France	−4.6	−1.3	−1.2	−0.7
UK	−2.4	−1.9	−3.3	5.2
Turkey	15.6	7.1	6.4	1.9
Japan	−1.5	−3.3	3.3	10.4
Mexico	43.0	13.0	−4.4	9.6
Spain	−1.6	3.1	−3.1	0.7
Belgium	−2.1	−1.8	−1.7	−0.8
Korea, Rep.	5.6	−2.5	3.5	3.9
Canada	6.0	1.8	−2.5	4.9
The Netherlands	−5.2	−4.3	−0.3	3
World	9.8	1.6	1.7	10.1

Source UN Comtrade

Table 2.8 Growth in import of clothing

Country	1990–1994	1995–2004	2005–2010	2010–2013
European Union	2.2	3.8	4.9	2.5
USA	10.2	6.9	−0.3	5.4
Germany	1.8	−1.4	5.1	4.8
Japan	15.1	1.5	3.4	11.8
Hong Kong, China	15.6	2.8	−3.2	−0.6
UK	0.6	8.9	1.2	4.7
France	1.5	4.5	4.4	3.1
Italy	9.5	9.3	5.5	−2.0
The Netherlands	0.3	1.1	7.5	15.1
Belgium	1.4	5.7	1.7	2.5
Spain	6.9	12.5	7.5	3.9
Canada	2.4	7.6	6.0	9.4
Switzerland	−0.4	0.9	3.9	5.7
Austria	2.9	1.8	4.6	4.2
Denmark	6.9	4.8	4.1	3.4
Sweden	−5.7	1.8	4.8	9.0
World	9.6	4.7	3.7	14.1

Source UN Comtrade

2.1.1 *Sources of Textile and Clothing Imports to EU and USA*

It is clear from the above discussion that the European Union and the USA are the major markets for exporters of textiles and clothing. Between textiles and clothing, these two markets accounted for the larger share for clothing than textiles. Thus, it would be interesting to look at the major sources of imports to these markets during 1995, 2006 and 2012.

Figure 2.1 depicts the source of textile imports to EU. Intra-EU imports seem to have dominated the total imports to the European Union. Among ten largest suppliers to EU, intra-EU trade accounted for over 55% of total imports in 1995. However, the share of intra-EU trade has declined in 2006 and 2012. Outside the EU, China and India accounted for 12 and 4%, respectively, of total imports in 2012.

In clothing, China has improved its market share from 8% in 1995 to 22% in 2012 (Fig. 2.2). As noticed in textile imports, the intra-EU trade in clothing has also declined over time. The market share of India has remained constant. The import share of others category has declined considerably. It might be due to capture of EU markets for imports by developing countries like Bangladesh, Romania and Turkey during recent years after the removal of quota regime.

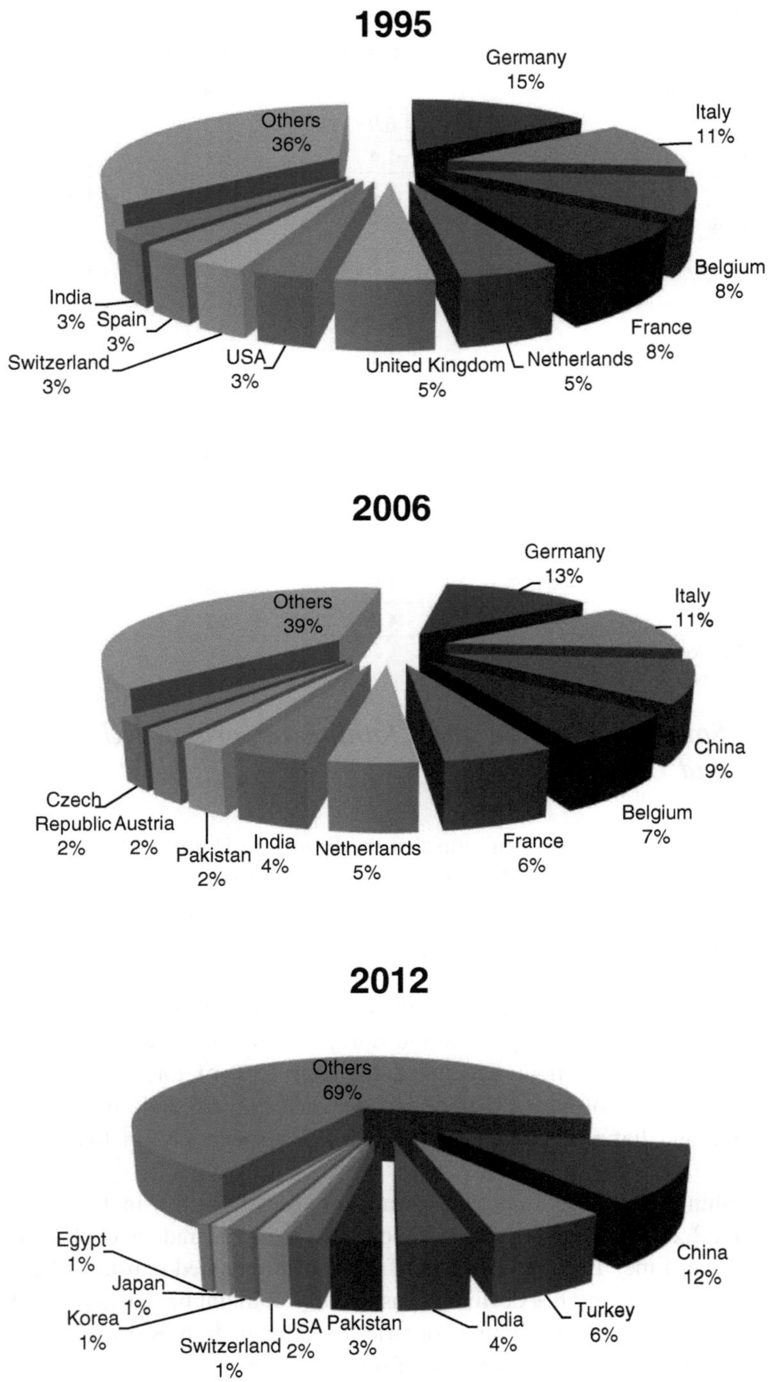

Fig. 2.1 Sources of textile imports to EU (1995, 2006 and 2012)

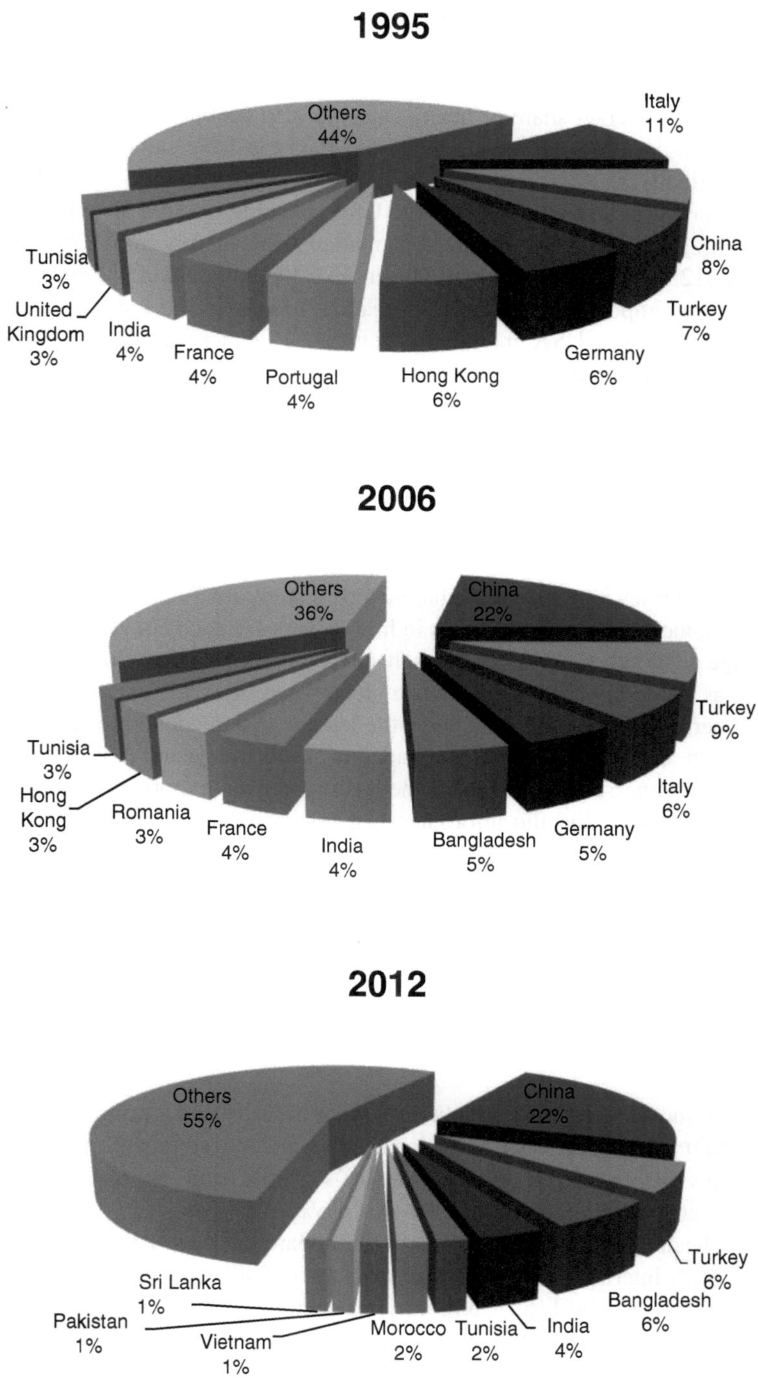

Fig. 2.2 Sources of clothing imports to EU (1995, 2006 and 2012)

Figure 2.3 shows sources of textile imports to the USA. China has improved its market share in remarkably from 11 to 39%. China's entry into the USA market has affected the market share of other large exporters. These included Mexico, Taiwan and Japan. The market share of others category also declined sharply from 36% in 1995 to 24% in 2006. However, India and Pakistan have improved their import share marginally.

As observed in textile imports to the USA, clothing imports also dominated by China (Fig. 2.4). China has improved its market share sharply from 15% in 1995 to 39% in 2012. In recent years, small players like Vietnam, Honduras and Cambodia have captured import share of the USA market. Indonesia and India have increased their imports to the USA marginally between 1995 and 2006. Bangladesh has market share of 5% in 2012. In clothing also, the share of others category has declined over time.

2.2 Comparative Advantages of Asia's Leading Players

Based on interviews of sixteen global buyers, a study by Tewari (2008) shows that there are some important differences in how buyers see each country's comparative advantage in South Asia. Even though all countries produce clothing and some textiles, as Table 2.9 shows, each has a niche where it excels over others from the buyer's perspective. Figure 2.5 shows the leading Asian economies in the apparel value chain and the industrial upgradation over the years. Table 2.10 shows strengths, weaknesses and threats of the leading apparel exporters. The subsequent discussion provides specific information of textile industry some of India's competitors in more detailed manner.

2.2.1 Textile Sector in Leading Export Competitors of India

2.2.1.1 China

The textile industry is China's traditional pillar industry and a principal exporter. It has contributed a great deal to China's economic development. With about 20 million people employed in the country's textile and apparel industry, the year-on-year growth reported in 2009 was 8.6%.

China leads the world in exports of both apparel and textiles. According to the WTO's 2008 International Trade Statistics, the country's apparel exports in 2007 were valued at US$115.2 billion, representing a 33.4% share in world exports. Of those, US$32 billion was exported to Asia, US$28.4 billion to Europe, US $27.4 billion to North America, US$13.7 billion to the Commonwealth of Independent States (CIS) and the remainder to the Middle East, Africa and South and Central America. Its textile exports in 2007 were valued at US$56 billion,

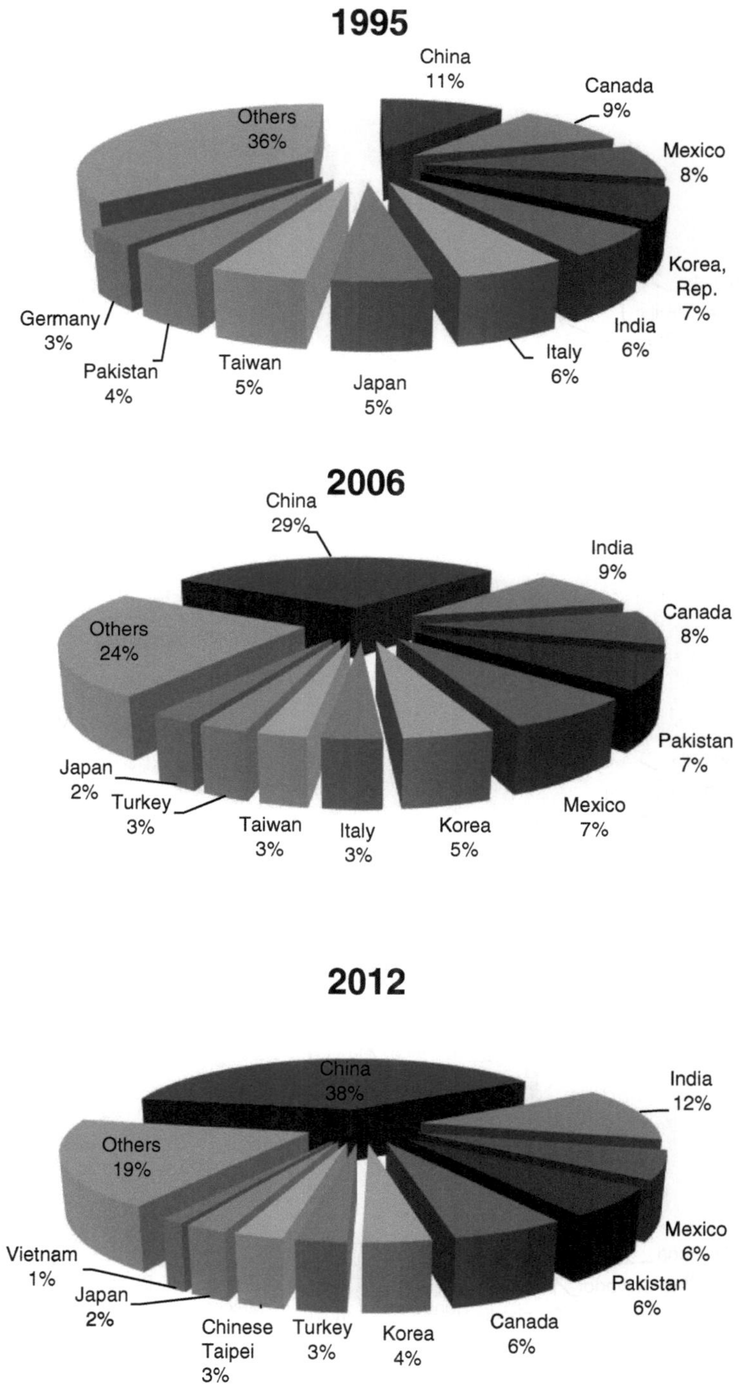

Fig. 2.3 Sources of textile imports to USA (1995, 2006 and 2012)

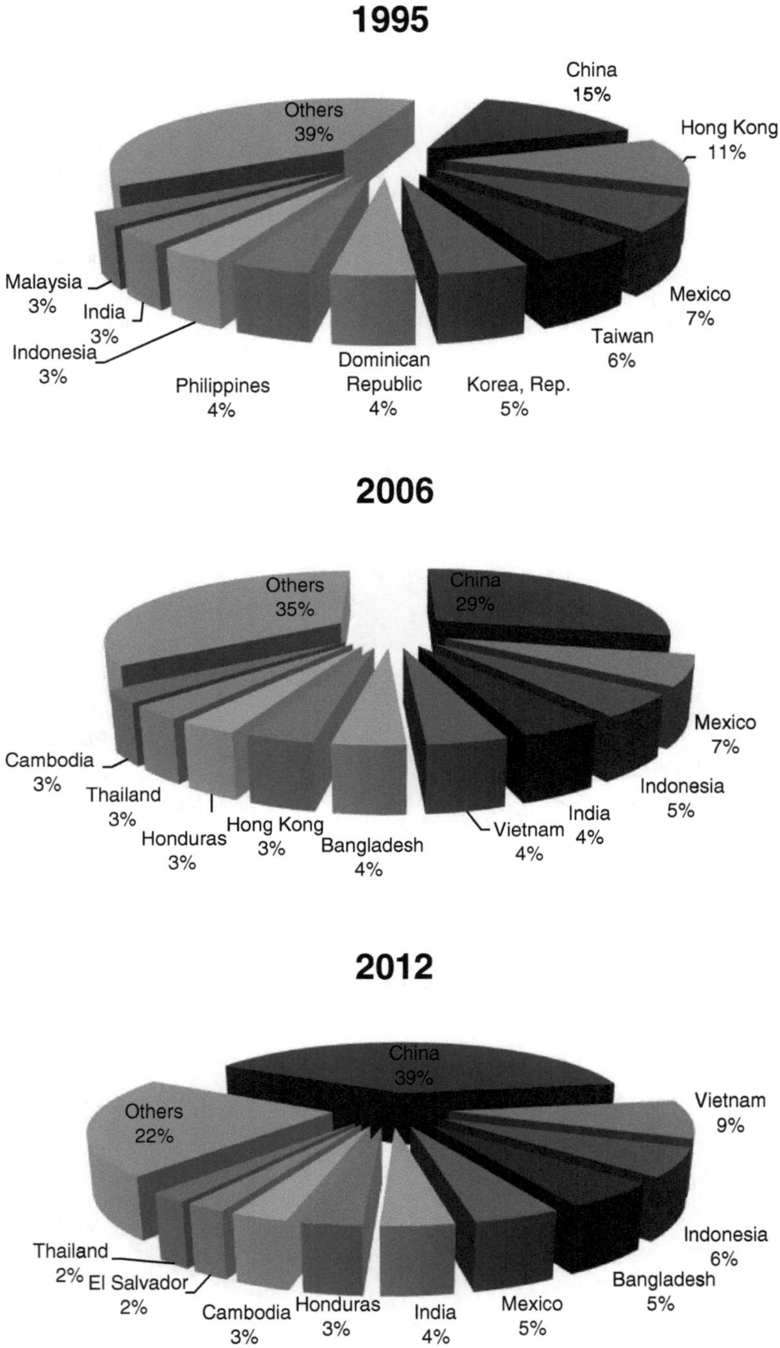

Fig. 2.4 Sources of clothing imports to USA (1995, 2006 and 2012)

Table 2.9 Product level specializations: comparative advantage of South Asia's leading players in the T&C sector

	Comparative advantage—global buyer's perspective	Share of top five items in total T&C exports[a] (%)
Pakistan	Mid-to-course gauge cotton yarn. Bedlinen, home furnishings, carpets, basic menswear and hosiery	54
Sri Lanka	Lingerie, swimwear of man-made fibres and cotton blends, formals	30
Bangladesh	Knit and woven menswear, sports and casual wear (shirts, trousers, T-shirts), pullovers	46
India[b]	Cotton knit and woven women's tops, blouses and skirts, embellished and embroidered, fine-yarn	44

Source Tewari (2008)
[a]Export shares include shares to the US and EU markets only
[b]Share to the world market

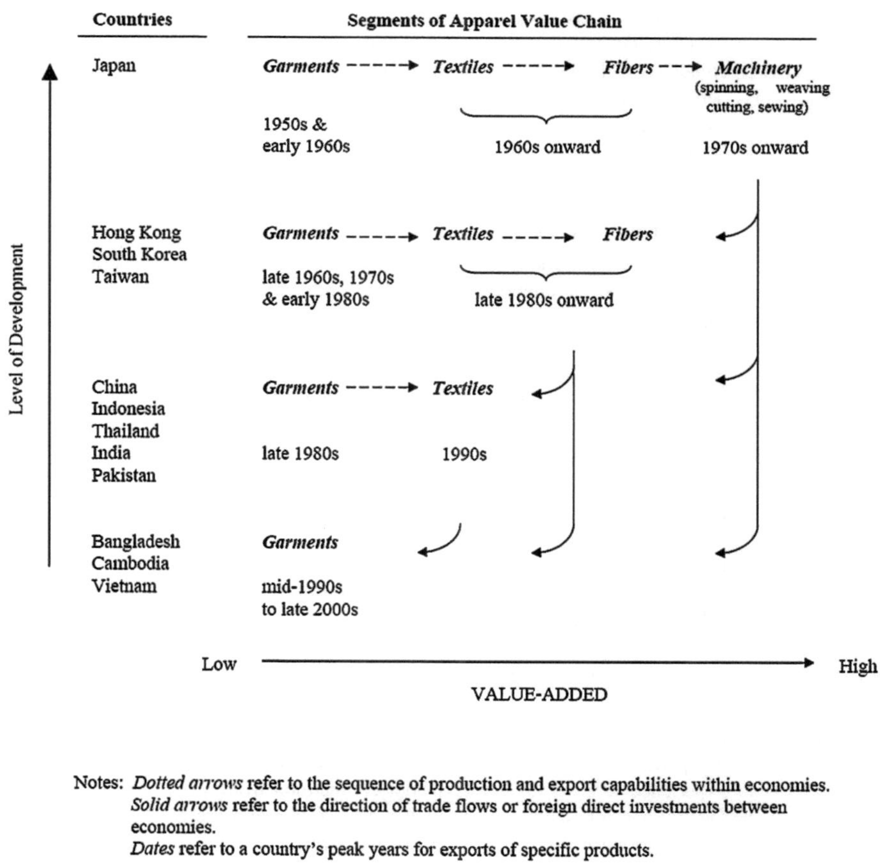

Fig. 2.5 Industrial upgradation by Asian Economies—apparel value chain. *Source* Cattaneo et al. (2010)

Table 2.10 Leading apparel exporters: strengths and weaknesses/threats

Country	Strengths	Weaknesses/threats	Labour rate
Bangladesh	• Low-cost and firms' willingness to keep margins low while investing in new technology to improve productivity and to reinforce relationships with buyers • Improvements in terminal handling and customs: clearance has gone from 12 to 13 days as recently as last year to clear goods within 3 days • Low labour costs and availability • Low energy costs • Currency depreciation: coincided with post-ATC period. More of an advantage to knit exports • Growing textile industries: Taiwanese and Korean investors are setting up fabric/fibre operations	• Lack of design, soft skills, and technology • Currency fluctuation (mainly Euro) causing losses in previously arranged letters of credit • Shortage of skilled workers and middle management • Human capital (poor) and worker unrest and strikes over poor pay and conditions • Energy reliability: power interruptions in the national power grid are common, and stand-alone generators are often needed (more expensive) • Inefficient infrastructure: port and transportation	$0.31/hour
Indonesia	• Large domestic market • Large installed production capacity • Low labour costs and relatively low turnover rates • Long, refined textile tradition (batik techniques, embroidery)	• High energy costs • Outdated machinery • General business climate: unfavourable bureaucracy, taxes, corruption, security and cooperation	$0.44 hour
Cambodia	• Labour: low cost, availability and standards • Government support • Economies of Scale (2005): 7% of the garment manufacturing entities employ over 5000 people	• Labour: unskilled, low productivity • All FDI; lack of local firms • Lack upstream textile industry • Lack of infrastructure in transportation and communication	$0.33 hour
China	• Labour: high productivity, competency and experience • Quality and reliability: fabric and garments • Technology investment (logistics)	• Inflation (increases producer prices) and labour competition from higher paying, non-apparel sector industries • Labour costs and labour laws: rising domestic	$1.44–$1.88 hour

(continued)

Table 2.10 (continued)

Country	Strengths	Weaknesses/threats	Labour rate
	• Product diversity: fabric and finished goods • Mentality and management: 'can do' business approach • Government support	wages, expected to increase further as a result of new labour laws • Currency appreciation • Energy costs: increasing • Shipping cost: major increases • Product safety	
Sri Lanka	• Diversification of product exports • Focus on niche apparel and enterprising nature of the private sector to position country in niche markets • Quality, on time deliveries and service • Compliance and emphasis on international labour and environmental standards	• Higher labour costs • Uncertainty of EU-GSP benefits • Dependence on apparel exports	\$0.46/hour (2004)
Pakistan	• Low labour cost • Government support and liberal FDI policies • Currency depreciation against the US dollar and other Western currencies	• Energy access and reliability • Political instability—security and safety issues • Mediocre quality and colour consistency of textiles and clothing • Low labour productivity • Lack of design skills and global market knowledge	\$0.56/hour
India	• Product diversity—most diversified exporter of T&C products in South Asia • Low cost, flexibility and speed—especially when compared to China • Growing domestic market	• Procedural hurdles to international trade • Lack of scale economies with almost 80% of T&C units labelled as small/cottage units typically employing fewer than 11 workers • Inflation in raw material costs compared to competitors • Higher manufacturing costs (power, operating and transaction) compared to competitors	\$0.51/hour

Source Cattaneo et al. (2010)

representing a 23.5-% share in world exports. Of those, US$21.4 billion was exported to Asia, US$10.5 billion to Europe, US$9.9 billion to North America, US$4.8 billion to Africa and the remainder to the Middle East, South and Central America and the CIS.

Because China's textile industry is so dependent on exports, it has been significantly impacted by the global economic downturn. The China General Administration of Customs released statistics indicating the country's January–June 2009 textile and apparel exports fell 10.9% year-on-year compared to the same period in 2008. Textile exports declined 15.2% to US$26.9 billion, and apparel exports dropped 8.5% to US$45.9 billion. The administration noted, however, that the decline in textile exports was smaller than that of overall nationwide exports.

The price paid for the quota puts the Chinese producer at a clear disadvantage than other Southeast Asian countries. The cost of quotas may be forcing Chinese producers to engage in illegal practices, e.g. transshipping through Southeast Asian countries or the exploitation of workers by providing a less than appropriate work environment. Considering the appreciation of the yuan renminbi since the middle of 2006 (it has reportedly appreciated about 10% since China adjusted its exchange rate policies in July 2005), it is obvious that Chinese producers at the low end of the garment industry are being squeezed out of their profits and thus a decline in exports of lower-end products. The growth in the export of shirts (knitted or crocheted) in 2005/2006 was far higher than the sector average, i.e. 83.3% compared with the average of 23.1%. However, non-knitted shirts (HS6205) literally stagnated (−1.3%) in 2006.

China's labour cost advantage in low-end garment products, particularly men's shirts and trousers, is being lost to other producers in the region. The advantage of producing its own fabrics is also not strong enough to compete with producers of neighbouring countries. Increasing labour costs, coupled with an added quota cost and an appreciating currency, is forcing China's producers to move production to smaller cities or to outsource them completely to cheaper manufacturers in other countries. The future of China's garment industry lies in higher-end products that involve fabrics, designs and technology that are more sophisticated. The good news is that the industry is developed enough to meet these challenges. The modernization of its factories over the past two decades, and the clustering of firms in the textile and garment industry through government-directed efforts, can sustain China's position as the 'tailor to the world'.

For garment producers in competing countries, particularly developing and emerging economies in Southeast Asia, greater linkages with Chinese garment producers are critical. These linkages, for example by being part of China's supply chain, could open markets in the developed countries and, more importantly, the growing Chinese market.

The development guidelines and main goal for the future of China's textile industry are to implement a science-led approach to bringing about an improvement in the economic growth mode and to build up an innovative, resource-saving, environmentally friendly industry. Greater efforts are to be made to increase the contribution by science and technology as well as brands to the economic growth of the textile industry by:

- Introducing an overall brand strategy for boosting brand sophistication, sharpening the competitive edge of domestic brands in domestic and international markets, and strengthening exchanges and cooperation with international brands;
- Expanding and improving energy saving processes, reducing energy consumption and effluents and increasing environmental protection in the textile industry in order to meet the various restrictive targets stipulated in the Eleventh Five-Year Plan;
- Strengthening industrial self-discipline and regulation in order to build up the industry in harmony with the environment. This includes introducing an improved service system for quality control, enhanced IPR protection and a system of social responsibility; and
- To maintain the policy of collaboration with the aim of achieving a win–win effect through broad bilateral and multilateral cooperation in the areas of science and technology, branding, trade and investment, exhibitions, training, information, etc., as part of a joint endeavour to sustain and strengthen the new global textile economy.

2.2.1.2 Pakistan

The textile sector holds a lead role in the development of the manufacturing sector in Pakistan. It comprises almost 30% of the manufacturing value added, provides employment to more than 40% of the manufacturing sector labour force, and it is a major foreign exchange earner for the country. Nearly 63% of the total exports of Pakistan comprise textile products. The trade in textiles is directly affected by the phenomenon of globalization that is leading to lower tariff barriers and removal of quantitative trade restrictions. Multi Fibre Arrangement adopted in the early 1970s by the developed countries to protect their domestic textile industry was replaced by the Agreement on Textiles and Clothing in 1994. The ultimate objective of the ATC is to phase-out the quota restrictions on the import of textiles by 2005.

T&C industry is dominated by the textiles sector. Although Pakistan exported $3.6 billion in clothing in 2005, it exported more than double that value in textiles —nearly $8 billion. Pakistan imports little fabric and has a quite comprehensive cotton-based T&C value chain. Textiles and clothing contribute 68% to export earnings, 9% to GDP and 38% to employment (roughly 15 million people) (Centad 2005; Taneja 2007). Pakistan's main markets are the USA (where it has preferential market access, especially post-9/11) followed by the European Union. Pakistan's top exports are dominated by textiles and made-ups: bedlinen (HS630231), toilet and kitchen linen (630,260), cotton yarn (520,512), men's/boys' cotton knitted shirts (610,510), woven fabrics of cotton (520,819), men's and boys' cotton trousers non-knit (620,342) and plain weave cotton fabrics (521,051).

2.2.1.3 Bangladesh

Bangladesh's textile and clothing sector began to grow in the mid-1970s and has grown dramatically in the past 20 years. Its total exports have grown rapidly post-MFA contrary to widespread predictions that quota elimination would harm its clothing exports. By some accounts, Bangladesh's T&C exports nearly doubled from $6.2 billion in 2004 to an estimated $12 billion in the first quarter of 2007. Ready-made garments dominate the structure of output in Bangladesh's T&C industry. Clothing accounts for 80% of Bangladesh's exports, contributing 10% to GDP, 30% to manufacturing output and 17% to total imports (James 2007; World Bank 2005). The sector employs 2 million people, mostly women, directly and another 8 million indirectly.

Bangladesh's main markets are the EU (64% share) and the USA (30% share), together accounting for nearly 95% of the country's clothing exports. Tariff-free access to the European and Canadian markets are important drivers of growth in the sector. Bangladesh has been quite successful in fostering backward linkages into spinning and weaving in its economy, and today, about 25% of the country's woven textile needs and nearly 80% of its knitwear inputs are generated locally. The sector overall used to be split between 80% woven exports and 20% knitwear, but knitwear has grown rapidly in the last five years, at the rate of 33% per year so that today the sectoral composition is nearly 50–50 knitwear and woven, and industry analysts expect knitwear exports to overtake woven clothing exports in 2007–2008. This has important implications for local linkages and multiplier effects from the sector's growth, since knitwear is much more deeply integrated into the domestic textile value chain and the growth of this sub-sector will also ensure much better value retention under EU's General System of Preferences (GSP) schemes. Cotton dominates the regions' fibre base, but there is a mix of blends, impregnated, coated and other man-made fibres through imported inputs. Five product categories dominate Bangladesh's exports to the world market: knit T-shirts (HS610910), men's and boys' cotton shirts knit (620,520) and non-knit (610,510), men's and boys' trousers (620,342) and pullovers of wool (611,300) and man-made fibre (611,010). Bangladesh is one of the biggest exporters of ready-made garments (RMG).

Bangladesh is heavily dependent on the RMG sector for its export earnings. Mostly due to the growth of this particular industry, Bangladesh has been able to maintain trade and macroeconomic balances during the past two decades or so, despite the shrinking significance of foreign assistance in the domestic economy. However, the abolition of the quota regime has exposed Bangladesh to a fierce competition with countries that were constrained by QRs.

The performance of the export sector has been one of the most notable success stories of the Bangladesh economy during the past 20 years. The phenomenal growth of the RMG industry has been the main driver of this significant development. Such growth has generated job opportunities, particularly for women, and created direct and indirect investment opportunities in various backward and forward linkage sectors. The government initiated some positive efforts in enhancing the competitiveness of T&C in order to put the sector on a par with competing countries. As a result, a large investment has been made during the past few years, mainly in spinning. With the increase in investment, the level of productivity has also risen, providing support for local export-oriented RMG units in competing on international markets.

The performance of the public sector is gradually going down in terms of yarn production and total stoppage in fabric production. During recent years, exports of knitwear items have almost overtaken woven garments. Although woven garments, knitwear, home textiles and textile fabrics all achieved persistent growth during the past five years, the growth rate in knitwear has been phenomenal compared with the other categories. This growth pattern has been attributed to the expanding domestic availability of raw materials due to the expansion of the spinning sub-sector as well as an active marketing approach by entrepreneurs, supported by a favourable policy package.

The weak backward linkage of the RMG sector is also recognized as a major constraint for sustaining RMG export growth in Bangladesh. Since prices of apparels are likely to decline considerably and the relatively advanced developing countries with substantial capacity to produce intermediate inputs have been freed to export without restrictions, it will be difficult for Bangladesh to compete and survive in the post-ATC period. A number of empirical studies on Bangladesh predicted that RMG exports could fall between 5 and 20% as a direct consequence of the phasing out of T&C quotas under ATC, which, in turn, could contract GDP by 0.5–2.3%. Predictions were also made that these adverse effects might cause employment to fall by 2–13.1%.

The overwhelming importance of RMG implies that a modest export loss in this sector may be difficult to offset, even by some strong growth in other export items. Against these pessimistic views, there are strong arguments for export diversification in the country, as an effectively diversified export portfolio can ensure undisrupted export earnings for the country in the medium to long run.

Bangladesh follows internationally recognized labelling. In this regard, the Product Labelling Policy, 2006, was adopted by the Government of Bangladesh. Recognized ISO standards are being developed and implemented. To ensure marketing of quality products of standard specification, the registration and prior approval of labels for certain products of T&C have been made compulsory.

2.2.1.4 Cambodia

Cambodia has 2073 garment factories and employs more than 270,000 people. It earns more than $2 billion in exports annually and contributes about $400 million per year to the country's GDP. Cambodian economy is expected to grow 6% this year over 8.5% last year 2006 expected value of foreign direct investment to reach US $3.036 billion.

The RMG industry plays a significant role in the Cambodian economy. The industry has attracted about 30% of the country's FDI and generated various direct and indirect employment opportunities. Cambodia's RMG export performance did not suffer even after the phasing out of T&C quotas under ATC; RMG exports reached US$2.2 billion in 2005 with a growth rate of about 12% over the 2004 figure. The economy also attracted 53 new investment projects in the RMG sector in the first year following the elimination of T&C quotas.

Over the last one decade or so, the RMG industry has been expanding rapidly in Cambodia. The number of RMG firms increased from almost nil in 1995 to about 250 in 2005, and export earnings from this sector also increased dramatically during this period. The RMG industry also has spillover effects on other auxiliary sectors. An estimate, based on the input/output model, suggests that an increase of US$100 in RMG exports would result in an additional demand of US$205 in the whole economy. Though most studies came out with pessimistic conclusions for Cambodia's RMG industry, the situation is not as dramatic as was predicted. Trade figures have revealed that Cambodia's share of apparel products continued to increase in the US market from 2.2% in 2004 to 2.5% in 2005, though in the case of the EU market, it slightly decreased from 0.9% in 2004 to 0.7% in 2005.

The expiry of ATC indirectly affects workers' livelihoods. Perceptions of workers during and post-ATC period are mixed, as these depend on various factors. In the post-ATC era, many firms preferred to give short-term contracts to their workers. In general, the real wages of workers have decreased during the post-ATC period. For instance, though RMG exports increased by over 20% in volume in 2005 (compared to 2004), the workers' earnings decreased by 8.5% over the same period.

On the other hand, the duty-free scenario assumes that the US preferential treatment would result in a unit retail price cut for Cambodian RMG exports. Based on expert opinions, it was assumed that the US consumers would directly gain 75% of the unpaid tariffs, which means that Cambodian exporters could raise their export price by about 25% of the US tariff. As for the EU market, Cambodia is able to derive limited benefits from the EU's EBA initiative due to complex ROO and supply-side constraints that the country faces. As noted above, in 2005, RMG exported to the EU at zero duty accounted for about 67% of RMG exports to this market and almost all made use of the ASEAN accumulation method.

The RMG industry also has a positive impact on human development in Cambodia; it generates employment, improves working conditions and empowers workers, and increases rural household incomes. In 2005, the RMG sector directly employed 270,000 people, and the number of indirect jobs created by the industry could be as high as 242,000, suggesting that one RMG worker has been creating another indirect job. Almost half of the indirect jobs are concentrated in services sectors such as transportation and trade.

2.2.1.5 Laos

The textile and garment industry is of great importance to the Lao economy. Currently, the industry comprises ninety-six factories and employs more than

25,000 workers. In 2003, garment exports, valued at US$115 million, accounted for approximately a third of total exports, second to electricity. Currently, 59 export-oriented RMG firms and 57 sub-contractors are operating in Lao PDR. The National Statistics Centre (NSC) of Lao PDR undertook a Garment Factory Survey in 2006, which covered 44 large- and medium-sized firms. The survey findings suggest that almost half of the RMG firms operating in Lao PDR are foreign-owned, slightly more than 30% are Lao-owned, and the rest are joint ventures. Foreign-owned firms account for almost half of the total employment creation and volume of production and thus play a very important role in the industry.

Laos exports ready-made garments to forty-two countries. As one of the forty-nine least-developed countries, Laos is granted duty-free and quota-free market access to certain developed countries under the generalized system of preferences (GSP). However, the garment industry benefits very little from the GSP due to strict rules of origin, particularly related to local content requirements (Thephavong et al., WTO).

The phasing out of quotas at the end of 2004 has significant implications for smaller least-developed countries including Laos. In the post-ATC era, inefficient ports can raise the cost of doing business in Lao PDR. Being a landlocked country, its foreign trade is highly dependent on transit routes through neighbouring countries to seaports, namely Bangkok, Da Nang and Cua Lo, and transportation cost turns out to be high. One of the biggest challenges for the RMG factories in Lao PDR is the low skill of workers. The current provision of training in vocational and technical schools is not directly suitable or sufficient for industrial garment production.

The Lao textile and clothing industry will face fierce competition in its export markets, particularly the European Union (EU), its main market for garments. Laos is not yet a member of the WTO, and thus its textile and clothing trade is dependent on bilateral trade arrangements with its trading partners; membership of the WTO would give Laos its necessary predictable market access to major markets.

In general, the Lao textile and garment industry is not in the right position to face the coming competition. It is expected that global exports of textiles and garments will expand when the quotas are abolished. Lao garment companies are likely to face a considerable level of competition from larger economies such as China, Vietnam, India and Pakistan, which have the comparative advantage of a large pool of cheap labour and the production of high-quality garments. Mr Bounma said that ‘In recent years, Lao Fashion Garment has received fewer and fewer orders compared with the late 1990s’, expressing his concern about his own factory. This has become a sign of the keen competition in the world textile and garment market.

On the other hand, the government authorities are not very aware of the impact of global competition, which requires short lead times, low prices, good-quality products and good-quality services. The garment factories expect to receive support from government authorities, particularly to provide timely import–export clearance. One area of support for productivity enhancement in the Lao garment industry is improvement in import procedures of raw materials and prompt service for the export of ready-made garments.

2.3 Supply Chain of Indian Textile Industry

In today's world of globalization, many apparel retailers are building strong supply chains to gain advantage over their competitors by offering the best value to their customers. The supply chain management (SCM) has become very critical to manage risk, dynamism, and complexities of global sourcing. A totally integrated supply chain is required for the company to get gain the maximum benefits.

A supply chain is characterized by the flow of goods, services, money and information both within and among business entities including suppliers, manufacturers and customers. It also includes all types of organizations engaged in transportation, warehousing, information processing and materials handling. Sourcing, procurement, production scheduling, manufacturing, order processing, inventory management, warehousing and, finally, customer service are the functions performed throughout the supply chain. The ultimate goal of SCM is to meet customers' demand more efficiently by providing the right product, in the right quantity, at the right location, on the right time and in the right condition.

The aim of SCM is to gain an advantage in terms of customer service and cost over competitors. Traditionally, performance measurement is defined as the process of quantifying the effectiveness and efficiency of action. It plays a critical role in monitoring performance, enhancing motivation and communication and diagnosing problems. Furthermore, performance measurement helps identifying the success and potential of management strategies and facilitating the understanding of the situation (Koprulu and Albayrakoglu 2007).

The Textile and Apparel Supply Chain comprises diverse raw material sectors, ginning facilities, spinning and extrusion processes, processing sector, weaving and knitting factories and garment (and other stitched and non-stitched) manufacturing that supply an extensive distribution channel (see Fig. 2.6). This supply chain is perhaps one of the most diverse in terms of the raw materials used, technologies deployed and products produced.

In the Indian context, the supply chain depicted above supplies about 70% by value of its production to the domestic market. The distribution channel comprises wholesalers, distributors and a large number of small retailers selling garments and textiles. It is only recently that large retail formats are emerging thereby increasing variety as well as the volume on display at a single location. Another feature of the distribution channel is the strong presence of 'agents' who secure and consolidate orders for producers. Exports are traditionally executed through Export Houses or procurement/commissioning offices of large global apparel retailers (Chandra 2007).

Critically analysing the components in the supply chain, cotton remains the most significant raw material for the Indian textile industry. For instance, in 2003–2004,

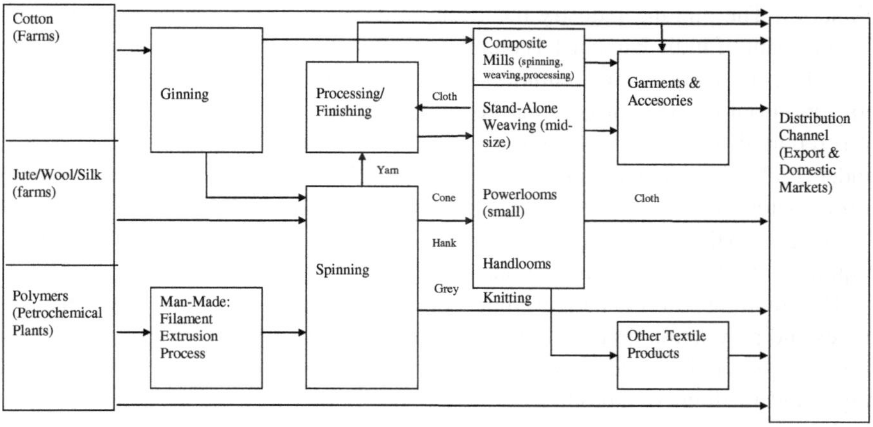

Fig. 2.6 Textile and apparel supply chain. *Source* Chandra (2007)

3009 million kg of cotton was grown over 7.785 million acres. Other fibres produced are silk (15,742 tonnes), jute (10,985,000 bales), wool (50.7 million kg) and man-made fibres (1100.65 million kg). Cotton grows mostly in western and central India, silk in southern India, jute in eastern and wool in northern India. Significant qualities of cotton, silk and wool fibres are also imported by the spinning and knitting sectors.

Indian cotton prices have been lower than international cotton prices of comparable varieties due to ban on imports and control on exports of cotton. In the 1980s, for each of the varieties of cotton, Indian prices were lower than their international counterpart. This gave a cost advantage to Indian textile and garment exporters. Cotton being preferred by the common people, the prices were not allowed to move up (trade control and buffer state operations); synthetic fibre was deliberately priced uncompetitively (it was viewed as a luxury fibre for higher income group) against cotton.

The ginning process is the most important mechanical treatment that cotton undergoes before it is converted into yarns and fabrics. Any damage caused to the quality of fibres during ginning cannot be rectified later in the spinning or subsequent processes. There are over 3500 factories in India dispersed in nine major cotton-growing states. Out of these, over 2600 factories perform only ginning operation and over 2000 factories have installed capacity of as small as 6–12 double roller gins.

Over the years, comparisons have always been made between ginning practices in India and abroad, and the difference observed in quality of ginned lint, particularly in terms of trash content and presence of contaminants. Though the fibre properties of Indian cotton are excellent, it was marred by excessive trash and contamination. Ginneries faced difficulty in addressing these issues due to the seasonal nature of activity, which does not ensure consistent employment of workers. Modernization through technological upgradation was the only solution to ginneries. The ginning industry has been on a modernization spree ever since the Government of India launched Technology Mission on Cotton. It is reported that as on today, as many as 860 ginning and pressing factories have completed modernization out of 1000 projects approved by Technology Mission on Cotton. It is also reported that about 500 ginning and pressing factories are being modernized under Technology Upgradation Fund Scheme. With these developments, ginning infrastructure in the country seems to be well on its way to secure a firm foundation. The cotton textile industry in India can look forward to meet its major raw material requirements through the indigenous supply of clean cotton.

The spinning sector is perhaps most competitive globally in terms of variety, unit prices and production quantity. Though cotton is the fibre of preference, man-made fibre (polyester fibre and polyester filament yarn) is also produced by about 100 large- and medium-size producers.

Spinning is done by 1566 mills and 1170 small and medium-sized enterprises (SME). Mills, chiefly located in North India, deploy 34.24 mn spindles and 0.385 mn rotors, while the SME units produce their yarn on 3.29 mn spindles and 0.119 mn rotors producing 2270 mn kg of cotton yarn, 950 mn kg of blended yarn and about 1106 mn kg of man-made filament yarn every year. Worsted and non-worsted spindles (producing woollen yarn) have also progressively grown to 0.604 and 0.437 mn, respectively. Spinning sector is technology intensive, and productivity is affected by the quality of cotton and the cleaning process used during ginning. During the year 2007–2008, the total number of installed spindles in both spinning and composite mills accounts for 39.07 million apart from 6.21 lakh rotors.

The data reported in Confederation of Indian Textile Industries (CITI) handbook correspond to medium and large-scale units. It may be noted that although there are many marginal and small-scale spinning units, these units are not accounted for in the CITI handbook data as their contribution to value addition and value of output are small. The share of medium and large units in total value added of the sector is 92.8%, whereas their share in value of output is 90.2%. These units employ around 66% of the total labour engaged in the spinning sector. Apart from cotton spun system, wool yarn and wool acrylic blend are produced on worsted spun system. Silk yarn is spun on different kind of spinning system. The installed capacity of woollen yarn is approximately 30 million kilogram and that of silk yarn 0.6 million kilograms. Table 2.11 shows the average capacity utilization of spinning mills. In recent years, the capacity utilization of most of the spinning mills dropped to below 90% due to slowdown in demand and large finished goods inventory.

Processing is another important activity in this chain where more than 80 thousand units are involved in the non-factory sector. Most of these units are OAME type. Large numbers of such units (58.8%) are working without the aid of power. This shows the condition of processing units in India. The total value of output produced by processing units is estimated at 11,494 crores during 2005–06, including both factory sector and non-factory sector units. Table 2.12 shows the value of output of units undertaking processing activity in both factory and

Table 2.11 Average capacity utilization of spinning mills

Year	Capacity utilization (%) (based on prowess data)	Capacity utilization (%) (Textiles Commissioner's Office)
1990–1991	79.9	80
1991–1992	79.4	76
1992–1993	78.7	78
1993–1994	82.9	84
1994–1995	87.1	81
1995–1996	85.6	86
1996–1997	82.2	86
1997–1998	72.7	86
1998–1999	74.2	79
1999–2000	76.3	83
2000–2001	70.0	85
2001–2002	69.8	82
2002–2003	75.8	80
2003–2004	77.2	83
2004–2005	81.4	87
2005–2006	81.6	88
2006–2007	89.9	89
2007–2008	–	90
2008–2009	–	88
2009–2010	–	86
2010–2011	–	90
2011–2012	–	85

Source Derived from Prowess: CMIE data and Ministry of Textiles

Table 2.12 Value of output of units undertaking processing activity in both factory and non-factory sectors

NIC 2004	Industry specification	Non-factory sector	Factory sector	Total
17121	Finishing of cotton and blended cotton textiles	1870	5684	7553
17122	Finishing of silk and blended silk textiles	12	46	58
17123	Finishing of wool and blended wool textiles	17	53	70
17124	Finishing of man-made and blended man-made textiles	82	202	285
17125	Finishing of jute, Mesta and other vegetable textiles fabrics	0	0	0
17126	Activity related to screen printing	62	0	62
17141	Bleaching, dyeing and finishing of cotton cloth and yarn by hand	332	797	1129
17142	Printing of cloth by hand	515	1238	1753
17143	Bleaching, dyeing and finishing of woollen textiles by hand	0	0	0
17144	Bleaching, dyeing, printing and finishing of silk textiles by hand	31	74	105
17145	Bleaching, dyeing, printing and finishing of artificial/synthetic textile fabrics by hand	122	292	414
17149	Finishing of textiles (khadi/handloom)	19	45	64
		3062	8433	11,494

Note The estimates of output are based on several assumptions at aggregate level in the absence of unit-wise ASI data and problem in output data for the NSSO 62nd round on unorganized manufacturing sector. NAS, CSO makes corrections for underreporting of data in both factory and non-factory sectors and publishes aggregate value of output for all NIC classifications. These corrections for NIC17 & 18 are taken into account and values at each NIC are adjusted. In certain cases, it may be leading to certain overestimations/underestimations need to be kept in mind while doing the analysis

Source Derived using NSSO, unorganized manufacturing sector, 62nd round, 2005–2006 and estimates of factory sector for the year 2005–2006 using results from 2000 to 2001 and 2004 to 2005 ASI data and adjusting with value of output for organized sector and unorganized sector from NAS, CSO

non-factory sectors. Based on this, NCAER (2009) projected the value of output for the year 2008–2009 as Rs 16,148 crore.

Weaving, using power looms, one important component in the chain was traditionally done by composite mills that combined it with spinning and processing operations. Over the years, government incentives and demand for low cost, high volume, standard products (especially sarees and grey cloth) moved the production towards power loom factories and away from composite mills (that were essentially full line variety producers). While some like Arvind Mills or Ashima transformed themselves into competitive units, others gradually closed down.

In 2010–2011, there remained 183 composite mills that produced 62,559 million sq. mts of fabrics. Most of these mills are located in Gujarat and Maharashtra. Most of the woven cloth comes from the power looms (chiefly at Surat, Bhiwandi, NCR, Chennai). In 2005, there were 425,792 registered power loom units that produced 26,947 mn sq. mts of cloth and employed about 4,757,383 workers. Weaving sector is predominantly small scale, has on an average 4.5 power looms per unit, suffers from outdated technology and incurs high coordination costs. Knits have been more successful especially in export channels. Strong production clusters like Tiruppur and Ludhiana have led to growth of accessories sector as well, albeit slowly. The hosiery sector, on the other hand, has largely a domestic focus and is growing rapidly.

In the textiles sector, handloom segment enjoys a special status as it provided the highest amount of employment in the non-farm sector before independence. In the post-independence period though its share in both total fabric production and total employment in the textiles sector is declining, it still supports the livelihood of a very large number of people. The decline in the share of handlooms in total production is associated with the rise of the power loom sector. Major difference in the product mix of handloom and power loom is that piece materials for end use such as sarees, bed sheets, table mats, table linen, curtains and dusters are prepared at handlooms, while yardage materials such as long cloth are produced at power looms. But many times, power looms also produce the piece materials for end use. Most of the clusters/states have some specialization in specific products—for example, Nuapatna (Orissa) and Pochampally (Andhra Pradesh) in Ikat Sarees, Karur (Tamil Nadu) and Bijnore (Uttar Pradesh) in home furnishings, Panipat (Haryana) in Khes, Amritsar (Punjab) in woollen furnishings and Chennimalai-Erode (Tamil Nadu) and Nalbari (Assam) in silk sarees. Average size of the handloom units in most of the clusters is generally small or medium except in Kerala where only medium- and large-sized units are usually found due to the existence of cooperatives. The problems faced by export-oriented handloom clusters include stiff non-tariff barriers. The buyers make frequent objections to even use of family child labour, livestock rearing near the location of looms in household unit, on the suspicion that such factors affect quality.

Other problem faced by handloom weavers includes improper implementation of government schemes, with dormant members (or those who no longer owning looms) taking benefits of handloom cooperatives schemes in states like Tamil Nadu and Delhi. If handloom sector is to withstand the competition from power loom sector, there is an urgent need for handloom upgradation. There is also need to increase the varieties of designs and modernize the dying and processing activities and to strengthen the handloom cooperatives and remove the loopholes in government schemes in the states where it is not properly functioning.

A value chain analysis was undertaken recently by NCAER (2009) to assess the various intermediary stages involved, value addition at varying stages and shortcomings in the supply chain for textiles and clothing products. The traders at the wholesale level purchase fabrics/garments through factory agent, directly from power loom and ready-made garments household units, whereas a small wholesaler purchases from large wholesaler and sometimes an agent exists between big wholesaler and small wholesaler. There are no fixed criteria for forecasting demand for fabric/garments. Almost all the traders forecast demand based on trend of the market. Traders generally are not encountering many problems of contract failure, renegotiations after contract, breach of forward contract on the part of buyers/sellers; in rare cases only contracts failed. All the traders in the sample reported that the producers play a major role in determining the price of fabrics/garments, whereas major decisions in determining the quality of fabrics/garments are taken by traders. The study findings indicate the key features of the supply chain as follows:

- About 31% of the supply chain involves 'factory to first intermediate agent, to second intermediate wholesaler, to third intermediate retailer and to final consumer';
- Around 31% of traders operate in the chain involving 'factory to 1st intermediate agent, to 2nd intermediate wholesaler, to 3rd intermediate small wholesaler, to 4th intermediate retailer and to final consumer';
- Close to 8% of traders operate in the chain consisting 'factory to 1st intermediate agent, to 2nd intermediate wholesaler, to 3rd intermediate agent, to 4th intermediate small wholesaler, to 5th intermediate retailer and to final consumer';
- About 8% of traders operate in the chain, 'factory to 1st intermediate agent, to 2nd intermediate retailer and to final consumer';
- Around 15% exist in the chain, 'factory to 1st intermediate wholesaler, to 2nd intermediate retailer and to final consumer';
- Close to 7% of traders exist in the chain, 'factory to 1st intermediate retailer and to final consumer'; and
- All large retailers (especially in malls) follow the chain, 'factory to own retailer (factory outlets) and to final consumer', with no intermediate players.

Lastly, the textile firms need to develop managerial capabilities required to manage large workforce and to develop appropriate supply chain. There is a need in building up a highly skilled workforce which can bring about a change throughout the supply chain and execute the tasks with precision. The upper management and middle management, including merchandiser, should be able to make sound plans, make realistic deadlines and procure right shade and texture of material timely. The designers should be such who can understand international consumers' requirements and skilled and semiskilled workers.

The exporters have to contend with logistical issues too. For example, there could be a six-month gap between samples being sent to the buyer country and the final order being placed. In this time period, the cloth, buttons, etc., could have been exhausted and prices could have spiralled, leading to a need for revision of prices. Thus, a seamless supply chain, control over retail and distribution, meticulous attentions to quality are issues that manufacturers will have to take care of.

Textile supply chains compete on low cost, high quality, accurate delivery and flexibility in variety and volume. Several challenges stand in the way of Indian firms before they can own a larger share of the global market. Competitive strategies developed by sector level firms, their individual and collective initiatives, help in achieving higher market share in global trade. While one has to be ever vigilant of non-tariff barriers in the post-MFA world, the new market will be won on the basis of capabilities across the supply chain. Policy will need to facilitate this building of capabilities at the firm level, and the flexible strategies that firms will need to devise periodically.

Chapter 3
India's Comparative Advantage in Export of Textiles and Apparel Products

Elumalai Kannan

3.1 India's Trade in Textile and Clothing

India's value of exports of textiles and clothing has increased tremendously from $5.2 billion in 1990 to $39.3 billion in 2014 (Table 3.1). However, share of textile and clothing exports in total merchandise exports has declined over time. Export of textile and clothing constituted 29.1% of total exports in 1990 and has declined to 12.6% in 2014. This might be due to increase in the value of exports of other items like gems and jewellery in the Indian export basket. It can also be noticed that textile exports dominate clothing exports during the study period.

Composition of India's textile exports at SITC three-digit levels is presented in Table 3.2. Textile yarn emerged as the topmost commodity, constituting about 25.8% of total textile exports. The declining share of textile yarn was offset by increase in the exports of made-up textile articles, which included carpets, curtains and bed sheets. In fact, the share of made-up textiles increased from 12.7% in 1990 to 25% in 2006. However, surprisingly, exports of made-up textiles registered negative growth rate during the post-ATC period. It is also interesting to observe that growth in export of raw cotton showed growth of 58.3% during the same period. Floor coverings and man-made woven fabrics each constituted about 10% of total textile exports. The share of man-made fabrics has consistently increased over time and has registered growth rate of 12.1% in 1990–2007 and 11% during the post-ATC period.

However, it would be more revealing to look at the composition of exports at further level (SITC four digits) of disaggregation. The export of top twenty textile products is presented in Table 3.3. Cotton yarn constituted the highest share of 15.4% of total textile exports followed by raw cotton excluding linters (14.1%) and curtains (10.9%) during 2007. All the products of man-made woven fabrics

E. Kannan (✉)
Centre for the Study of Regional Development, School of Social Sciences,
Jawaharlal Nehru University, New Delhi, India

K.S.K. Kumar (ed.), *A Study of India's Textile Exports and Environmental Regulations*, https://doi.org/10.1007/978-981-10-6295-7_3

Table 3.1 Share of export of textiles and clothing in total exports in India ($ ‘00 million)

Year	Textiles		Clothing		Textiles and clothing	
	Value	Share (%)	Value	Share (%)	Value	Share (%)
1990	27	15.0	25.3	14.1	52.2	29.1
1991	27	15.0	25.3	14.1	52.1	29.1
1992	30	14.7	31.0	15.0	61.3	29.6
1993	31	14.1	29.7	13.4	61.1	27.5
1994	39	14.8	37.0	14.1	76.1	28.9
1995	44	14.0	41.1	13.0	85.6	27.0
1996	54	16.2	42.2	12.6	96.3	28.8
1997	55	15.8	43.4	12.5	98.5	28.3
1998	46	14.0	47.8	14.4	94.3	28.4
1999	52	14.1	51.5	14.1	103.2	28.1
2000	61	13.5	61.8	13.7	123.0	27.2
2001	54	12.3	54.8	12.4	109.2	24.6
2002	61	11.7	60.4	11.5	121.6	23.2
2003	72	11.4	66.3	10.5	137.9	21.9
2004	72	9.1	66.3	8.3	138.7	17.4
2005	93	9.0	92.1	8.9	184.8	17.9
2006	105	8.4	94.2	7.5	199.7	15.8
2007	116	8.0	99.3	6.8	215.4	14.8
2008	124.0	6.8	109.7	6.0	233.7	12.9
2009	106.2	6.0	120.1	6.8	226.3	12.8
2010	165.8	7.5	112.3	5.1	278.1	12.6
2011	128.4	5.1	146.7	5.8	275.1	10.9
2012	191.1	6.3	138.3	4.5	329.4	10.8
2013	180.9	6.0	168.4	5.6	349.3	11.6
2014	210.4	6.7	182.7	5.9	393.1	12.6

Source UN Comtrade

(653) falling under top twenty products have registered higher growth rates during 1990–2007 and 2005–2007. Among made-up textile articles, bed/table/toilet linen has shown positive growth rates, and its export share has increased from 0.6% in 1990 to 4.2% in 2007.

Composition of India’s clothing exports at SITC three-digit levels is given in Table 3.4. Among clothing exports, women/girl clothing woven (29.9%) constituted the highest share followed by articles of apparel (25.5%) and men’s/boys’ wear woven (15.9%). Though, shares of women/girl clothing woven and men’s/boys’ wear woven have declined over time, but it is offset by increase in the export share of articles of apparel, which has grown at 16.3% in 1990–2007 and 16.7% in 2005–2007. Among clothing items, only exports women/girl clothing woven has shown negative growth in 2005–2007.

Table 3.2 Composition of India's textile exports (%)

SITC Rev.3	Items	1990	1995	2000	2005	2007	Growth (%)	
							1990–2007	2005–2007
263	Cotton	17.3	1.4	0.9	7.2	14.3	5.8	58.3
651	Textile yarn	13.4	30.3	32.7	24.6	25.8	10.3	14.5
658	Made-up textile articles	12.7	14.5	19.0	25.7	20.0	13.0	−1.1
659	Floor coverings, etc.	16.9	14.0	10.6	12.1	10.5	4.3	4.1
653	Man-made woven fabrics	5.8	9.4	8.3	10.6	10.4	12.1	11.0
652	Cotton fabrics, woven	21.2	21.6	18.0	9.3	8.1	2.1	4.7
654	Woven textile fabrics	7.3	4.6	6.1	5.3	4.0	6.6	−2.9
657	Special yarns/fabrics	0.6	1.4	1.5	1.8	1.9	13.1	13.3
656	Tulle/lace/ember, etc.	0.5	0.5	1.3	1.3	1.4	12.9	17.0
655	Knit/crochet fabrics	2.7	1.5	0.6	0.5	0.7	−1.1	26.8

Source UN Comtrade

Clothing exports at further disaggregated level of SITC four digits reveals a broader picture of India's clothing exports. Share of export of India's top twenty clothing exports is presented in Table 3.5. The share of T-shirts/singlets knit/crochet has increased remarkably from 1.9% in 1990 to 16.4% in 2007. The share of women's/girls' blouse woven has declined over time, and it has constituted 10.8% of total clothing exports. The export of men's/boys' shirts woven has also fallen over time. Women's/girls' dresses woven and men's/boys' trouser, etc. woven constituted about 6 and 5.3% of total clothing exports in 2007. Further, exports of babies' garments, women's/girls' under/night wear, men's/boys' underwear, etc. knit/crochet and men's/boys' suits, etc. knit/crochet have consistently increased through 1990–2007.

3.2 India's Textile and Clothing Export Destinations

International market was opened for textile and clothing exports from developing countries after the elimination of quotas in 2005. This has helped Indian exporters to expand their export markets over time. Figure 3.1 depicts the destination for India's textile exports during 1995 and 2013. It is presented for ten largest importing countries and for rest of the markets as others category. India has increased exports of textiles from 14% in 1995 to 18% in 2013 to the USA. However, textiles export to UK, Germany and Bangladesh has declined in 2013. Interestingly, about 11% of total textiles particularly raw cotton was exported to China during 2013. The share of India's exports to others category has stable with

Table 3.3 Share of export of India's top twenty textile products (%)

SITC Rev.3	Items	1990	1995	2000	2005	2007	Growth (%)	
							1990–2007	2005–2007
2631	Raw cotton, excluding linters	16.6	1.1	0.2	6.9	14.1	4.9	60.2
6513	Cotton yarn	10.0	21.7	22.5	15.8	15.4	9.2	10.7
6585	Curtains, etc.	7.1	10.8	11.3	13.9	10.9	11.1	−1.0
6531	Woven synthetic filament yarn fabric	3.0	5.3	4.5	6.2	5.9	13.0	9.2
6518	Yarn of staple fibres, <5 mm	0.8	3.2	3.9	4.0	4.7	16.1	21.7
6584	Bed/table/toilet linen	0.6	0.2	0.9	3.3	4.2	30.1	27.0
6595	Carpets, woven	8.6	6.2	4.9	4.9	3.5	2.7	−5.2
6589	Made-up textile articles	2.0	1.0	5.0	6.4	3.3	19.9	−18.9
6523	Woven cotton finished	5.1	5.7	3.6	2.9	3.0	3.4	13.4
6541	Woven silk fabrics	4.2	2.7	4.5	4.0	2.9	8.5	−5.4
6592	Carpets knotted	7.7	3.6	2.9	3.2	2.8	3.2	4.9
6522	Woven unbleached cotton fabrics	11.9	9.7	6.6	3.1	2.7	−1.2	4.7
6596	Carpets, etc.	0.2	3.6	1.8	2.4	2.3	8.8	10.5
6534	Woven synthetic staple fibres blends	0.2	1.5	1.7	2.3	2.3	22.8	11.1
6516	Synthetic filament yarn, untextured	0.4	1.0	1.5	1.7	2.2	17.5	29.4
6594	Carpets, tufted	0.2	0.5	0.8	1.6	1.9	22.4	19.8
6524	Woven cotton finish	1.7	2.8	3.7	1.6	1.7	7.5	14.7
6532	Woven synthetic staple fibre fabric	0.0	0.3	0.5	0.6	1.4	34.9	67.9
6515	Synthetic filament yarn, textured	0.0	0.7	1.2	0.8	1.4	19.1	46.5
6565	Embroidery, in piece/strip	0.4	0.3	0.9	0.9	1.1	13.1	21.2

Source UN Comtrade

an increase during 2007 over time. It might be due to the expansion of India's exports to small importing countries.

Figure 3.2 shows export destination for India's clothing products. The USA accounted for the largest market for the Indian clothing exports. About 24–30% of textiles is exported to the USA. India has improved marginally its market share in the UK and United Arab Emirates. The export to Germany has declined from 14% in 1995 to 8%. Exports to France, the Netherlands, Italy and Canada also showed a marginal decline over time.

Table 3.4 Composition of India's clothing exports (%)

SITC Rev.3	Items	1990	1995	2000	2005	2007	Growth (%)	
							1990–2007	2005–2007
841	Men's/boys' wear, woven	19.0	22.7	21.9	16.3	15.9	6.7	2.7
842	Women's/girls' clothing woven	39.4	37.6	32.9	36.1	29.9	6.5	−5.5
843	Men's/boys' wear knit/crochet	9.3	11.4	9.8	8.6	8.8	8.0	5.3
844	Women's/girls' wear knit/crochet	6.0	4.9	6.2	8.1	9.5	11.8	12.3
845	Articles of apparel	9.3	8.7	15.7	20.2	25.5	16.3	16.7
846	Clothing accessories	4.5	3.8	5.2	4.8	4.8	9.1	3.6
848	Headgear/non-text clothing	12.6	10.8	8.3	6.0	5.6	2.2	0.4

Source UN Comtrade

3.3 Revealed Comparative Advantage

To measure comparative advantage in export of textile and clothing from India, a widely used measure of revealed comparative advantage (RCA) and its alternative index of Revealed Symmetric Comparative Advantage (RSCA) are used. RCA was developed by Balassa (1965) and is based on observed trade pattern. On the assumption that the commodity pattern of trade reflects relative costs as well as differences in non-price factors, the revealed comparative advantage indicates the relative trade performance of individual countries in particular commodities.

Revealed comparative advantage based on relative export shares was obtained by dividing a country's share in the exports of a given commodity category by its share in the combined exports of manufactured goods of the countries under consideration. The normalized relative export share is expressed as follows:

$$\text{RCA}_{ij} = \left(X_{ij}/X_{wj}\right)/\left(X_{it}/X_{wt}\right)$$

where X refers to exports, i is a country, j is a commodity, t is total exports and w represents world.

The RCA of a commodity greater than one indicates that India is efficient in exporting that commodity in world market. Meanwhile, Dalum et al. (1998) argued that Balassa's revealed export advantage index is asymmetric and the use of which in the econometric analysis results in biased estimates. They suggested that Balassa index should be made symmetrical, because the RCA is not comparable on both sides of unity as it varies from one to infinity if a country has a comparative advantage in product groups and from zero to one for those if the country has

Table 3.5 Share of export of India's top twenty clothing products (%)

SITC Rev.3	Items	1990	1995	2000	2005	2007	Growth (%) 1990–2007	Growth (%) 2005–2007
8454	T-shirts/singlets, knit/crochet	1.9	2.8	8.1	12.8	16.4	24.0	17.4
8427	Women's/girls' blouse, woven	19.5	16.1	12.3	14.2	10.8	4.9	−9.3
8415	Men's/boys' shirts, woven	15.7	18.3	14.2	8.6	7.9	3.3	−0.1
8424	Women's/girls' dresses, woven	5.7	9.1	8.4	4.1	6.0	5.5	25.7
8414	Men's/boys' trouser, woven	1.1	1.9	3.7	4.5	5.3	19.4	12.8
8481	Leather clothing accessories	12.4	10.3	8.1	5.6	5.2	2.0	0.2
8437	Men's/boys' knit/crochet shirt	8.0	9.5	6.4	4.7	4.9	4.4	6.3
8461	Clothing accessories not knit/crochet	4.1	3.4	4.2	4.2	4.2	8.4	3.9
8451	Babies' garments, etc.	0.6	1.3	2.9	2.8	4.0	20.8	22.9
8425	Women's/girls' skirts, woven	4.5	4.9	3.6	8.7	3.8	8.6	−31.1
8447	Women's/girls' blouses, knit/crochet	2.9	1.7	1.8	3.8	3.7	11.7	3.3
8426	Women's/girls' trousers, woven	3.6	2.4	3.3	2.8	3.6	9.2	17.6
8422	Women's/girls' suit/ensemble, woven	3.6	1.4	1.2	2.9	3.3	8.7	11.0
8442	Women's/girls' outerwear, knit/crochet	2.3	1.6	2.5	2.0	2.8	8.8	25.0
8448	Women's/girls' under/night wear, knit/crochet	0.7	1.6	1.7	2.3	2.8	16.6	14.8
8453	Jerseys/pullovers, etc.	4.2	2.9	2.8	2.2	2.6	5.6	12.3
8438	Men's/boys' underwear, knit/crochet	0.6	1.0	1.7	1.9	2.3	18.0	14.4
8432	Men's/boys' suits, knit/crochet	0.3	0.9	1.0	1.3	1.5	16.4	10.0
8428	Women's/girls' under/nightwear, woven	0.7	1.8	2.2	1.4	1.2	10.3	−5.1
8458	Garments, not knit/crochet	0.7	0.8	1.3	1.0	1.1	9.1	7.0

Source UN Comtrade

comparative disadvantage in it. Because of this asymmetric problem, the mean of the index tends to be higher than median, thus resulting in the skewed distribution of the index towards right. This leads to overstating the relative weight of sectors with the value of index greater than one when compared to the sectors with the value of index less than one (Dalum et al. 1998; Laursen 1998). To overcome this problem, Dalum et al. proposed an alternative index called "Revealed Symmetric

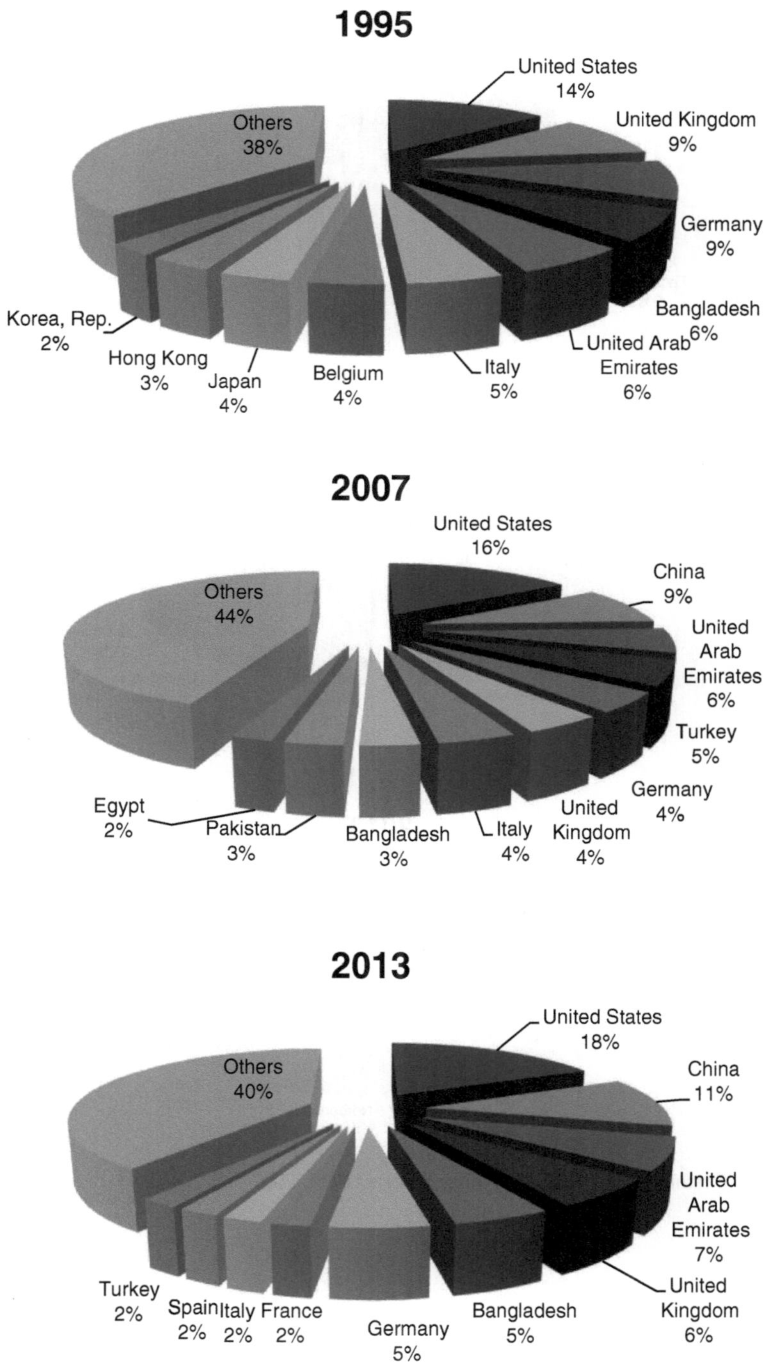

Fig. 3.1 Destination for India's textile exports (1995, 2007 and 2013)

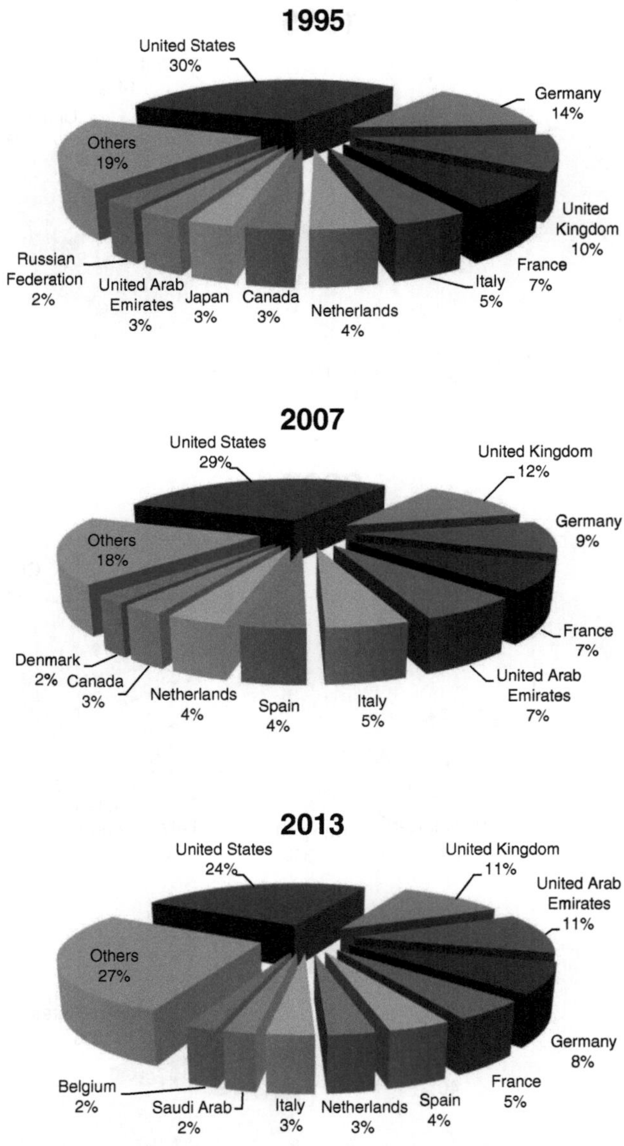

Fig. 3.2 Destination for India's clothing exports (1995, 2007 and 2013)

Comparative Advantage (RSCA)". The value of RSCA ranges from −1 to +1 and avoids the problem of zero values.

$$\mathrm{RSCA}_{ij} = \left(\mathrm{RCA}_{ij} - 1\right) / \left(\mathrm{RCA}_{ij} + 1\right)$$

3.3.1 Revealed Comparative Advantage of India's Textiles Products

Comparative advantage in export of textiles at SITC three-digit levels is presented in Table 3.6. In general, textiles can be grouped into two categories, namely textile fibres (26) and textile yarn/fabric/articles (65). India has comparative advantage in textile yarn, cotton fabrics woven, man-made woven fabrics, woven textile fabric, tulle/lace/embroidery/trimmings, etc., man-made textile articles and floor coverings, etc. consistently during study period. Among these products, comparative advantage seems to be stronger in floor coverings, etc. Within textile fibres (26), except wool/animal hair and worn clothing, etc., India has started to gain comparative advantage in other products during the recent years. A similar pattern of comparative advantage can also be observed through RSCA. The positive value of RSCA for a commodity indicates that India has comparative advantage, while the negative value indicates comparative disadvantage in that product.

However, a closer look at disaggregate level will reveal a broader picture of efficiency of India's export of textiles. Table 3.7 presents revealed comparative advantage in textile fibres at SITC four-digit levels. The value of RCA was greater than one consistently for the products like silkworm cocoons/waste, cotton waste, cotton carded/combed and coconut fibres/wastes during triennium ending 1995–2007. It indicates that India is the efficient competitor for these products in world market. Meanwhile, RCA value has improved for various commodities during the recent years. These products included raw cotton excluding linters, jute/bast fibre raw/retted, sisal, etc. unspun, vegetable textile fibre unspun, synthetic fibre not processed, artificial spinning fibre and waste of man-made fibre. However, India has lost comparative advantage during recent years in certain products like jute, towed/waste, synthetic filament yarn and horse hair etc.

In case of textile yarn/fabrics/articles (Table 3.8), India is the efficient exporter of several products. Among them, revealed comparative advantage was stronger for curtains, carpets knotted, carpets woven and carpets, etc., during the study period. Cotton yarn, woven unbound cotton fabrics, woven silk fabrics, woven jute, etc. fabrics, woven cotton fabrics, woven synthetic blends, man-made textile articles and hand woven rugs have also a relatively strong comparative export advantage. Of total 59 commodities, 28 commodities have RCA value greater than one during the study period. Similar pattern of comparative advantage can be observed through values of RSCA index.

Table 3.6 Comparative advantage in export of textiles (triennium ending)

SITC Rev.3	Items	RCA				RSCA			
		1995	2000	2004	2007	1995	2000	2004	2007
261	Silk	0.73	4.01	1.18	1.91	−0.20	0.60	0.07	0.27
263	Cotton	3.87	0.96	1.41	11.78	0.35	−0.05	−0.05	0.83
264	Jute/bast fibres raw/processed	0.98	10.25	2.63	7.43	−0.04	0.64	0.45	0.34
265	Vegetable textile fibres excluding cotton/jute	0.18	0.73	1.18	2.61	−0.70	−0.15	0.08	0.42
266	Synthetic spinning fibres	0.56	1.02	1.32	1.99	−0.29	−0.02	0.12	0.29
267	Other man-made fibres suitable for spinning	0.23	0.28	0.67	1.18	−0.63	−0.57	−0.20	0.07
268	Wool/animal hair	0.05	0.14	0.39	0.44	−0.91	−0.76	−0.44	−0.39
269	Worn clothing, etc.	0.06	0.23	0.70	0.14	−0.88	−0.66	−0.18	−0.76
651	Textile yarn	5.73	7.91	6.22	5.63	0.70	0.77	0.72	0.70
652	Cotton fabrics, woven	7.13	6.98	4.19	2.89	0.75	0.75	0.61	0.49
653	Man-made woven fabrics	1.70	2.01	3.48	2.99	0.26	0.33	0.55	0.50
654	Other woven textile fabric	2.89	4.45	4.85	3.95	0.48	0.63	0.66	0.59
655	Knit/crochet fabrics	0.95	0.34	0.27	0.29	−0.03	−0.50	−0.57	−0.55
656	Tulles/lace/embroidery/trimming, etc.	1.18	1.98	1.54	1.46	0.07	0.32	0.21	0.19
657	Special yarns/fabrics	0.46	0.62	0.52	0.54	−0.37	−0.24	−0.32	−0.30
658	Made-up textile articles	7.43	8.69	7.74	6.51	0.76	0.79	0.77	0.73
659	Floor coverings, etc.	12.03	10.84	8.58	8.87	0.85	0.83	0.79	0.80

Source UN Comtrade

Table 3.7 Comparative advantage in export of textile fibres (triennium ending)

SITC Rev.3	Items	RCA				RSCA			
		1995	2000	2004	2007	1995	2000	2004	2007
2613	Raw silk (not thrown)	0.36	0.44	0.53	0.80	−0.49	−0.39	−0.32	−0.21
2614	Silk worm cocoons/waste	1.88	16.26	4.58	7.22	0.23	0.88	0.55	0.75
2631	Raw cotton, excluding linters	4.04	0.57	1.23	12.44	0.31	−0.32	−0.09	0.84
2633	Cotton waste	3.24	3.95	1.18	3.25	0.44	0.58	−0.08	0.52
2634	Cotton, carded/combed	–	6.04	6.39	1.81	–	−0.28	0.22	−0.07
2641	Jute/bast fibre, raw/retted	0.44	17.52	2.71	10.49	-0.42	0.63	0.46	0.37
2649	Jute, etc., tow/waste, etc.	5.06	5.81	2.01	0.64	0.47	0.70	0.28	−0.30
2652	True hemp/waste	–	0.06	0.03	0.07	–	−0.89	−0.94	−0.88
2654	Sisal, etc., unspun/tow	0.11	2.25	1.98	1.04	−0.81	0.31	0.31	−0.03
2657	Coconut fibres/wastes	5.44	13.13	10.40	37.76	0.56	0.82	0.82	0.92
2658	Vegetable textile fibres	0.20	0.86	3.70	3.15	−0.69	−0.33	0.44	0.31
2665	Synthetic fibres, not processed	0.48	1.04	1.26	2.30	−0.36	−0.02	0.10	0.34
2666	Synthetic filament tow	0.26	0.40	1.77	0.67	−0.61	−0.43	0.21	−0.23
2667	Synthetic fibres, processed for spinning	1.80	2.01	1.39	0.43	0.19	0.33	0.15	−0.40
2671	Artificial spinning fibres	0.21	0.25	0.60	1.10	−0.66	−0.60	−0.25	0.04
2672	Waste of man-made fibres	0.41	0.61	1.47	2.14	−0.43	−0.33	0.18	0.35
2681	Wool, greasy	0.01	0.07	0.04	0.02	−0.98	−0.87	−0.93	−0.96
2685	Horse hair, etc., uncombed	2.15	1.22	0.42	0.43	0.36	0.06	−0.42	−0.50
2686	Waste wool/animal hair	0.43	0.55	0.87	0.74	−0.42	−0.31	−0.07	−0.17
2687	Combed/carded wool/hair	0.06	0.21	0.91	1.14	−0.89	−0.65	−0.05	0.06
2690	Worn clothing, etc.	0.06	0.23	0.70	0.14	−0.88	−0.66	−0.18	−0.76

Source UN Comtrade

Table 3.8 Comparative advantage in export of textile yarn/fabrics/articles (triennium ending)

SITC Rev.3	Items	RCA				RSCA			
		1995	2000	2004	2007	1995	2000	2004	2007
6511	Wool/animal hair yarn	1.93	1.61	0.97	0.96	0.32	0.19	−0.01	−0.02
6512	Cotton sewing thread	7.54	8.94	18.66	12.75	0.76	0.77	0.90	0.85
6513	Cotton yarn	18.73	23.80	15.78	14.66	0.90	0.92	0.88	0.87
6514	Man-made sewing threads	1.12	0.60	0.58	0.70	0.06	−0.26	−0.27	−0.18
6515	Synthetic filament yarn, textured	1.07	1.69	1.45	2.13	0.02	0.22	0.18	0.35
6516	Synthetic filament yarn, untextured	1.09	1.46	1.64	2.01	0.04	0.18	0.24	0.33
6517	Artificial filament yarn	6.09	6.60	5.92	4.38	0.71	0.73	0.69	0.63
6518	Yarn of staple fibres, <5 mm	2.95	5.07	6.65	5.78	0.47	0.66	0.74	0.70
6519	Yarn-textile fibres	3.05	4.13	3.13	1.68	0.51	0.61	0.51	0.25
6521	Cotton gauze/pile/chenille	1.11	9.79	1.51	0.39	0.05	0.80	−0.04	−0.46
6522	Woven unbleached cotton fabrics	18.40	15.12	10.11	7.29	0.90	0.88	0.82	0.76
6523	Woven cotton, finished, weighing <200 g/m^2	4.98	5.04	3.26	2.91	0.66	0.67	0.53	0.49
6524	Woven cotton, finished weighing >200 g/m^2	3.36	4.69	3.08	1.91	0.54	0.65	0.49	0.31
6525	Woven cotton blend, weighing <200 g/m^2	5.58	5.31	3.35	0.46	0.69	0.68	0.52	−0.38
6526	Woven cotton blend, weighing >200 g/m^2	11.38	3.20	4.17	2.38	0.83	0.52	0.59	0.26
6529	Woven cotton fabrics	2.37	7.18	4.81	5.10	0.10	0.72	0.65	0.66
6531	Woven synthetic filament yarn fabric	2.18	1.99	4.00	3.06	0.37	0.33	0.60	0.51
6532	Woven synthetic staple fibre fabric	0.54	2.11	2.59	4.47	−0.35	0.35	0.44	0.61
6533	Woven synthetic staple fibre cotton fabric	1.77	2.74	2.15	1.28	0.27	0.46	0.36	0.09
6534	Woven synthetic staple fibre blends	2.39	4.33	7.31	7.31	0.39	0.62	0.76	0.76
6535	Woven artificial filament yarn fabric	2.15	1.03	1.73	2.14	0.36	0.01	0.25	0.35
6536	Woven artificial staple fibre fabric	0.23	0.63	1.03	0.53	−0.64	−0.24	0.01	−0.33
6538	Woven artificial staple fibre blend fabric	0.20	0.38	0.54	1.07	−0.67	−0.45	−0.31	0.03
6539	Pile/chenille man-made fabric	0.22	0.31	0.21	0.38	−0.64	−0.54	−0.66	−0.45
6541	Woven silk fabrics	8.09	20.13	21.46	14.71	0.78	0.90	0.91	0.87
6542	Woven animal hair fabrics	0.65	1.03	0.54	0.48	−0.21	0.01	−0.30	−0.35
6543	Woven wool, hair	0.33	0.45	0.44	0.62	−0.52	−0.38	−0.39	−0.24
6544	Woven flax fabrics	0.08	0.16	0.17	0.40	−0.86	−0.73	−0.72	−0.44

(continued)

Table 3.8 (continued)

SITC Rev.3	Items	RCA				RSCA			
		1995	2000	2004	2007	1995	2000	2004	2007
6545	Woven jute, etc. fabrics	44.28	54.83	47.44	46.22	0.96	0.96	0.96	0.96
6546	Woven glass fibre fabric	0.02	0.01	0.02	0.13	−0.96	−0.99	−0.97	−0.77
6549	Woven fabrics	0.42	1.64	1.72	2.25	−0.41	0.20	0.20	0.38
6551	Knit/crotch pile fabric	0.54	0.39	0.77	0.83	−0.30	−0.46	−0.14	−0.10
6552	Knit/crotch fabric	1.04	0.33	0.18	0.21	0.02	−0.52	−0.69	−0.66
6561	Narrow woven fabrics	0.12	0.19	0.28	0.33	−0.78	−0.68	−0.56	−0.50
6562	Textile badges, etc.	0.39	0.53	0.39	0.44	−0.45	−0.31	−0.45	−0.39
6563	Gimped yarn/tassels, etc.	0.56	1.19	1.60	1.34	−0.29	0.06	0.21	0.14
6564	Tulles/nets/laces	1.45	1.30	0.56	0.54	0.18	0.12	−0.29	−0.30
6565	Embroidery, in piece/strip	3.09	7.34	5.07	3.85	0.50	0.76	0.67	0.59
6571	Felt fabric	0.13	0.42	0.38	0.39	−0.76	−0.42	−0.45	−0.43
6572	Non-woven fabrics	0.01	0.01	0.02	0.01	−0.98	−0.98	−0.96	−0.97
6573	Coated/impregnated fabric	0.44	0.32	0.37	0.50	−0.39	−0.52	−0.47	−0.34
6574	Quilted textile products	0.50	0.17	0.87	2.12	−0.39	−0.71	−0.12	0.36
6575	Twine/cords/cables/nets	1.63	3.52	2.31	2.65	0.24	0.55	0.39	0.45
6576	Hat shapes/forms/bodies	1.53	6.26	5.35	4.20	0.21	0.72	0.68	0.61
6577	Industrial wadding/wicks/fabrics	0.33	0.55	0.48	0.35	−0.51	−0.29	−0.35	−0.48
6578	Rubberized thread/cord	0.02	0.11	0.12	0.10	−0.95	−0.81	−0.79	−0.82
6579	Special textile products	1.44	1.64	1.23	0.69	0.18	0.24	0.10	−0.18
6581	Textile sacks/bags	11.25	5.70	5.57	4.35	0.84	0.70	0.69	0.63
6582	Tarpaulins/tents/blinds	0.37	0.95	0.88	0.52	−0.47	−0.03	−0.07	−0.33
6583	Blankets/travelling rugs	3.82	4.12	3.55	2.88	0.58	0.61	0.56	0.47
6584	Bed/table/toilet linen	0.25	0.68	1.67	2.68	−0.60	−0.22	0.24	0.45
6585	Curtains, etc.	37.32	34.81	22.83	18.50	0.95	0.94	0.92	0.90
6589	Made-up textile articles	3.72	10.99	10.98	6.91	0.57	0.83	0.83	0.73
6591	Linoleum, etc.	1.15	1.13	0.86	0.03	−0.01	0.06	−0.23	−0.94
6592	Carpets knotted	19.20	17.29	13.47	20.94	0.90	0.89	0.86	0.91
6593	Hand woven rugs	0.45	5.82	5.77	6.19	−0.45	0.56	0.70	0.70
6594	Carpets, tufted	0.65	2.02	1.92	2.55	−0.22	0.33	0.31	0.43
6595	Carpets, woven	25.27	20.05	18.48	16.23	0.92	0.90	0.90	0.88
6596	Carpets, etc.	26.72	18.74	12.29	13.00	0.93	0.90	0.85	0.86

Source UN Comtrade

3.3.2 *Revealed Comparative Advantage of India's Clothing Products*

Revealed comparative advantage in export of clothing is presented in Table 3.9. The RCA value of all the products was greater than one indicating that India is efficient in exporting its clothing items in the international market. Among clothing items, the comparative advantage appears to be relatively strong in men's/boys' wear knitted/crochet and women's/girls' clothing woven. However, worrying feature of India's garments exports is that comparative advantage in most of these products has started showing declining trend during recent years.

Revealed comparative advantage of clothing products at more disaggregate level, SITC four digits are shown in Table 3.10. Of total 38 items, value of RCA was greater than one consistently for 23 items indicating that India is efficient in exporting these products. However, as noted before, value of RCA is declining for most of the products during recent years. There is an urgent need for focusing policy attention on these products to maintain their competitiveness in world market. India is having relatively strong revealed comparative advantage in the products like women's/girls' blouse woven, women's/girls' dresses woven, women's/girls' suit woven, women's/girls' skirts woven, men's/boys' shirt woven and men's/boys' knit/crochet shirt.

Table 3.9 Comparative advantage in export of clothing (triennium ending)

SITC Rev.3	Items	RCA				RSCA			
		1995	2000	2004	2007	1995	2000	2004	2007
841	Men's/boys' wear, woven	3.71	4.24	3.11	2.74	0.57	0.62	0.51	0.46
842	Women's/girls' clothing, woven	6.23	6.96	4.34	4.42	0.72	0.75	0.62	0.63
843	Men's/boys' wear, knit/crotch	9.03	7.45	7.23	4.43	0.80	0.76	0.75	0.62
844	Women's/girls' wear, knit/crotch	2.59	2.99	2.95	2.57	0.44	0.50	0.49	0.44
845	Articles of apparel	1.25	2.19	2.09	2.06	0.11	0.37	0.35	0.35
846	Clothing accessories	2.78	2.88	2.40	2.30	0.47	0.47	0.41	0.39
848	Headgear/non-textile clothing	5.55	5.22	2.90	2.47	0.69	0.68	0.49	0.42

Source UN Comtrade

Table 3.10 Comparative advantage in export of clothing (triennium ending)

SITC Rev.3	Items	RCA				RSCA			
		1995	2000	2004	2007	1995	2000	2004	2007
8411	Men's/boys' coats, woven	0.40	1.25	1.43	0.71	−0.43	−0.05	0.17	−0.21
8412	Men's/boys' suits, etc., woven	1.28	1.40	1.15	1.40	0.12	0.15	0.07	0.17
8413	Men's/boys' jackets/blazer, woven	1.61	1.83	1.57	1.92	0.23	0.29	0.22	0.32
8414	Men's/boys' trouser, etc., woven	0.75	1.77	1.61	2.00	−0.15	0.28	0.23	0.33
8415	Men's/boys' shirts, woven	11.37	12.94	8.27	6.65	0.84	0.86	0.78	0.74
8416	Men's/boys' under/night wear, woven	3.79	4.54	4.40	2.73	0.58	0.64	0.63	0.44
8421	Women's/girls' coats, woven	0.75	0.87	0.64	0.31	−0.15	−0.07	−0.23	−0.55
8422	Women's/girls' suit/ensemble, woven	2.51	2.79	3.37	8.57	0.43	0.47	0.53	0.79
8423	Women's/girls' jacket, woven	2.09	2.41	1.83	1.54	0.35	0.41	0.29	0.21
8424	Women's/girls' dresses, woven	13.56	19.60	11.23	8.68	0.86	0.90	0.83	0.79
8425	Women's/girls' skirts, woven	9.04	9.32	4.84	7.81	0.80	0.80	0.66	0.76
8426	Women's/girls' trousers, woven	1.97	2.27	1.24	1.20	0.33	0.39	0.10	0.09
8427	Women's/girls' blouse, woven	13.10	15.58	13.07	12.58	0.86	0.88	0.86	0.85
8428	Women's/girls' under/nightwear, woven	5.23	7.99	6.77	5.28	0.68	0.78	0.74	0.68
8431	Men's/boys' coats, knit/crochet	1.29	5.15	14.40	3.68	0.04	0.47	0.84	0.40
8432	Men's/boys' suits, etc., knit/crochet	2.97	2.50	2.55	1.79	0.50	0.42	0.43	0.27
8437	Men's/boys' shirts, knit/crotch	15.32	11.78	11.04	7.26	0.88	0.84	0.83	0.75
8438	Men's/boys' underwear, etc., knit/crotch	3.61	5.96	6.91	5.44	0.57	0.71	0.75	0.69
8441	Women's/girls' coats, etc., knit/crotch	4.24	2.09	3.28	0.33	0.60	0.30	0.47	−0.50
8442	Women's/girls' outerwear, knit/crotch	2.06	2.42	1.93	1.56	0.34	0.40	0.31	0.21
8447	Women's/girls' blouses, knit/crotch	3.63	4.13	4.07	4.77	0.57	0.61	0.60	0.65

(continued)

Table 3.10 (continued)

SITC Rev.3	Items	RCA				RSCA			
		1995	2000	2004	2007	1995	2000	2004	2007
8448	Women's/girls' under/nightwear, knit/crotch	2.40	2.86	3.42	2.70	0.41	0.48	0.54	0.46
8451	Babies' garments, etc.	2.40	4.85	4.61	4.56	0.41	0.65	0.64	0.64
8452	Felt/coated textile clothes	0.80	0.46	0.59	0.37	−0.13	−0.38	−0.28	−0.51
8453	Jerseys/pullovers, etc.	1.11	1.08	0.69	0.62	0.05	0.03	−0.19	−0.24
8454	T-shirts/singlets, knit/crotch	1.82	4.65	5.04	4.70	0.29	0.64	0.66	0.65
8455	Bras/girdles/corsets, etc.	0.05	0.11	0.20	0.21	−0.90	−0.81	−0.68	−0.66
8456	Swimwear	0.53	0.40	0.30	0.47	−0.31	−0.43	−0.54	−0.38
8458	Garments, not knit/crotch	1.27	2.34	1.10	1.19	0.12	0.40	0.04	0.09
8459	Apparel, knit/crochet	0.89	0.91	1.09	1.47	−0.06	−0.07	0.02	0.18
8461	Clothing accessories, not knit/crotch	5.61	5.85	5.19	5.89	0.69	0.69	0.68	0.71
8462	Panty hose/hosiery, knit/crotch	0.35	0.69	0.63	0.41	−0.49	−0.19	−0.24	−0.41
8469	Made-up/part cloth accessories	0.96	0.97	0.95	0.61	−0.04	−0.07	−0.04	−0.24
8481	Leather clothing accessories	10.99	11.60	6.22	5.97	0.83	0.84	0.72	0.71
8482	Plastic/rubber clothing accessories	1.19	0.69	0.68	0.53	0.09	−0.19	−0.19	−0.31
8483	Natural/artificial fur apparel/accessories	–	0.01	0.03	0.00	–	−0.98	−0.94	−0.99
8484	Headgear/fittings	0.19	0.12	0.13	0.20	−0.68	−0.79	−0.77	−0.67

Source UN Comtrade

Chapter 4
Global Environmental Requirements—Textile Industry

Zareena Begum and K.S. Kavi Kumar

The textile industry affects the environment in various ways. Some environmental aspects that are generally applicable to textile industry include: energy consumption using fossil fuels directly or indirectly through power (which is generated by fossil fuels), contributing to the green-house gas (GHG) emissions; usage of fossil fuels like petroleum and coal for producing some synthetic fibers and auxiliary chemicals, usage of water that could have been otherwise used for drinking, etc; displacement of agricultural and forest lands; methyl bromide, which is used for cotton growing, introduces most of the bromine content to stratosphere, depleting ozone layer; noise pollution; chemical hazards etc.

Some ways in which textiles affect the environment uniquely are: wet treatments like desizing and scouring using oxygen-depleting substances reduce the cleanliness of the water; adsorbable organic halides (AOX) emissions caused by less biodegradable organic halogenated compounds result from bleaching processes; high chemical oxygen demand (COD) arising from cotton desizing; strong alkaline effluent from mercerization; dyeing process produces effluent with high COD, metals, toxic substances, salts, etc., originating from the dyes and dispersing agents. Such effluent is released to water sources such as river, resulting in pollution (Schönberger and Schäfer 2003).

Therefore, the main environmental concern in the textile industry is wastewater, both in terms of its volume and the pollutants it carries, because the textile industry largely employs wet processes to treat textile goods. Some emissions stem from substances that are already present on the raw materials before they reach the processing stage, including pesticides, impurities, knitting oils and preparation agents. Removing these substances produces a very high chemical oxygen demand (COD) as well as various non-biodegradable and to some extent hazardous substances (Kahlenborn et al. 2009).

Z. Begum · K.S. Kavi Kumar (✉)
Madras School of Economics, Chennai, India
e-mail: kavikumar@gmail.com

K.S.K. Kumar (ed.), *A Study of India's Textile Exports and Environmental Regulations*, https://doi.org/10.1007/978-981-10-6295-7_4

Figure 4.1 provides an overview of the textile processing stages and the various environmental concerns that emerge at each stage. Annexure I provides an overview of the environmental concerns for various stages of textile processing. Generally speaking, harmful substances in textiles and clothing products include the following categories:

- Formaldehyde, fluorescent bleacher, and softener (may cause allergies)
- Residues of pesticides, antiseptics, and mold inhibitors in cotton and in wool fiber, such as pentachlorophenol (e.g., PCP)
- Residues of heavy metals
- Residues of azo monomers, formaldehyde, and halide carrier in chemical fiber
- Residues of pesticide and fertilizer used in cotton farming

4.1 Textile Industry and Environment—Global Challenges

Since the 1990s, many countries have adopted environmental standards and requirements restricting the use of harmful chemicals in the production of textiles and clothing. Some of these standards and requirements are imposed by laws and regulations. The best known is the *Second Amendments to the Consumer Protection*

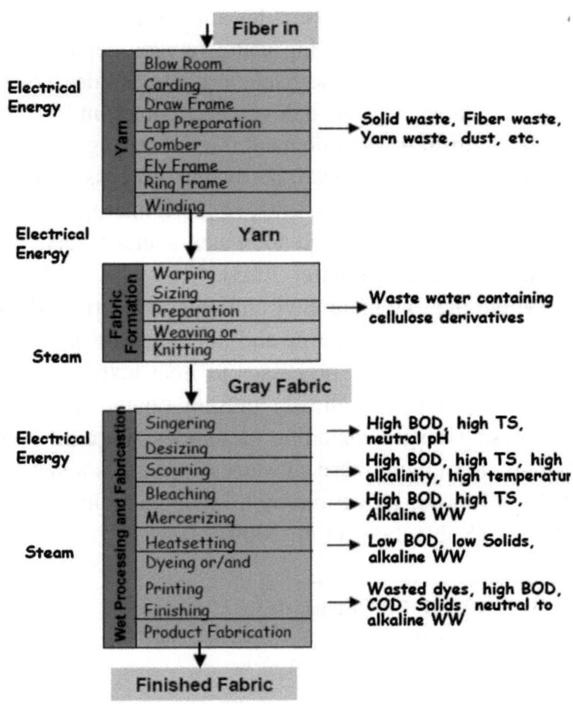

Fig. 4.1 Environmental pollution—stages of textile processing (Color figure online)

Act enacted by the German government in 1994 prohibiting the use of azo dyes. In 1996, the Netherlands also enacted a law prohibiting the use of certain azo dyes. The contents of this legislation are similar to the list of banned substances in the German law. In this context, Germany basically leads the European Union.

In addition to mandatory environmental standards and requirements for textiles, there are some eco-labeling schemes imposing environmental requirements for textile products on a voluntary basis. The most well-known programs include Milieukeur and Eko of the Netherlands, and Oeko-Tex Standard 100 and Toxproof of Germany. Generally speaking, the German Act of 1994 forbidding azo dyes and some eco-labeling standards for textiles such as Oeko-Tex Standards 100 are the ones that have the most trade implications.[1] They have had both positive and negative impacts on the world textile trade, imposing a great challenge for textile exports of India as well as other developing countries.

4.1.1 Global Environmental Requirements

Many federal countries, like the USA, Canada, and Australia, have national environmental legislation, which, like those in Europe, establishes the limit values to comply. Many countries, like Thailand, have followed the American system. Others have followed the European model, like Turkey or Morocco. In some countries, for example India, Pakistan, and Malaysia, the emission limits are recommended, but not mandatory, limit values.

While limits exist for a large number of parameters, the discussion here focuses on the six most important parameters of the textile industry (Green Textiles and Apparel 2008; Hessel et al. 2007). These parameters are: biochemical oxygen demand of 5 days (BOD_5), chemical oxygen demand (COD), suspended solids (SS), salinity (chloride or sulfate), color, and detergents.

4.1.1.1 Color

In some countries like France, Austria, and Italy, there are limit values for the effluent coloration. However, these countries use different units, which make comparison difficult. The oldest unit is the Hazen, in use since the beginning of the

[1]The original intent of the German law is to protect consumer health rather than protecting trade (so-called green protectionism). From a positive perspective, the German law has to some degree also promoted environmental protection in the textile industry in India. But it has also brought about some obstacles to India's textile trade. Before the law was enacted and during its implementation, Germany did not fully consider providing necessary and relevant information, technical assistance as well as any special treatment to developing countries. To a large extent, these are the factors that have brought about some obstacles to textile exports from developing countries including India.

twentieth century. In France, the current unit is mg L^{-1} Pt–Co units. The coloration values are determined by a comparative analysis with model solutions prepared according to perfectly defined procedures. In France, a sample of the colored effluent is diluted by a factor 30; if there is no visible coloration after dilution, the effluent is said to be complying with the norm.

4.1.1.2 BOD

The Australian limit value for BOD_5 is outstanding—it shows a far higher tolerance for discharge into municipal wastewater treatment plants (4000 mg L^{-1}) than in other countries. For the other countries for which numerical values were obtained (Hong Kong, France, and other European countries), it can be seen that the first dyeing baths are not accepted by municipal wastewater treatment plants due to their high organic load. This explains why dye manufacturers mix their different baths before sending the mixture to municipal wastewater treatment plants. As for discharge into the environment, the limits are in most cases lower than 40 mg L^{-1}, which indicates that protecting the environment from biodegradable compounds has become a matter of general concern.

4.1.1.3 COD

In France, the same can be concluded about the efficiency of treatment plants concerning COD. Four European countries and Hong Kong impose high limit values for discharge into municipal wastewater treatment plants. All the cotton ennoblement baths can, thus, be directly discharged. A great many countries authorize emissions with COD limit values as high as 600 mg L^{-1}.This means that the different dyeing baths must be mixed before being sent to treatment plants. Regarding discharge into the environment, the COD limit value is about 200 mg L^{-1} in all countries except Chile, Czechoslovakia, and Thailand, which have high limits.

4.1.1.4 Suspended Solids

For discharge into municipal wastewater treatment plants, only Thailand imposes a high suspended solid limit value. Three other countries have relatively high limits, South Africa, Australia, and Portugal. Most of the other countries have limit values about 500 mg L^{-1}. Regarding discharge into the environment, all these countries have relatively low limits, around 50 mg L^{-1}.

4.1.1.5 Salinity

Dyeing effluents contain two types of salt: sodium chloride and sodium sulfate. In many countries, there is no NaCl emission limit for discharge into a municipal wastewater treatment plant (Japan, Austria) or into the environment (Morocco) or whatever the destination of the effluent (Austria, India, France, Mexico, and Argentina). However, countries that have normalized discharge to treatment plants have set their limits between 0.5 and 2000 mg L^{-1}. Discharge location seems to have little influence on limit values, which are of the same magnitude whether the effluents are discharged into municipal wastewater treatment plants or into the environment.

4.1.1.6 Detergents, Oil, and Grease

There is no direct relation between the amount of detergents and the amount of oil and grease in effluents. Nevertheless, a correlation between total oil and grease and fatty alcohol-based detergents has been established in Canada: the "total oil and grease" parameter seems to reflect the amount of fatty acid- and fatty alcohol-based detergents. Some countries impose a limit for detergents (Portugal, Argentina), for oil and grease (Belgium, Switzerland), and for both parameters (China, Indonesia). On average, the limit values for oil and grease are lower than 50 mg L^{-1}. The limit values for detergents are often the same whatever the discharge location, lower than 10 mg L^{-1}.

Table 4.1 provides general standards for various effluents from the textile industry.

4.2 Consumers' Environmental Demand

Consumers' awareness of environmentally friendly products has increased in the past few years, as more products are labeled with "green" terminology. Consumers are today more sensitive to the protection of the environment. Four out of five European consumers would like to buy more environmentally friendly products, provided they are properly certified by an independent organization. For instance, in a survey conducted twice in 2006 in Europe, one-third of consumers said they were more aware of organic apparel and home textiles "today" than "a year ago." However, the choice to actively seek out environmentally friendly clothing remains restricted to a small niche group of consumers. When asked how much effort they put into finding environmentally friendly clothing, only 5% of consumers said they put a lot of effort into finding such clothing, statistically the same share as in an earlier survey the same year. Broadly, consumers are concerned about chemicals from non-organic clothing and bedding affecting their health and the world. Retailers are taking the eco-movement seriously, too.

Table 4.1 Environmental standards—textiles industry

Parameter	Maximum value [if not specified, units are milligrams per liter (mg L^{-1})]
pH	6–9
BOD_5	50
COD	250
AOX	8
Total suspended solids	50
Oil and grease	10
Pesticides (each)	0.05
Chromium (total)	0.5
Cobalt	0.5
Copper	0.5
Nickel	0.5
Zinc	2
Phenol	0.5
Sulfide	1
Temperature increase	<3 °C
Coliform	400 most probable number/100 mL

(a) The effluent should result in a temperature increase of no more than 3 °C at the edge of the zone where initial mixing and dilution take place. Where the zone is not defined, use 100 m from the point of discharge; (b) the liquid effluent should not be colored; (c) effluent requirements are for direct discharge to surface waters

Environmental issues are now becoming a part of the development in production field and services, and an important aspect of international cooperation. Environmental requirements such as charges and taxes for environmental purposes, requirements related to products, including standards and technical regulations, eco-labeling, packaging and recycling requirements used for the achievements of global as well as national environmental objectives have natural impact on market access and competitiveness of products. While not exclusively a developed-country phenomenon, consumers in OECD countries increasingly want the goods and services they purchase be protected by environmental requirements. Governments have reacted by developing regulations and standards, and non-governmental organizations (NGOs) are taking on a new role in the development of standards and codes of conduct. At the same time, a large number of companies have begun imposing strict requirements on their suppliers. Companies that do not understand their market conditions and trends risk going out of business. The trend of environment requirements is an increasingly important market reality and must not be seen simply through the eyes of protectionism. Because trade with developed countries makes up an ever-increasing share of the gross domestic product (GDP) of many developing countries, environmental requirement can increase the vulnerability of developing countries economy to market conditions beyond their control and capacity to address. Particularly as tariff barriers and quantitative restrictions become dismantled in multilateral and bilateral trade liberalization agreements, there is concern that product and related process requirements have the potential to be misused by countries to create technical barriers to trade. This has led to concerns that some environment requirements are designed not so much to protect the environment or health, as to protect domestic trade interests in OECD countries. Experience has demonstrated that trade interests can be significantly affected by the establishment of environmental requirement. As such requirements in developed countries are mushrooming—increasing in both stringency and complexity. Environmental requirements are also becoming more stringent as a result of increased knowledge of the risk and harm to health and the environment, in particular of certain chemicals. For example, threshold limits for certain substances may be set so low (e.g., some maximum residue levels are already expressed in parts per billion) that they are no longer detectable except with the latest equipment, which may not be available or affordable in developing countries. Standards and regulations concerning maximum residue levels (MRLs) for pesticides and other chemicals are thus an issue of concern to developing countries, which, even if they wanted to comply, may not have access to the equipment needed to monitor and demonstrate compliance. In some cases, previously accepted substances are being banned outright, such as mercury regulations in the USA, which have also influenced regulations in Canada. For Guatemala and Honduras, difficulties in complying with their obligations under the Montreal protocol with regard to methyl bromide have affected their melon exports. These countries have recently obtained funding support from the multilateral fund of the Montreal protocol to overcome this problem. Not only are ERHRs becoming more stringent, they are also becoming more complex. Recent examples of this trend are the draft chemical safety regulation in the European Union (EU) concerning registration, evaluation and authorization of chemicals (REACH), the draft EU regulation on eco-design for energy-using products (EUPs), and mandatory requirements on recycling and phasing out of hazardous substances for electrical and electronic equipment in the EU, Japan, and Switzerland. Whereas in the past, most standards and regulations focused on specific sectors, recent legislative projects, such as the draft REACH and EUP Directives, or the recycling-oriented policy framework in Japan, have a much broader, cross-sectoral impact that is more complicated to assess and more difficult to address. This complicates the planning and implementation of adjustment measures, especially for developing countries. The often sophisticated technical issues are beyond the ability of many individual companies to address and require sectoral cooperation and government action. In sectors dominated by small and medium-sized enterprises (SMEs), this problem is even more acute.

4.3 Global Environmental Standards for Textile Products

4.3.1 The ISO 14000

The ISO 14000 family addresses various aspects of environmental management. The very first two standards, ISO 14001:2004 and ISO 14004:2004, deal with environmental management systems (EMS). ISO 14001:2004 provides the requirements for an EMS, and ISO 14004:2004 gives general EMS guidelines. An EMS meeting the requirements of ISO 14001:2004 is a management tool enabling an organization of any size or type:

- to identify and control the environmental impact of its activities, products or services,
- to improve its environmental performance continually,
- to implement a systematic approach to setting environmental objectives and targets, to achieve these and to demonstrate that they have been achieved.

ISO 14001:2004 does not specify levels of environmental performance. If it specifies levels of environmental performance, they would have to be specific to each business activity and this would require a specific EMS standard for each business. However, that is the not the intention of ISO 14000 standards.

4.3.2 Eco-Labeling

Eco-labeling guarantees certain ecological criteria for all sorts of textile items and their manufacturing processes. It identifies whether:

- Products are environmentally safe
- Manufactured by eco-friendly material, and
- Avoids harmful chemicals
  Oekotex 100 is one of its classified standards.

4.3.3 Bluesign®

The bluesign® standard starts from the ground up. It's not about testing finished products. Instead, before production begins components and processes are selected to ensure they meet the specified criteria. This is the only way to guarantee maximum implementation of resource productivity and EHS—that's environment, health and safety—in the most efficient and cost-effective way for everyone involved.

The bluesign® standard is practice-oriented. Instead of working with bans and restrictions, the bluesign® standard provides solutions for EHS issues at all levels, from raw material and chemical components suppliers to manufacturers and retailers. The bluesign® standard is widely recognized within the complete textile production chain. To assure efficient and economical solutions, the bluesign® standard includes all levels of the manufacturing chain. It is recognized by leading chemical companies, numerous textile manufacturers as well as well-known retailer and brand companies.

4.3.4 Made in Green®

Made in green is a special symbol for all those who provide or who are seeking textile products manufactured with the guarantee that they are free from substances harmful to health. This certifies that the product, throughout its traceability chain, has been manufactured in factories which respect the environment and the universal rights of workers. The object, therefore is, free from harmful substances, respect for the environment and respect for human rights.

4.3.5 Impact of REACH

Other initiatives include registration, evaluation and authorization and restriction of chemicals (REACH) legislation which aims to encourage safe and eco-friendly chemical production. In the USA, the Toxic Substances Control Act (TCSA) enables the US Environmental Protection Agency (EPA) to track industrial chemicals produced in or imported into the country. Some man-made fibers, such as Lenzing's lyocell fiber Tencel, have a minimal impact on the environment. Also, organic cotton production is growing rapidly but still accounts for only a small fraction of global cotton output. Nonetheless, organic cotton is being adopted by high profile companies such as C&A, Coop, Nike, Wal-Mart, and Woolworths. And a growing number of brand and manufacturing companies are pursuing environmentally friendly strategies. Such companies include American Apparel, Gap, Interface, Patagonia, and Wal-Mart in the USA as well as Rohner Textil in Switzerland, and a small knitwear company in India, MaHan, which was founded by an ex-teacher from the Netherlands (see Nieminen et al. 2007 for more details).

4.3.6 Textile/Clothing Eco-Labeling Schemes

Environmental labels are attached to a variety of products to attract the attention of consumers about the environmentally positive features of the products. Generally these labels are voluntary and mostly used for the promotion of the products on the basis of their environmentally friendly characteristics. In the case of textiles and clothing, there are currently no eco-labels, the use of which has been enforced by mandatory rules.

Eco-labels are normally issued either by government supported or private enterprises once it has been proved that the product of the applicant has met the criteria set by them for the label. Eco-label generally represents a holistic judgment, giving an overall assessment of a product's environmental quality relative to other products in the same category. In other words it is a claim which indicates the environmental aspects of a product or service. Environmental labels operate as informative and voluntary market instruments. Environmental labeling programmes are becoming popular world over. At least, 15 countries including India have launched the eco-labeling schemes that are sponsored either by the governments or by the voluntary organizations that receive technical and financial support from their government.

4.3.7 Types of Eco-Labels

Independent or Private Eco-labels
Institution Related—Eco-Tex 100, Eco-Tex, 1000, eco-tex®, AKN Trademark
Producer's association—AKN members, Company eco-labels (e.g., Steilmann, Otto, Versnad, Hess Natur, Green Cotton)
National and International Labels
Multinational: EU-label, Nordic Swan
National: Green Mark (China-Taiwan Province), Environmental Eco-Mark (Japan), Eco-Mark (India), EKO-Seal (Netherlands), etc

Table 4.2 provides an overview of various eco-labeling schemes followed by different countries for textile products.

4.4 Comparison of India with Her Competitors on Pollution Abatement

Most countries in the world have comprehensive environmental regulations. China has been increasing its environmental standards in the recent years, particularly from late 1990s, although it has had discharge standards pertinent to textile processing industry since late 1980s.[2] Though China's overall surface water quality is poor even in 2011, it has reduced COD discharge by 2.04% compared to the previous year, by closing firms with outdated technologies, improving supervision systems and developing ETPs.[3]

[2]http://english.mep.gov.cn.

[3]http://english.mep.gov.cn/standards_reports/soe/soe2011/201307/t20130715_255509.htm.

Table 4.2 Eco-labeling schemes of different countries for textile products

Country	Organization	Name of eco-label	Product categories
Republic of China-Taiwan	EPA	Green mark	Cloth diapers, non-bleached towels
Thailand	Thailand environment institute	Thai green level	Products made from cloth: hat, bag, shirts, trousers, cloth accessories, home and household textile fabrics
Korea	Korean ministry of environment	KELA	Washable products in babies, men and ladies clothing and constant skin-contacting products
Japan	Japanese environmental association	Eco-mark	Cloth diapers for infant(24 products – 9 companies)
India	Government of India	Eco-mark	Cotton, wool, man-made fiber and blends of jute and jute products, silk and silk products
Australia	New Zealand government and international accreditation new Zealand manages it on behalf of the ministers for the environment	New Zealand mental choice	Wool pile carpets Wool-rich pile carpets
European union		Eco-label flower scheme	Bed mattresses (4 companies) Textile products (37 companies)
Nordic countries (Norway, Sweden, Finland Denmark, and Iceland)	Nordic council of ministers (the ministers of consumer affair	Nordic swan	Textile Washable diapers
Austria	Government of Austria	Austrian eco-label	Textile Floor coverings
Croatia	Ministry of environmental protection & environmental planning	Environmental label	Linen towel on the rail
The Netherlands	Stitching Milieukeur (the eco-label foundation)	Milieukeur	Footwear Hand dryers (cotton)
Sweden	(SSNC) Swedish for nature conservation	BRA MILJOVAL (good environmental choice)	Fiber production textile manufacture

Bangladesh had drafted the East Pakistan Water Pollution Control Ordinance even before it came into existence in 1970,[4] imposing penalties on polluters. This was repealed by more stringent standards in 1977 and then in 1995. Most of the standards laid for large textile processing plants (with an investment of more than 30 million Taka) are similar to Indian standards.[5] However, most of the Bangladeshi textile processing units are small and CETPs are yet to be set up for them.

While the Pakistani environmental policy does highlight aspects such as clean production and industrial wastewater treatment plants,[6] millions of gallons of untreated wastewater is released to various water resources every day owing lack of enforcement.[7] Thai industrial wastewater discharge standards are well-defined, and they are comparable to Indian standards.[8] In short, it may be safe to conclude that environmental standards and pollution abatement are pretty similar for India and her competitors, although there is no concrete evidence for this given the variations in the quality of data and reporting across these countries.

---

[4]http://www.moef.gov.bd/html/laws/env_law/273-276.pdf.

[5]Schedule 12, Rule 13 of The Environment Conservation Rules, 1997, available online at http://www.moef.gov.bd/html/laws/env_law/178-189.pdf.

[6]National Environmental Policy 2005, available online at http://www.environment.gov.pk/nep/policy.pdf.

[7]Report of Sub-Group on Pollution Control, 2009, available online at http://www.environment.gov.pk/NEP/Sub%20Working%20Group%20on%20Environment%5B1%5D.pdf.

[8]http://www.pcd.go.th/info_serv/en_reg_std_water04.html#s1.

Chapter 5
Non-tariff Barriers in Textiles: Incidence and Perceptions

K.S. Kavi Kumar, Zareena Begum and Sukanya Das

5.1 Introduction

Baldwin (1970) in his seminal work defines "non-tariff distortion as any measure (public or private) that causes internationally traded goods and services, or resources devoted to the production of these goods and services, to be allocated in such a way as to reduce potential real world income". A more commonly understood phrase is non-tariff barriers (NTBs). The NTBs have the following stylized characteristics, namely reduction in quantity of imports, increase in the price of imports, change in elasticity of demand for imports and variability and uncertainty in their implementation.

UNCTAD's TRAINS (Trade Analysis and Information System) classification defines over 100 different types of non-tariff measures (NTMs), and a much smaller subset called "hard core measures" that includes quantity control measures excluding tariff quotas and enterprise specific restrictions; finance measures excluding regulations concerning terms of payment; and price control measures. However, this classification excludes many internal regulatory measures that can also discriminate against imports such as production subsidies, tax concessions and discriminatory government procurement. Yet another problem with this classification is that it does not distinguish between NTMs that are GATT consistent and not GATT consistent.

There is also the WTO inventory of NTMs based on notifications collected from national sources, which in the view of notifying contracting parties constituted non-tariff measures. This inventory includes licences, quotas, prohibition, voluntary

K.S. Kavi Kumar (✉) · Z. Begum
Madras School of Economics, Chennai, India
e-mail: kavikumar@gmail.com

S. Das
Department of Policy Studies, TERI University, New Delhi, India

K.S.K. Kumar (ed.), *A Study of India's Textile Exports and Environmental Regulations*, https://doi.org/10.1007/978-981-10-6295-7_5

export restraints, plus information related to custom surcharges, minimum import prices, additional taxes and charges and approval process for imports and exports.

Thus, there is no single internationally agreed list of NTMs. In general, NTMs cover all measures affecting trade, other than tariffs, and hence, any list of NTMs will be very long and is probably continuously growing as governments invent new and new measures. Being non-transparent, NTMs are difficult to identify and analyse. Since NTMs cover all measures affecting trade other than tariffs, what then are NTBs. Are the two terms synonymous? In the literature, both the terms are used interchangeably, and the distinction is quite vague. The rationale for using the term "measure" instead of "barrier" is sometimes held on the ground that in some cases, policies that stimulate the volume of trade rather than retard trade such as export subsidies cannot be held as a barrier. A barrier means prevention of something—in this case trade. Exports subsidies do not prevent trade, and hence cannot be a barrier. This interpretation will keep many internal regulatory measures out of the NTB bundle. Agricultural production subsidies, for instance, will be out of this NTB bundle. Global agriculture is riddled with national subsidies to farmers that perpetuates a widely criticised disarray in agricultural production and generates substantial trade conflicts—the large agricultural production surpluses in rich countries maintained by a heavily subsidized agriculture lowers the export opportunities of developing countries such as India. Though the GATT—Uruguay Round of negotiations began to address agricultural distortions with agreed disciplines on domestic agricultural support measures, only modest progress is achieved in reducing support and protection levels. Several studies have analysed the impact of these subsidies on developing countries like India. Notwithstanding these differences, the present discussion uses the terms non-tariff measures and non-tariff barriers interchangeably.

The Non-Tariff Barriers as defined by the GATT allows an importing country to introduce measures, which are necessary to protect human, animal or plant life or health. It may be noted that the WTO agreement on technical barriers to trade also allows for the imposition of technical requirements on products by an importing country. NTBs are typically associated with:

Environmental issues—one allowance to regulate imports is the concern that such product will have a detrimental affect on the environment of the importing country. As there is no international standard on what qualifies as harmful, countries are free to make up their own standards such as certain AZO-free fabrics, nickel-free buttons or zippers. Exporters have been responsible for abiding by these requirements and as such have had to assume the cost. There are apprehensions that several small-scale exporters may not be in a position to bear such costs and hence become less competitive.

Social issues—major concerns being focused on child labour, forced labour, health and safety, disciplinary practices, working hours and remuneration. These are currently being addressed in such voluntary standards/certification schemes as SA 8000, Worldwide Responsible Apparel Production (WRAP) certification scheme, and Compliance and Supply Chain Management (CSM) system.

Anti-dumping Actions—dumping happens when a company sells a product in a foreign country at a price lower than the one in its own home market. To prove dumping a country needs to establish three things: (1) Dumping test: that imported goods are being sold at "below the normal price"; (2) Injury test: that a domestic firm is being injured by these exports; and (3) Causality test: that dumping is causing injury.

Safeguard measures—while both safeguard and anti-dumping measures are aimed at import surges, safeguard measures act in a blanket non-discriminatory manner, whereas anti-dumping measure is against a specific company in the exporting country. When a safeguard measure is applied, the country applying the measure shall endeavour to maintain a substantially equivalent level of concession through mutual agreement with the country affected. As opposed to anti-dumping actions, no compensation is required.

5.1.1 Characteristics of Non-tariff Barriers

Compared with tariffs and quotas, NTBs have several advantages (viewed from the country imposing such barriers). With the development of the world economy and technology, NTBs tend to be more varied and unpredictable with the same result of tariffs and quotas. NTBs are more flexible and pertinent: while tariff barrier settings must be agreed to by legislation, usually over a drawn-out period of time, NTBs can be carried out by an administrative process very quickly, and it is much more convenient in urgent cases where the importing country needs to take a quick action on one importing item from one certain country. For example, Tara Materials Inc. (Tara), an US company applied for an anti-dumping appeal to the United States Department of Commerce (DOC) and International Trade Commission (ITC) regarding painting fabric imported from China on 31 March 2005 with a request to levy an anti-dumping tariff on certain painting fabric made in China. ITC accepted the appeal from Tara on 21st April and judged the painting fabric from China injured the existing same industry in the USA. DOC launched an investigation and levied a 244% import tax (compared to a general level of 6%). The entire process took only three weeks.

NTBs are more efficient in limiting imports. Tariff barriers indirectly restrict importing by weakening the rival's competition with higher tariff collection to increase the cost and price of importing product. At the same time, if an export country has a tax refund for stimulation exports, such as China, or exporting country uses dumping sales strategies to decrease the cost and price, then high taxation will not have the desired effect. NTBs, however, can have an immediate effect on this situation.

NTBs are also more concealable. Tariffs once set are not easily changed and are usually not difficult to understand. For NTBs, however, prior notification is not required and given their arbitrary nature, it can be very difficult to understand what is being restricted. NTBs vary from year to year and from country to country and can often be quite contradictory making a concentrated response difficult and frustrating.

5.1.2 Measuring Incidence of NTBs

Two different indices (or methods) are generally used in the literature to measure the extent of protection accorded by NTBs. These indices estimate the "frequency ratio" (i.e. how many lines or products) of imports is subject to NTBs and "coverage ratio" of NTBs (i.e. how much of imports of a country are subject to NTBs). Since both these indices have some advantages and at the same time some limitations, we will rely on estimates of both these indices.

1. Index of Coverage Ratio (C_j) is defined as

$$C_j = \left(M_{j,T}/M_j\right) * 100$$

   where "$M_{j,T}$" is the value of import subject to reported NTBs in the given product class (or commodity group) and "M_j" is the total value of import of commodities in that class.
2. Index of Frequency Ratio (F_j) is defined as

$$F_j = \left\{n_{T,j}/n_j\right\} \times 100$$

   where "$n_{T,j}$" is the number of products (or lines) subject to reported NTBs in the given class (or commodity group), and "n_j" is the total number of commodities in that class.

Besides these inventory-based approaches, some studies have also used price wedge methods. Price wedge methods rely on the idea that NTMs can be gauged in terms of their impact on the domestic price in comparison with a reference price. This method has been used to provide a tariff equivalent or ad-valorem equivalent (AVE) measure. The tariff equivalent measure can be estimated by calculating the price wedge between the imported good and the comparable product in the domestic market. The correct measure would be to compare the price that would prevail without the NTM to the price that would prevail domestically in the presence of the NTM if the price paid to suppliers were to remain unchanged. However, these prices usually are unobservable, and actual measures focus instead on a comparison of the domestic and foreign price in the presence of the NTM.

5.1.2.1 NAMA Negotiations and NTBs

Recognizing their importance in distorting international trade, the Non-Agricultural Market Access (NAMA) negotiations launched pursuant to the Doha Round

Ministerial meeting (2001) agreed to discuss textual proposals to deal with NTBs in particular on products of export interest to developing countries. As per the present status of the NAMA negotiations on NTBs, member states have so far submitted around 14 proposals. These proposals have been grouped under two broad categories viz.

- Horizontal Proposals (Related across sectors)
- Vertical Proposals (Related to specific sectors)

Among the Horizontal Proposals are:

- Ministerial Decision on Procedures for the Facilitation of solutions to Non-Tariff Barriers (known as the Horizontal Mechanism)
- Decision on the elimination of Non-Tariff Barriers imposed as unilateral trade measures
- Ministerial Decision on Trade in Remanufactured Goods

The vertical proposals relating to specific sectors have been further classified into export-related proposals and proposals related to technical barriers to trade (TBT). While the export related proposals cover areas like: revised submission on export taxes and protocol on transparency in export licensing to the General Agreement on Tariffs and Trade 1994, the proposals relating to technical barriers to trade cover specific sectors like chemical products, electronics, automotive textiles, clothing, footwear and travel goods.

The NAMA text has stated that 7 of the 14 proposals merit attention. While most proposals have little support, three of them are under active discussions. They are:

- Ministerial decision on procedures for the facilitation of solutions to NTBs known as the horizontal mechanism.
- Ministerial declaration on trade in remanufactured goods.
- Proposals related to the agreement on TBT.

5.2 Non-tariff Barriers and Indian Textile Exports

In the Indian context, textile and clothing sector, along with leather sector, has received considerable attention with regard to NTBs. Studies have shown that the textile and clothing sector has been subjected to the maximum types of non-tariff barriers. These barriers range from labelling restrictions, certification requirements, minimum import prices, import restrictions, additional documentation, rules of origin, labour and environmental standards. Within the textile and clothing sector, the cotton textile sector has attracted the maximum number of non-tariff measures followed by the apparel and clothing sector.

Among the importing countries, it is observed that highest number of non-tariff restrictions is imposed by EU, USA and Mexico, though other countries have also joined in recent times. Some examples of non-tariff measures/barriers imposed by the importing countries on Indian textile exports are shown below in Table 5.1.

Table 5.1 Examples of non-tariff measures/barriers—Indian textile exports

Country	Non-tariff measures/barriers
USA	Restrictions have been imposed in the form of rules of origin. Norms violating US child labour policies, issues relating to compliance with environmental norms and security checks of consignments. Indian exporters also face stringent compliance audits for ensuring maintenance of labour standards. The USA also imposes product characteristic requirements or labelling requirement in over 95% of apparel tariff lines.
EU	In the case of the EU, the current push being given to a separate agreement on labelling provisions for the textile and clothing sector has the potential to become a serious trade barrier in the years to come. Further, the EU's policy of granting special incentives for enforcing labour standards and environmental safeguards is a direct attempt to link non-trade issues with trade policy. The repeated attempts to initiate anti-dumping and anti-subsidy measures against the exports of bed linen from India, which have been well documented, are also part of the ECs efforts to impose non-tariff barriers on Indian exports. The recent legislation passed on use of certified chemical substances under the acronym REACH (Registration, Evaluation, Authorisation and Restriction of Chemical Substances) is being seen in many quarters, emerging as a serious barrier to trade in apparel and processed goods.
Other countries	Apart from the USA and EU, other countries have also imposed non-tariff barriers on Indian exports of textiles. Some of them are outlined here: • In recent months, Turkey has not only imposed safeguard measures on export of cotton yarn from India but has also placed special export registration arrangements only for textiles and clothing products which require cumbersome procedures to be followed by importers and exporters resulting in potentially high costs of compliance. • Safeguard measures on the import of cotton yarn from India were also sought to be imposed by Egypt and Peru. Both Egypt and Peru withdrew the measure following diplomatic pressure. However, Peru has recently put in place phytosanitary measures on imports of cotton from India, thereby restricting trade. • Argentina has also imposed minimum reference prices on imports of various textile products to safeguard against low-cost imports. • Labelling requirements for textile and clothing products have been imposed by the Mercouser Group of countries, namely Argentina, Brazil, Paraguay and Uruguay. • In South Asia, Pakistan has not granted most favored nation (MFN) status to India. Bangladesh, on the other hand, has been giving cash subsidy of 2% for use of local cotton yarn. Bangladesh has also not implemented the regional accumulation clause for SAARC countries, which would enable garments made in Bangladesh from Indian fabrics eligible for GSP benefits.

Saini (2009a, b) has recently studied in detail the impact of non-tariff measures on India's textile and clothing exports. While Saini (2009a) attempted to measure the incidence of NTMs on Indian textile and clothing exports, Saini (2009b) discussed the impacts of NTMs based on results from a primary survey of textile exporters from India. The Ministry of Commerce database shows that cotton sector received the maximum number of NTMs, followed by apparel and clothing

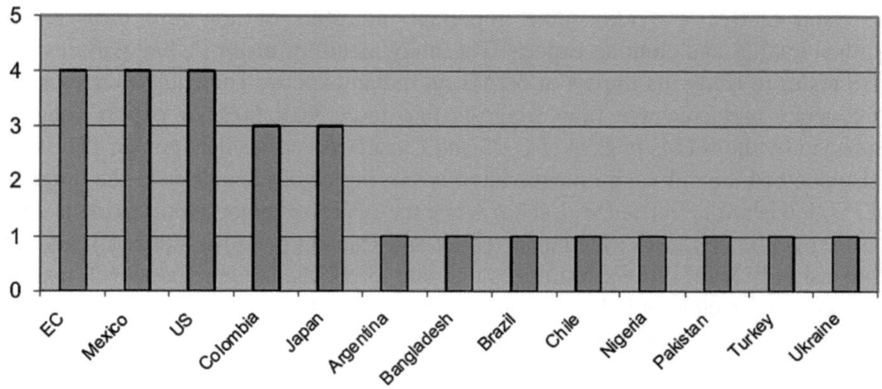

Fig. 5.1 Types of NTMs imposed by different countries on Indian textile exports (*Source* Saini, 2009b) (Color figure online)

accessories segment. Dividing NTMs into different types, Fig. 5.1 shows the types of NTMs imposed by various countries. The EU, USA and Mexico impose a maximum number of NTMs covering four different types, followed by Japan and Colombia that impose three types of NTMs. These NTMs include among other things measures related to labour environmental standards.

In terms of the types of NTMs, a maximum number of countries imposed measures related to minimum import price. This is followed by measures related to import restrictions. Figure 5.2 shows the distribution of types of NTMs on Indian textile exports. Though environment-related NTMs are relatively lower, there is significant potential for under-reporting of the same.

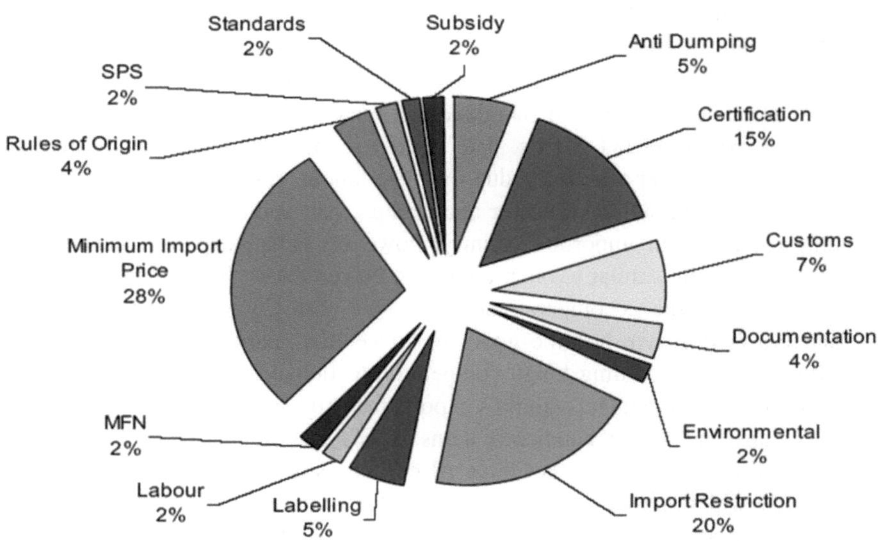

Fig. 5.2 Distribution of NTM types (*Source* Saini 2009b) (Color figure online)

Saini (2009a) provides some important indicators of non-tariff measures in Indian textiles and clothing exports. The study identifies major trading partners and HS codes to study the impact of NTMs on Indian exports. The count measures i.e. frequency and coverage ratio suggests that more than 60% of export value is affected by the NTMs in USA, EU-25 and Canada at various data points. The study also showed that ad-valorem equivalent is varying across countries in the range of 17% (Pakistan) to 340% (Sri Lanka) while the AVE for major export markets such USA (61%), EU-25 (52%), Japan (66%) and Canada (43%) is not too scattered. Interestingly Saini (2009a) estimates that due to NTMs, at aggregate level, textiles and clothing sector could have observed a total trade loss of about billion 2.34 US$ which is 16.8% of base trade value while on the other hand, the zero tariff gains are roughly billion 1.36 US$, which is 9.8% of base values. Among sectors, man-made filaments, staple fibres and other fibres and other are identified as textile articles that are highly affected due to NTMs.

Some of the important issues relating to the impact of the NTMs on textile and clothing exports from India include:

- Specification of testing and certification agencies—Buyers ask the exporter to use accessories from the suppliers and get certification from the agencies, nominated by them, which are usually outside the exporting country and hence, more time consuming and costly. Buyer nominates institutions/agencies such as SGS, BVQI, ITS and TUV for various types of testing and certification; Singapore for labels (in Coimbatore, most of the buyers send the model label and instruct exporters to manufacture accordingly); Hong Kong and China for the purchase of accessories such as zip, zip puller, handbags, badges, plastic strings, tape (cotton), cotton support (garment) and fabrics; and flammability test from countries other than India such as Canada and China. In such cases, buyer normally specifies the brand for a particular accessory and vendor for the same. Many a time, exporters need to pay royalties for the labels used.
- NTMs lead to loss of competitiveness—Indian exports are less competitive in price terms as compared to Bangladesh, China, Sri Lanka and Pakistan due to various export related NTMs. The prices of many export items from these countries are lower than India due to cheap labour, cheap and easy availability of raw material, sufficient power and cheap credit and/or due to other benefits they receive from importing country; however, Indian exporters usually face price bargaining similar to other countries. Nevertheless, India is unable to offer similar prices due to comparatively high-input cost. Countries such as Vietnam and Cambodia have become good export centres mainly due to proximity to China and are providing tough competition to Indian exports.
- Discriminatory treatment—India's exports face higher-import duty on bed linen, made ups and textile handicraft items in EU and South Africa than that of competing countries such as China. Also, there is often specification of the port through which goods are to be shipped; for example, exporters are asked to route their good through Chennai and/or Tuticorin ports instead of availing local

facilities of Tirupur ICD (Inland Container Depot), which increases their transport cost.

- NTMs promote efficiency and competitiveness—Studies based on field level observations argue that exporter often feel that NTMs in the form of quality and standard requirements are good for Micro, Small and Medium Enterprises (MSMEs) as these firms increase their competitiveness during the process of meeting standards. NTMs promote internal competition among exporters thereby increasing firm's efficiencies and competitiveness. For instance, the establishment of a water treatment plant is a capital expenditure, which is mainly for environmental requirements; however, at the same time, it saves regular expense on water, which varies according to the firm size.

5.3 Assessing Impact of Environmental Regulations on Textile Trade

As mentioned in Chap. 1, it is relatively easy to recognize the "potential" for the impact of non-tariff measures on trade prospects, but it is extremely difficult to systematically establish the presence of such measures and even more difficult to measure the impact of such measures on the trade and welfare. Literature has adopted at least three approaches to address this issue:

(a) Elicit the perceptions through primary survey of the exporters and use the survey data to quantify the impact of the environmental regulations and standards on trade;
(b) Use firm-level secondary data from exporting countries along with appropriate proxies to measure the additional costs incurred by the exporters to meet the growing environmental demands in the importing countries to analyse the influence of environmental regulation on the exit decisions of the exporters and on the productivity improvements; and
(c) Use estimates of the compliance costs (to meet the environmental standards imposed by the importing country) obtained from a critical review of the literature and incorporate them in large-scale computable general equilibrium models including trade component to analyse the welfare implications and trade prospects under various plausible scenarios.

This book explores the approaches (a) and (c) in this chapter and the next chapter, respectively. A recent study by Chakraborty (2011) analyzed the impacts of environmental regulation using firm-level data. Using a firm-level data set comprising of firms in leather and textile sectors in India for the period 1989–2003, the study analyzed the implications of stringent environmental regulations—both domestic and foreign, on the abatement costs, export revenues, and exit decisions of the firms. The results indicate that environmental regulations have increased the pollution abatement costs and have adversely affected the productivity of firms. The study suggests that both large and small exporters were successful (over the study period of 1989–2003) in adjusting to trade-related environmental standards. However, this was mainly resulted due to active support extended by the government in various ways to lower the cost of compliance. The support included technical assistance, adjustment of import duties and negotiating with the importing country in getting crucial additional time to facilitate the exporters to adjust.

5.4 Analysis of Impact of Pollution Abatement on India's Textile Trade

There has been an intense debate in the literature on whether or not to include international standards within the international trading frameworks like WTO. While studies such as Srinivasan (1996) argue against the inclusion of environmental standards in terms of welfare loss arising out of possible non-compliance by many industries in developing countries like India, those such as Rodrik (1997) deny any notion of protectionism in the linking of environmental standards with international trade. The latter opines that legitimacy of trade rests in part on its compatibility with domestic norms and social arrangements as it has implications on them.

Uimonen and Whalley (1997) observe that the argument of "unfair trade advantage" to the countries that have low-environmental standards neglects the likelihood that the environmental standards may reflect different approaches to attain similar levels of environmental protection and different priorities with respect to such protection. Efficient differences in standards in abatement costs argue against harmonization. However, in the absence of standards, there would be no incentive to undertake environmental policy interventions, which necessitates the importance of effective policy instruments. This study infers that the relative differences across the countries in environmental costs are low as compared to the other costs of production.

Parikh et al. (1995) conducted a questionnaire-based survey among the Indian exporters to understand the awareness of environmental standards, costs of compliance and impacts of eco-labelling on trade. Their results show a good awareness among the large-scale exporters, an increase of 3–5% of product cost with the compliance to environmental standards and a prominent notion among the garment exporters that environmental factors come only after fashion and feel even in Germany. Almost all exporters to EEC have complied with packaging standards. A study by ICICI (1996) based on interviews with Indian garment exporters and US buyers' throws light on the fact that the buyers are keen on Indian exporters to adopt the global standards in environment and labour.

In fact, highlighting the criticality of the issue of environmental standards and regulation in the textiles sector, in an assessment of the trade effects of eco-labelling, UN (1997) notes that textiles sector in India has been affected severely by the ban on Pentachlorophenol (PCP) and Azo dyes since the domestically available alternatives were incompatible with the production process or were inappropriate in their existing form. This study estimates the adjustment costs for complying with this ban to be 8–10% for large-scale companies and 15–20% for small-scale companies in terms of total cost. Further, it suggests that the Indian textile exports have been diverted away from Germany and the Middle East owing to these regulations. The problems inherent in the eco-labelling of Indian exports by Denmark, Germany and Italy are lack of relevant information and transparency, a large range of confusing concepts, terminologies and definitions, unsuitability, limited testing infrastructure in India, high costs and low-technical knowledge.

As for the possibility of inclusion of standards in the WTO, though Gstohl and Kaiser (2004) opine that WTO may not be able to link the standards with the free trade regime, Das (2004) points out that such standards may be observed by the non-governmental measures of the buyers in the importing countries, since the WTO can control only the governmental measures against free trade.

There have been two major developments in the history of pollution abatement in Indian textile industry. Firstly, Environment (Protection) Act, 1986 laid down the rules for releasing wastewater into the rivers. Secondly, Indian judiciary system (including the Supreme Court) set a precedent of stringent implementation of such rules by ordering the closure of several polluting textile units in 1998–1999. Clearly, of these two, the second development, entailing strict enforcement of the 1986 rules, is likely to have more severe impact on India's cost-competitiveness, production and hence exports.

Figures 5.3 and 5.4 show the trend in the export performance of the Indian textile sub-sectors. There has been an overall rise in the real value of exports of all commodities, but the growth has been enormous for the garments. This is surprising since many textile processing units were closed in 1998–1999 in Tiruppur, which accounts for more than half of India's exports of knit garments. Knit garment sector has remarkably seen no major decline from 1996–1997 to 2008–2009. Even other major

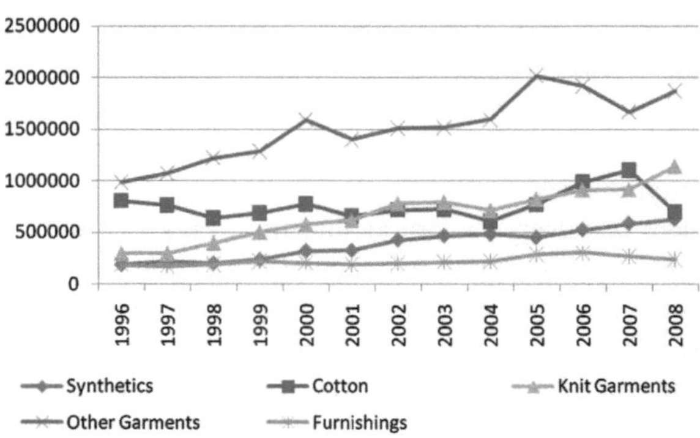

Fig. 5.3 Value of exports of major textile commodities. *Note* The values are in lakhs of INR, in constant prices with the base year of 1993–1994. *Source* Own calculations based on data from www.dgftcom.nic.in

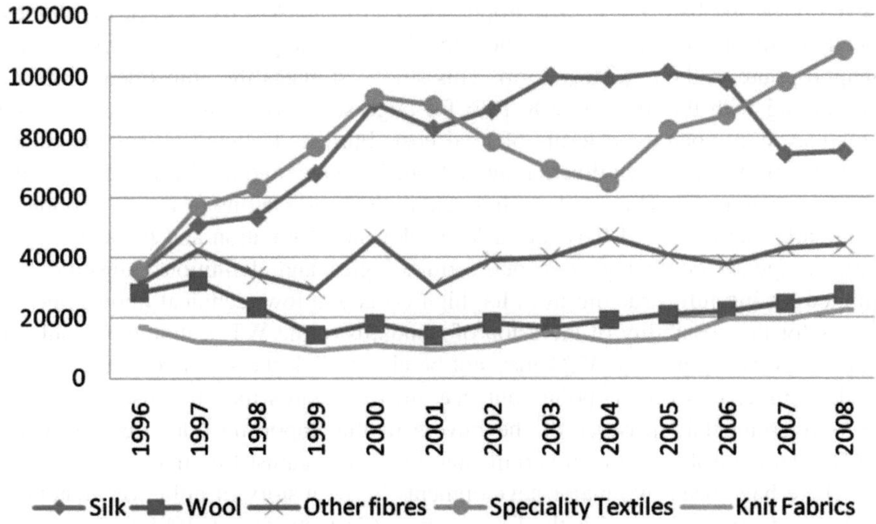

Fig. 5.4 Value of exports of minor textile commodities. *Note* The values are in lakhs of INR, in constant prices with the base year of 1993–1994. *Source* Own calculations based on data from www.dgftcom.nic.in

sub-sectors do not show any significant fall until 2001–2002. There is also a slight decline after 2005–2006, perhaps due to the increased competition resulting from the phasing out of MFA quotas. The global crisis of 2008–2009 has had considerable negative impact on cotton textiles, which includes cotton yarn and fabric.

Figures 5.5 and 5.6 show that the decline in cotton textile exports occurred in the years 1996–1997, 1998–1999, 2001–2002, 2004–2005 and most notably in 2008–2009. Knit garment exports fell in 2004–2005, but have hence picked up and are growing rapidly despite the global crisis. Knit fabric exports suffered in the late 1990s, in 2001–2002 and in 2004–2005, but they are growing since then. Exports of furnishings suffered a setback early this millennium, but have picked up after 2005–2006, but for a fall in 2007–2008. Other major sectors have been growing through the entire period considered. All these observations indicate that pollution abatement, which has been much more widespread in Indian textile sector since 1998–1999, has not had serious ramifications for the overall exports so far, other than for the cotton textiles sector.

However, there is a deep concern arising from Figs. 5.7 and 5.8, which shows that the shares of exports of textile commodities in total exports from India are indeed falling secularly over the years. For the cotton textile sector, such decline started in 1997–1998, while for most of the other sectors, it started early this millennium. Knit garment export share is relatively more stable, but it has not grown since 2003–2004. Given that textile sector has got a boost in 2005, from the removal of MFA quotas, this is a bit puzzling at the first sight because other sectors did not face as much of a boost. However, given the intense competition to which India is open to, after the quota regime, this is understandable. One way of facing

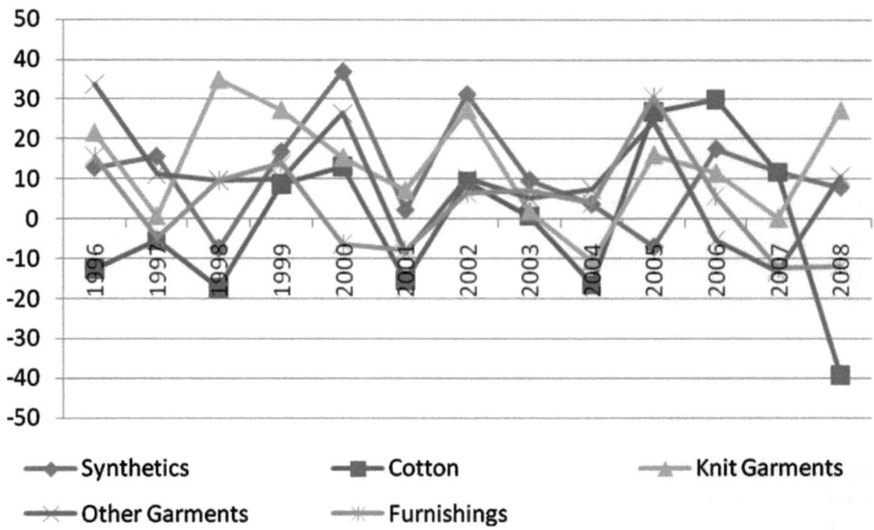

Fig. 5.5 Growth rates in the value of exports of major textile commodities. *Note* Growth is calculated in percentage on annual basis using data from Fig. 5.1. *Source* Own calculations based on data from www.dgftcom.nic.in

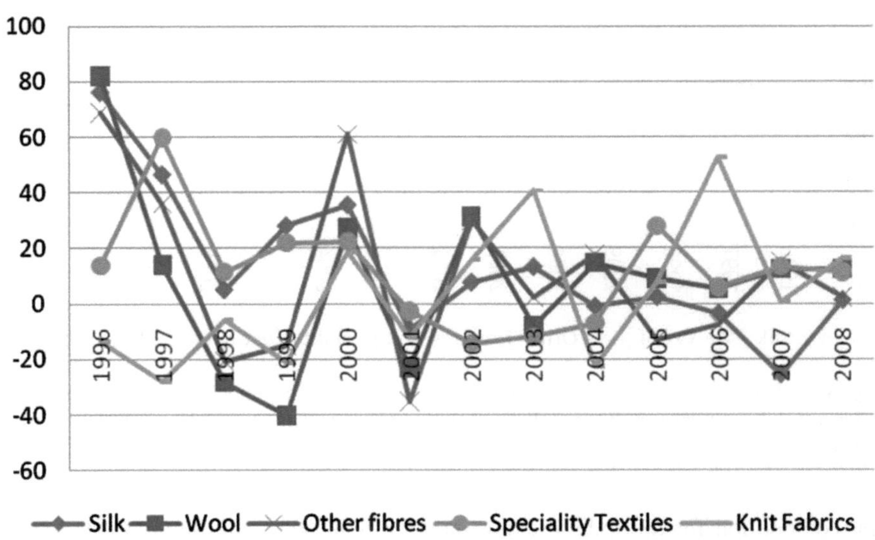

Fig. 5.6 Growth rates in the value of exports of minor textile commodities. *Note* Growth is calculated in percentage on annual basis using data from Fig. 5.2. *Source* Own calculations based on data from www.dgftcom.nic.in

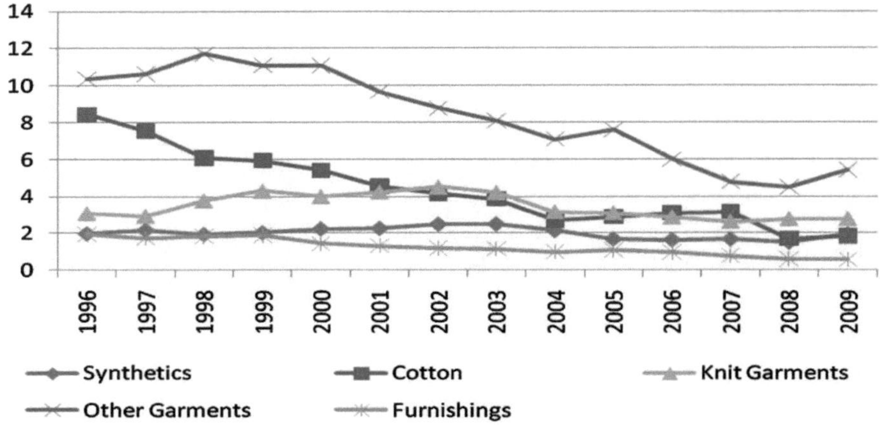

Fig. 5.7 Shares in the total value of exports of major textile commodities. *Note* Shares are a percentage of the total exports from India. *Source* Own calculations based on data from www.dgftcom.nic.in

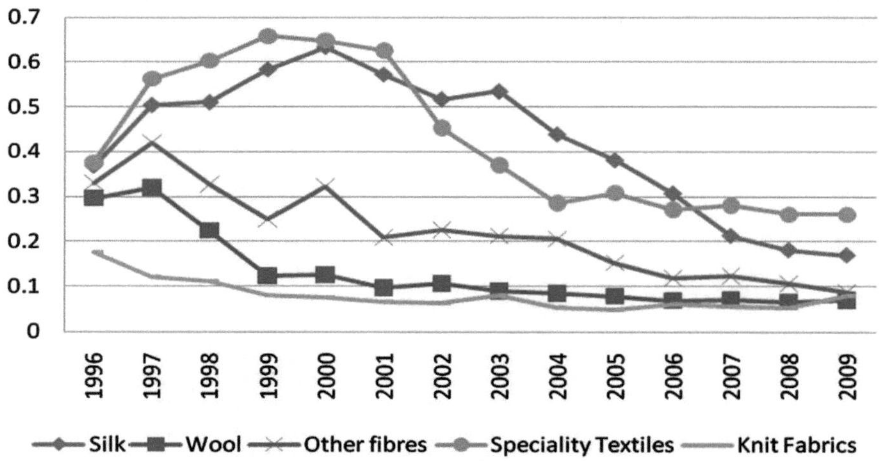

Fig. 5.8 Shares in the total value of exports of minor textile commodities. *Note* Shares are a percentage of the total exports from India. *Source* Own calculations based on data from www.dgftcom.nic.in

the competition for the Indian textile industry is to adopt all environmental standards, thereby improving its appeal to the world.

Since it is difficult to separate the textile processing industries per se from the analysis done so far, the trends in output and employment of the textile processing sectors are analyzed next, for which pollution abatement is really relevant. With a long-time series data from 1973–1974 to 2007–2008, an increasing trend is observed in the output of all the processing sectors.

As seen in Fig. 5.9, processing sectors for cotton and synthetic fibres have been growing until 2005–2006, when they started increasing their output rapidly. Some minor declines can be seen in the late 1980s and a flattening can be noticed in late 1990s and early in this millennium. Although more fluctuations have been seen in the smaller processing sectors (Fig. 5.10), the flattening trend in the late 1990s and early 2000s remain notable. One could interpret this as partly due to the stringent implementation in the late 1990s impeding the growth of these sectors. It could also be hypothesized that by 2005, most of the processing factories in the organized sector have got adjusted to the technological changes involved in setting up ETPs, which is the major form of pollution abatement in India today.

Figures 5.11 and 5.12, in conjunction with Figs. 5.9 and 5.10, indicate that these sectors have been becoming less labour-intensive since mid-late 1990s and have

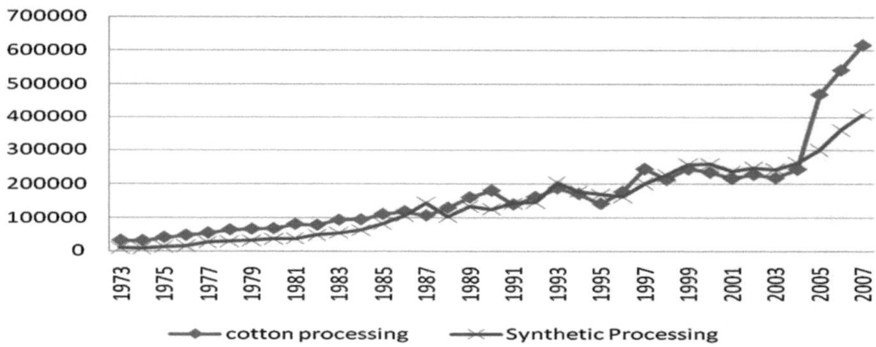

Fig. 5.9 Output trends in major textile processing sectors. *Note* Output is measured in lakhs INR at 1993–1994 constant prices. *Source* Own calculations based on data from EPWRF-ASI Data (1973–1974 to 1997–1998) and http://www.mospi.nic.in/stat_act_t3.htm (1997–1998 to 2007–2008)

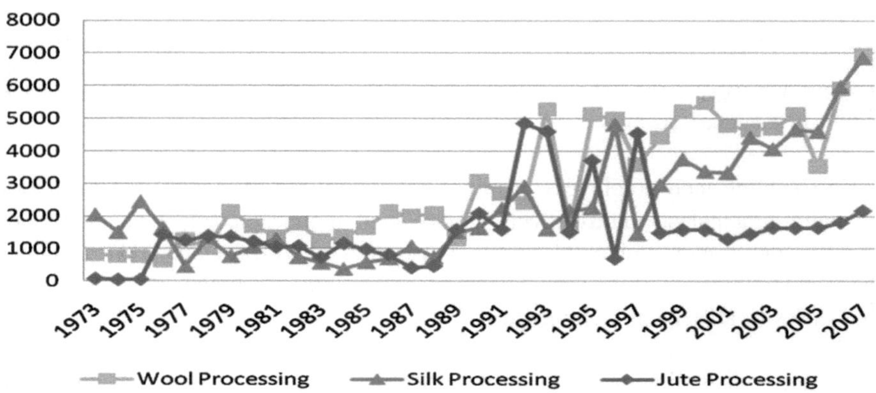

Fig. 5.10 Output trends in minor textile processing sectors. *Note* Output is measured in lakhs INR at 1993–1994 constant prices. *Source* Own calculations based on data from EPWRF-ASI Data (1973–1974 to 1997–1998) and http://www.mospi.nic.in/stat_act_t3.htm (1997–1998 to 2007–2008)

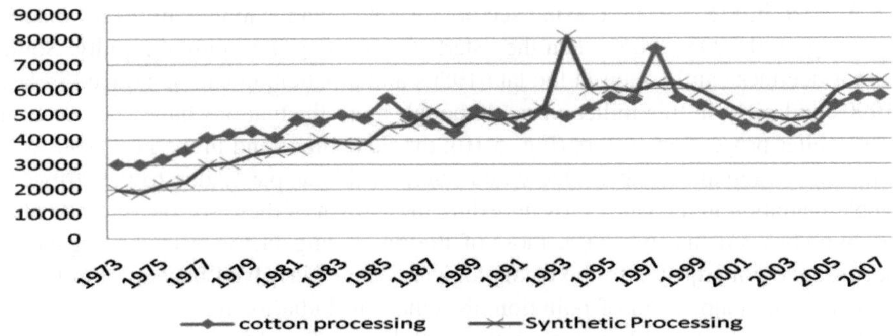

Fig. 5.11 Employment trends in major textile processing sectors. *Note* Output is measured in lakhs INR at 1993–1994 constant prices. *Source* Own calculations based on data from EPWRF-ASI Data (1973–1974 to 1997–1998) and http://www.mospi.nic.in/stat_act_t3.htm (1997–1998 to 2007–2008)

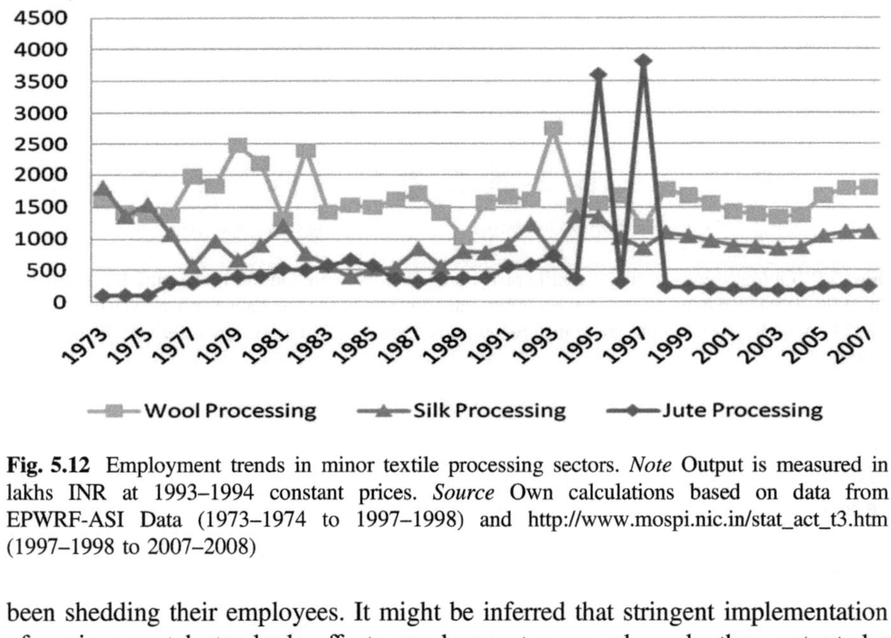

Fig. 5.12 Employment trends in minor textile processing sectors. *Note* Output is measured in lakhs INR at 1993–1994 constant prices. *Source* Own calculations based on data from EPWRF-ASI Data (1973–1974 to 1997–1998) and http://www.mospi.nic.in/stat_act_t3.htm (1997–1998 to 2007–2008)

been shedding their employees. It might be inferred that stringent implementation of environmental standards affects employment more adversely than output, by shutting down more vulnerable firms. A rise in employment since 2004–2005 can be seen in almost all of the processing sectors, possibly due to the adjustment of the industries to abatement technologies.

The main indicator of the competitiveness of an industry is the price of the goods it produces. It is difficult to obtain the price data for commodities that are exclusively produced by the textile processing mills that are involved in pollution. However, the price index data for synthetic textiles and synthetic dyed/printed cloth are available. The latter is the product of synthetic textile processing industries,

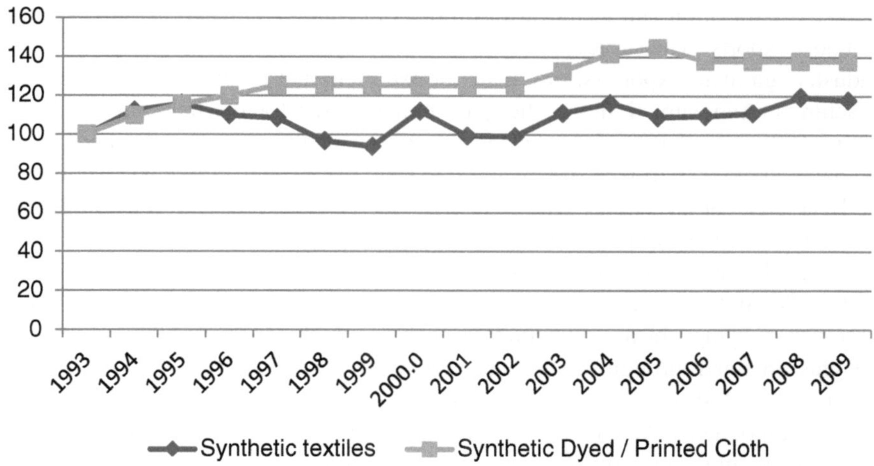

Fig. 5.13 Price indices of synthetic textiles. *Source* http://eaindustry.nic.in/ Base Year: 1993–1994 = 100

while former is that of the aggregate synthetic textiles. It is clearly seen from Fig. 5.13 that the prices have increased at a much faster pace for the synthetic dyed/printed cloth, since the mid-1990s. Since 2005–2006, the gap is becoming narrower. This is consistent with the story emerging from the analysis presented in Chap. 6, that the costs of abatement are seen more at the beginning than at the later stages. The findings from the primary survey of the textile exporters discussed below also provide similar insight.

5.5 Environmental Standards and Perceptions of Textile Exporters

As outlined above environmental standards are often specified as non-tariff measures by the importing country. Given the overall interest of the present study on interlinkages between trade and environment, an attempt was made to access the incidence and impact of NTMs on Indian textile exports based on field level study. This section provides a summary of findings based on the field level observations.

In an attempt to assess the stakeholders' perspective on implications of environmental standards on exports, a survey of exporters of textile and textile products was undertaken. The survey was administered in two ways—by sending a detailed questionnaire to several exporters all over India, and by administering the questionnaire to several exporters based largely in South India. Specifically, the survey attempted to address the following issues: Do the environmental standards abroad in the form of product specifications/packaging requirements, act as non-tariff barriers? Are Indian exporters aware of the requirements and if they are, what are the costs of compliance with the requirements? What are the roles of government, industry association and technical institutions in creating an enabling environment to boost exports? The survey was conducted among three different groups of textile industry: garment exporters, raw material exporters and textile and clothing manufacturers. Annexure II shows the questionnaire used for the field survey. While about 150 respondents acknowledged the receipt of the questionnaire and/or participated in the face-to-face survey, close to sixty respondents provided responses to at least 50% of questions. The responses largely provided information on the perceptions of the exporting firms on the environmental issues, but have not given clear insight into the influence of environmental regulations on the trade prospects and productivity. In the absence of such information, the survey data could not be used for carrying out any quantitative analysis. In the following paragraphs, the insights obtained through the primary survey are described.

Figure 5.14 shows the use of a type of effluent treatment facility among the survey respondents. While more than 50% of the respondents report the use of independent effluent treatment plant, close to 9% report dependence on the common effluent treatment plant.

Most of the respondents report possession of one or the other form of environmental certification, reflecting the need for the same to gain entry into the export market. ISO 9001 and 14001 certification accounts for more than 70% of the total sample, whereas 15% of the respondents report having eco-mark. Figure 5.15 provides distribution of respondents on the basis of certification.

It was observed that most of the firms who were engaged into garments manufacturing production export around 70% of their goods and they manufacture the required raw material on their own. Most of the companies are involved in manufacturing garments for men, women and inner wear, etc. Textile-exporting companies observed that largely environmental standards are specified on the products

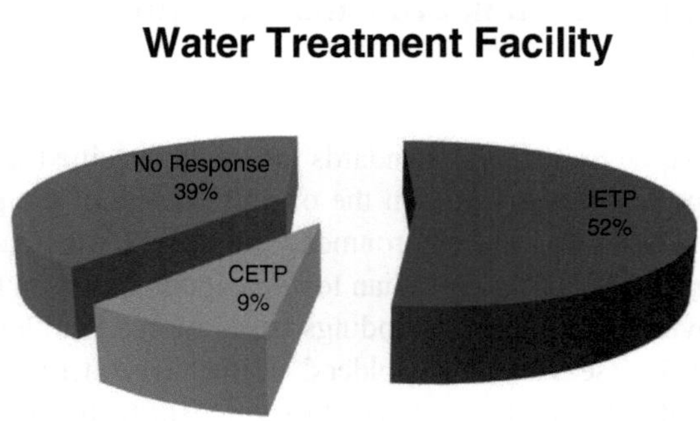

Fig. 5.14 Distribution of respondents on the basis of treatment plant

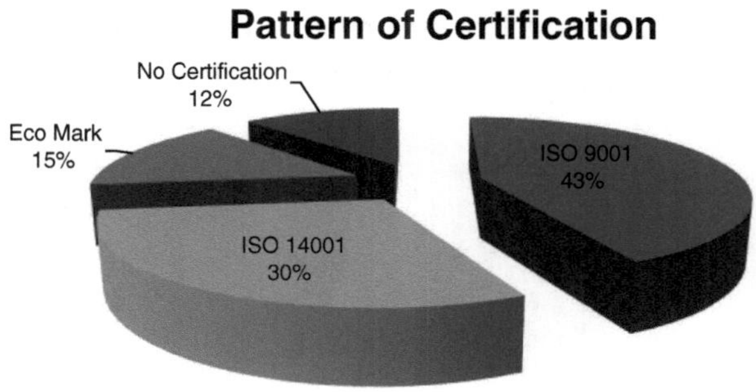

Fig. 5.15 Distribution of respondents on the basis of certification

only by the importing countries. Though some exporters have expressed concern that lack of access to the environmental testing facility in close proximity to the manufacturing hub is affecting them, by and large, most exporters feel that the testing facilities are adequate (Fig. 5.16). It was also observed during the survey that adherence to environmental regulations affects the price to an extent of 3% on an average. However, evidence from the survey (Fig. 5.17) is not categorical on whether adhering to environmental regulations adversely affects the exporter's competitiveness with close to 50% exporters feeling that such regulations had adverse effects on their trade prospects and the remaining 50% considering such regulations to have no significant effect.

One of the main points that emerged from the survey is the need for providing the cost-effective technological options by the publicly funded R&D to the textile and clothing manufacturers. Further, most of the respondents demanded government intervention in increasing the awareness among the exporters about the environmental standards—especially on product specifications and packaging

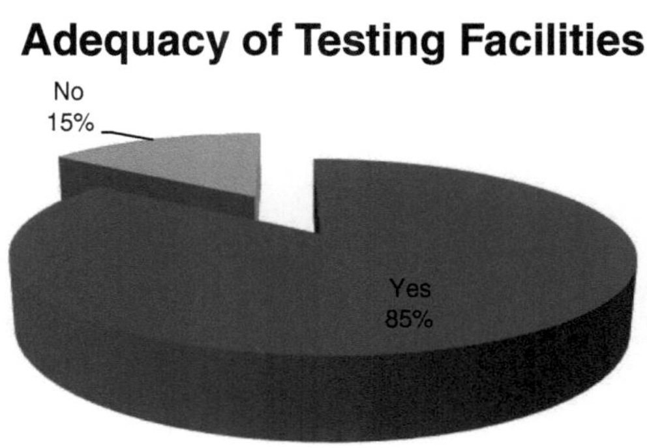

Fig. 5.16 Adequacy of environmental testing facilities

Fig. 5.17 Adverse impact of environmental regulations on competitiveness

requirements, demanded by the developed country markets. Among the companies who were into raw material supply, about 50% of them expressed the need for establishing more laboratories to test their products. They have noticed the increase in quality and price for their goods after compliance with export regulations. They also wanted more textile research facilities in their cities.

The survey findings suggest that raw material exporters had ventured into spinning, domestic sales, weaving, knitting, fabric bags, etc. Thus, the quality test is of utmost necessity for them to meet the expectations of customers. The garment manufacturing companies felt that adhering to the environmental standards resulted in the increased quality and pricing. This corroborates the general observation made above in Sect. 5.2 with regard to the positive impact of NTMs.

In summary, the analysis of the recent and past trends in exports, output, employment and prices indicate that there had been an initial adverse impact of the environmental regulations on the textile sector, but once the sector has had enough time to get adjusted to the changes required for environmental compliance, all the parameters in the sector started growing again. This is also in line with the expressed views of the exporters.

Chapter 6
Exploring Linkages Between Pollution Abatement and Trade in Textile Industry

G. Badri Narayanan

6.1 Introduction

This chapter investigates the features of pollution abatement in India, cost of compliance to international environmental standards and its impact on India's performance in terms of trade, economic growth and welfare. The chapter is organised as follows: the first section describes the current status of pollution abatement in Indian textile sector. The next section analyses the pollution abatement costs in Indian textile sector, mainly for natural dyes and ETPs. Impact of pollution abatement on India's textile exports is analysed in the subsequent section. The last section summarises the main findings.

6.2 Status of Pollution Abatement in Indian Textile Sector

There are well-defined regulations in India, prevalent since 1970s, for controlling air and water pollution. Textile industry causes both air pollution and water pollution. Water pollution is caused due to effluents released during textile processing, mainly dyeing. Air pollution is caused in terms of that associated with energy consumption in all textile processes and mixing of fibres and chromium in the air from the rollers that have chromium coating, in ginning and processing, which has mostly local impact. Textile industry pollutes the water much more significantly than it does the air. Most of the pollution caused by textile industry takes place at the stage of textile processing, primarily resulting in water pollution. Therefore, the regulations pertaining to water pollution are discussed in this section, although there

G.B. Narayanan (✉)
School of Environmental and Forestry Sciences, University of Washington, Seattle, WA, USA

K.S.K. Kumar (ed.), *A Study of India's Textile Exports and Environmental Regulations*, https://doi.org/10.1007/978-981-10-6295-7_6

are some other process standards in India—e.g. 112 harmful dyes and chemicals have been banned by the government.

The Water (Prevention and Control of Pollution) Act, 1974; the Water (Prevention and Control of Pollution) Cess Act, 1977; and its Amendment Act, 1988, are specially meant for curtailing water pollution. There are various features related to water pollution in Environment (Protection) Act, 1986, which followed the Bhopal tragedy of December 1984. This Act is implemented by the Central Pollution Control Board (CPCB), which was incorporated in 1974 originally to implement the Water (PCP) Act, and the State Pollution Control Board (SPCB). They require the firms to collect and treat the wastewater, using an ETP, before it is disposed on land or on surface waters. Minimising waste to conserve raw material by recovering solvents, which also leads to reduction of pollution at source, is encouraged by the boards. The Water (Prevention and Control of Pollution) Amendment Act, 1988, empowers the PCBs to close down industries or to deny essential services such as water and electricity to the polluting industries, if found necessary (Nagdeve 2004).

There are certain environmental standards put forth by the Central Pollution Control Board (CPCB), for the textile sector. Wastewater generation is limited to 120, 150 and 500 m^3 per tonne of nylon/polyester, viscose staple fibre and filament yarn, respectively. Table 6.1 shows some of the generic standards, relevant for

Table 6.1 Generic standards for wastewater discharge in India

Parameter	Inland surface water	Public sewers	Land for irrigation	Marine/coastal areas
Suspended solids, mg/l max	100	600	200	(a) For process wastewater (b) For cooling water effluent 10% above total suspended matter of influent
Particle size of total suspended solids (TSS)	Shall pass 850 micron IS Sieve	–	–	(a) Floatable solids, max 3 mm (b) Settleable solids, max 856 microns
pH value	5.5–9.0	5.5–9.0	5.5–9.0	5.5–9.0
Oil and grease, mg/l, max	10	20	10	20
Total residual chlorine, mg/l max	1.0	–	–	1.0
Biochemical oxygen demand (3 days at 27 °C), mg/l, max	30	350	100	100
Chemical oxygen demand, mg/l, max	250	–	–	250
Temperature	≤ 5 °C above the receiving water temperature			≤ 5 °C above the receiving water temperature

Source CPCB website (http://cpcb.nic.in)

textile dyeing effluents, laid out for the discharge of environmental pollutant. Table 6.2 shows specific standards meant for dyeing industry. CPCB also specifies standards (applicable to Rayon industry) for carbon disulphide (CS_2) and hydrogen sulphide (H_2S) as 21 kg/ton of fibre and 6.3 kg/ton of fibre, respectively. The ambient standards for these pollutants stand respectively at 100 and 150 $\mu g/m^3$. With regard to the particulate emissions that the boilers emit, the standards prescribed by CPCB are as follows: 1600 mg/Nm^3 for boilers of capacity less than 2 tons/h, 1200 mg/Nm^3 for boilers of capacity 2–5 tons/h and 150 mg/Nm^3 for boilers of capacity greater than 15 tons/h.

In addition, there are also sector-specific standards for different sub-sectors in the Indian textile industry and for small-scale industries (SSI), summarised in Table 6.3. For jute processing industry, there is also a recommendation that the colours should be as minimal as possible. For Rayon fibre manufacturing, there are air quality standards applicable to the level of hydrogen sulphide (e.g. 6.3 kg/t for new plants) and carbon disulphide (e.g. 21 kg/t for new plants). Almost all the standards mentioned here were laid down in 1986. Handling of Azo dyes was prohibited in 1997.

Though the wastewater may be treated to meet the standards, there are some remnants from the ETP process. They are collected into a solid chunk called sludge, which is dumped in bags by the industries in different places. Such dumping is restricted by the Ministry of Environment and Forests, using some regulations, such

Table 6.2 Dye and dye intermediate industry: wastewater discharge standards

Parameter	Concentration not to exceed, mg/l (except pH, colour and bio-assay test)
pH	5.5–9.0
Colour, Hazen unit	400
Suspended solids	100
Biochemical oxygen demand (BOD) (27 °C, 3 days)	30
Chemical oxygen demand (COD)	250
Oil and grease	10.0
Phenolic compounds as C_6H_5OH	1.0
Cadmium as Cd	0.2
Copper as Cu	2.0
Manganese as Mn	2.0
Lead as Pb	0.1
Mercury as Hg	0.01
Nickel as Ni	2.0
Zinc as Zn	5.0
Chromium as Cr hexavalent	0.1
Total chromium	2.0
Bio-assay test	90% survival after 96 h

Source CPCB website (http://cpcb.nic.in)

Table 6.3 Textile sub-sectors and SSI: wastewater discharge standards

Process parameter	Jute	Cotton	Semi-synthetic	Synthetic	Woollen	SSI
pH	5.5–9	5.5–9	5.5–9	5.5–9	5.5–9	5.5–9
BOD (mg/l)[a]	30	30	30	30	100	150
TSS (mg/l)	100	100	100	100	100	250
Oil and grease (mg/l)	10	10	–	–	10	10
Chromium (mg/l)	–	2	–	–	2	3
Sulphide (mg/l)	–	2	–	–	2	2
Phenolics (mg/l)	–	5	–	–	5	5
Zinc (mg/l)	–	–	5	5	–	5
Water consumption	1.5 m^3/ton	–	–	–	–	–
Bio-assay test	–	90% survival in 96 h			90% survival in 96 h	

Source CPCB website (http://cpcb.nic.in)
[a]All these standards are applicable if the wastewater is released to surface waters. This is 150 mg/l for cotton textiles if it is released to the land

as Hazardous Wastes (management, handling and transboundary movement) Rules, 2008, (which replaced similar rules framed in 1989) and its amendments in 2009. Textile chemical residue, process sludge and the sludge from wastewater treatment appear in the list of hazardous wastes mentioned in Schedule 1.[1] According to these rules, such waste materials should be recycled or disposed safely and in environmentally friendly ways in facilities authorised by the regulatory agency, which is mostly the State Pollution Control Board. If they are stored, it should not be more than ninety days.

All these standards, however, vary to some extent across the states and are implemented at varying degrees in different states. For example, Bedi et al. (2009) find that Punjab and Tamil Nadu are more stringent, while Uttar Pradesh is relatively flexible. A recent report by CPCB (2009a), however, develops guidelines for the development of location-specific stringent standards, based on local conditions as well as existing global standards. Given that pollution levels vary across the country, different degrees of stringencies are required for the standards to be effective. So in future, one could expect more stringent and location-specific standards. The extent to which the existing standards are complied with is a different issue, dealt with in the next sub-section.

[1]The list is available online at http://envfor.nic.in/legis/hsm/hwamdsch1.html.

6.2.1 Compliance to the Existing Environmental Standards in India

About 1–15% of the dyes applied to the textile yarns or fabrics are present in the effluent or wastewater, as they are unused in the process (Neelavannan et al. 2007). This results in heavy concentration of various hazardous chemicals in it, increasing the BOD, COD, etc. Table 6.4 shows the characteristics of wastewater from textile bleaching, dyeing and washing processes for various fibres, from different parts of the country.

A typical dyeing factory in India has two types of effluents one from the dye-bath process and one from washing and rinsing of the dyed fabric or yarn. The last column shows some features for the effluents from reactive dyeing wash and bath process, as an example for a particular type of synthetic dyes. In all other

Table 6.4 Typical characteristics of wastewater from textile processing units

Process parameter	Cotton bleach	Cotton dyeing	Synthetic dyeing	Wool washing	Wool dyeing	Reactive dyeing wash/bath
pH	10–13	9.3–13	8.3	5	2.7	8/9
BOD (mg/l)	300	350–380	302	170	469	–
COD (mg/l)	650	700	2547	6000	1040	400/6000
TSS (mg/l)	300	350	140–1610	1200	59	4000/2000
TDS (mg/l)	6560	9000–10,000	–	–	–	3200/52,000
DO (mg/l)	–	1	–	–	–	–
Colour	Whitish	Intense	Intense	Whitish	Intense	Intense
Oil/grease (mg/l)	<5	<5	<5	<5	<5	<5
Water consumption (m^3/ton)	2–4	2–4	2–4	2–4	2–4	2–4
Nitrite–nitrogen (mg/l)	–	6.50	–	–	–	–
Total phosphate (mg/l)	–	1.12	–	–	–	–
Total alkalinity (mg/l)	–	510	–	–	–	–
Lead (mg/l)	–	0.04	–	–	–	–
Cr, Co (mg/l)	–	Low	–	–	–	–
Zinc (mg/l)	–	0.38	–	–	–	–
Nickel (mg/l)	–	0.01	–	–	–	–
Cadmium (mg/l)	–	0.21	–	–	–	–
Copper (mg/l)	–	0.01	–	–	–	–
Iron (mg/l)	–	2.3	–	–	–	–

Source Compiled from NPC (1992) as cited in Kathuria (2007)

columns, the effluent from the dye-bath process alone is shown. It can be seen that the pollution intensity is much higher for the dye-bath effluent than for the effluent from washing or bleaching. When compared with the figures in Table 6.4, all these characteristics indicate that a lot of pollution abatement is required to comply with the standards set by CPCB. Even until as late as a decade ago, most of the textile processing firms were directly releasing such wastewater directly into rivers that are used for drinking, etc.

Compliance to the standards has been found to be very high in the case of exporters because they are required by the buyers to adopt even more superior standards (Parikh et al. 1995). In general, compliance to the environmental standards in the developing countries is known to be difficult in the light of its higher costs, lower access, less literate and skilled human and poorer financial resources. Further, compliance to the standards also varies across each country. Particularly in textile sector, compliance is easier for the large-scale industries (LSI) than for the SSI. It is a function of both the degree of stringency and constraints to technological change, which are due to the modified relationships between labour, capital and technology in the large- and small-scale industries. There are various aspects such as organisational, technological and economic barriers that are inherent to the firm size, lack of space and smaller investible capital.

Government of India encourages the growth of SSI sector because of its employment generation capacity, particularly of women and the backward communities. However, forcing the standards on SSI and closing them if they do not implement is detrimental for the masses in the economy. Therefore, a participatory system with incentives and penalties is recommended. As a step in this direction, Government of India has introduced some relaxations in the standards if the SSIs treat the effluent collectively in a terminal effluent plant.

In a common effluent treatment plant (CETP), many firms are involved in treating their wastewater together. For example, Tiruppur city has 830 units with merely 8 CETPs (Balasubramanian et al. 2006). Karur city has 43 dyeing units that have a single plant named Amaravathi CETP that treats 200 m^3 of effluents daily.[2] Therefore, in such CETPs, incentive incompatibility to minimise pollution arises due to the fact that the individual firms do not directly monitor the plant and might tend to free ride by polluting more. This, being a public sharing problem, requires setting up of new institutions, mutual monitoring and credible commitments. By not meeting these requirements and not following the polluters pay principle (PPP), a CETP at Kundli, Haryana, which involved textile dyeing units among others, failed. Since there were other industries, textile units had to do unit-level chemical pre-treatment, so that COD is reduced to the levels that exist in the wastewater from other industries. A more sustainable CETP in Ankleshwar, Gujarat, which met these requirements and created incentives for the polluters to reduce pollution at source, has been successful (Kathuria 2007).

---

[2]http://www.fibre2fashion.com/industry-article/3/215/textile-effluent-treatment-a-case-study-in-home-textile-zone1.asp.

As recently as a decade ago, 84% of the Indian textile processing units were aware of global environmental standards and requirements, on an average, as shown in Table 6.5. In this table, composite units are those that process textiles from the stage of fibres to finished fabrics. Semi-composite units have weaving and processing, comprising converting yarns to finished fabrics. Independent processing units do nothing other than textile wet processing and finishing.

Table 6.5 also shows that independent processing units and all SSI are least aware of eco-parameters, while semi-composite non-SSI units are most aware of them; 87% of all units have ETPs on an average, while 93% of composite units have ETPs. Tertiary ETP units are more comprehensive in terms of waste treatment than secondary units, which, in turn, are better than primary ones. Semi-composite SSI units mostly do primary treatment alone, while most of the other units have secondary ETPs. In all categories, less than 20% units do tertiary treatment.

It also clearly emerges from Table 6.5 that SSI units follow less comprehensive effluent treatment practices when compared with non-SSI and an average processing unit, probably because of being least aware of environmental requirements. In number, SSI units are predominantly independent processing units (97%), while non-SSI units are more diversified in terms of the type of units: 45% semi-composite, 31% composite and 24% independent units. All these numbers might have changed over the years and may look somewhat different more recently, but the percentage trends should not have changed a lot and this is just to get an overall picture as to which segments are most and least compliant to the environmental standards.

Most of the environmental regulations and the institutions that implement them (the State and Central PCBs) assume the "Command and Control" method of controlling pollution, which requires huge laboratories, comprehensive knowledge

Table 6.5 ETPs and eco-awareness in Indian textile processing sector

Type of units	SSI/non-SSI	% number of units with ETP (type of ETP: primary, secondary, tertiary)	% Eco-awareness
All	All	87 (34% Prim, 53% Sec, 13% of Teri)	84
Composite	All	93 (25% Prim, 60% Sec, 16% of Teri)	93
Semi-composite	All	85 (35% Prim, 50% Sec, 15% of Teri)	92
Independent	All	87 (34% Prim, 53% Sec, 13% of Teri)	83
All	SSI	– (39% Prim, 52% Sec, 9% of Teri)	83
Composite	SSI	No composite units exist in SSI sector	–
Semi-composite	SSI	– (69% Prim, 28% Sec, 3% of Teri)	84
Independent	SSI	– (38% Prim, 53% Sec, 9% of Teri)	83
All	Non-SSI	– (31% Prim, 54% Sec, 15% of Teri)	84
Composite	Non-SSI	– (26% Prim, 54% Sec, 20% of Teri)	93
Semi-composite	Non-SSI	– (38% Prim, 53% Sec, 9% of Teri)	95
Independent	Non-SSI	– (27% Prim, 53% Sec, 20% of Teri)	81

Source Own calculations from Census of Textile Power Processing Industry in India, 2001, Textiles Committee, Mumbai of the environmental problems and good monitoring and enforcement abilities. Priyadarshini and Gupta (2003) show the following reasons for less compliance in India: lack of flexibility (one-size-fit-all strategy), over-ambitiousness of law and standards, weak enforcement despite significant powers and judicial support, poor monitoring, lack of effective punitive measures, paucity of funds in the PCBs and "race-to-the-bottom approach" followed by several states to attract investments. Three scenarios of non-compliance are plausible in India: prohibitively high mitigation costs; over-ambitious laws causing high marginal abatement costs; and lower probability of being caught and punished.

While the enforcement of environmental regulations in textiles has not been very strong in India, judiciary has taken a lead in ensuring that firms reduce pollution to acceptable levels, even at the cost of closing them down against their appeals. For example, the textile processing industries in Tiruppur used to directly discharge 500 tons of effluents from the 1800 tons of dyes consumed annually in late 1990s. Owing to obsolete technologies, typical water consumption in Tiruppur is around 200–400 l/kg of finished product, compared with the international norm of 120–150 l/kg, despite widespread lack of water supply in this region. This polluted the Noyyal River dam used for irrigation, surface water sources, tube wells and borewells in this area. Based on the litigation from the Noyyal River irrigation farmers' association, Chennai High Court ordered all the hosiery units to clean up the dam or shut down (Narayanaswamy and Scott 2001). In 1997–1998, about 270 units were closed due to this, with further support from the Supreme Court. Such a strict enforcement by PCBs and the Judiciary has led to the presence of ETPs in more or less all processing units in Tiruppur and elsewhere in the country.[3]

The government also assists the firms in abating pollution in various ways. For example, in a centrally sponsored scheme for the SSIs, the central government provides up to 25% of the capital cost of setting up a CETP, if the state government offers 25%. MoEF also provides guidelines that 20% should be shared by the entrepreneurs involved and 30% from financial institutions. However, more recently in January 2010, 600 dyeing units in Tiruppur have gone on an indefinite strike to protest against the failure of the government in sharing costs of the CETPs.[4]

In many of the textile factories that have ETPs, they do not spend enough money and care in ensuring that the parameters of the treated water are well within the limits required. Even when they do have the required infrastructure, some of them ensure full compliance only when they anticipate inspections from the PCBs. Therefore, the literature suggests a participatory approach that involves the industrialists to identify the constraints to abate pollution, prioritise and address them, iterative technological changes and demonstration, using firms well chosen, of the

[3]http://www.indianexpress.com/ie/daily/19980519/13950204.html.

[4]India: apparel production could be hit by dyers' strike, 5 January 2010. Available online at http://www.just-style.com/article.aspx?id=106312.

economical and environmental benefits of pollution abatement, wherever it is technologically and economically feasible.

National Environmental Policy (2006) addresses the constraints in pollution abatement, by proposing the consideration of various aspects, such as local relevance, reduction related to health, ecosystem and man-made assets, societal costs of compliance, concentration as well as mass-based standards and techno-economic feasibilities, for setting environmental standards.

In the recent years, there have been phenomenal improvements in the monitoring procedures followed by the PCBs. Many project studies are carried out in water laboratories, through various SPCBs all over India by CPCB, since 1991, when there were merely 20 of them. In 2007, there were 150 such laboratories evaluating 1019 water quality monitoring stations, spread across various sources of water in all states and union territories of India. The performance of these laboratories was evaluated 23 times, and the water was found acceptable in 58–81% in terms of 30 physico-chemical parameters.[5] CPCB also participates in the international proficiency testing (PT) programme for various physico-chemical parameters, including BOD, COD, oil and grease, TSS, TDS and various minerals. It has been accredited with National Accreditation Board for Testing and Calibration Laboratories (NABL), Department of Science of Technology, as per ISO 17025 for 85 chemical and 6 biological parameters.[6]

CPCB (2009b) developed a comprehensive environmental pollution indicator (CEPI) that is based on pollutant, pathway and receptor. This is applied in various pollutants in 88 industrial clusters all over India. Penalties are strictly fixed, based on CEPI. The report finds 43 of them critically polluted. As a remedial action, CPCB would analyse the spatial and temporal data for these 43 clusters, so as to identify the extent of damage and to evaluate alternative plans and procedures, along with other stakeholders and policymakers, to abate the pollution and restore environmental quality (CPCB 2009c).

Environmental planning is increasingly being stressed by CPCB. Currently, the industries are not set up with due consideration of the sites in relation to environmental sensitivities and mitigation capacities, but they rather go for various clearances after choosing a site. This makes pollution mitigation difficult to implement. To avoid this, CPCB has been proposing "zoning atlas", which pinpoints industrial areas within each district in India. This would enable the government to notify such areas, deciding the type of industrial development with due importance given to environment and economic factors and restricting the growth of certain industries in different areas. Industries would benefit from the ease in choice of location offered by the economic feasibilities discovered by the government in the notified industrial areas. PCBs would be able to plan well ahead of time and act on quick clearances, setting industry-specific standards and monitoring facilities and resources (including manpower), provision of CETPs if applicable.

---

[5]http://cpcb.nic.in/project_studies_in_water.pdf.

[6]http://cpcb.nic.in/QAandQC.pdf.

With the zoning atlas, even the public can have their say well in advance about the type of industries that could be set in their neighbourhoods. Such an initiative stems from successful studies in Pondicherry (1988) and Hassan (1992).[7]

With all these advances in the planning, evaluation, monitoring and implementation procedures in the PCBs in India, the compliance is likely to increase in the foreseeable future. Further, the charter on corporate responsibility for environmental protection (CREP), launched in March 2003, urges the industries to voluntarily go beyond the standards set by the government.[8]

Many more efforts are being taken by the government and its autonomous agencies to improve compliance to environmental standards. In its 1992 Environmental Policy Statement, Ministry of Environment and Forests (MoEF) included cleaner production and waste minimisation as environmental protection measures. National Productivity Council (NPC) has developed a project named as "waste minimization circles" (WMC). Every such circle consists of a cluster of industries that collectively minimise waste by a participatory approach supported by NPC. NPC also hosts a National Cleaner Production Center (NCPC), established by United Nations Environment Programme (UNEP) and United Nations Industrial Development Organization (UNIDO) to demonstrate cleaner production concept in Indian industries by conducting demonstration projects and training workshops, disseminating sector-specific information and policy-level intervention.[9] Among its efforts, NCPC has partnered with Wuppertal Institute in Germany to publish a website resource (http://www.e-textile.org/) that explains the practical benefits of cleaner production.

Even the industries that manufacture chemicals for the textile industry play a role in helping the industries comply with the regulations by minimising the pollution load in the effluent itself. For example, Clariant textile chemicals have many environmentally friendly dyes and finishing chemicals. They also comply with international regulations such as registration, evaluation, authorisation and restriction of chemical substances (REACH) of the EU.[10]

North Indian Textile Research Association (NITRA) has been conducting surveys among textile units to improve energy efficiency in textile firms, in a project sponsored by Japanese Government in consultation with India's Ministry of Textiles. In this project, the firms are also given an opportunity to identify the areas where they can maximise energy efficiency and modify their processes accordingly.[11] However, despite all these efforts by the governmental and regulatory bodies to improve compliance in terms of the treatment of wastewater, most of the textile industries in India do not comply with the 2008 hazardous waste rules on

---

[7]http://cpcb.nic.in/Env_Planning.php.

[8]http://cpcb.nic.in/crep.php.

[9]http://www.npcindia.org/NationalCleaner.aspx.

[10]www.clariant.com.

[11]http://nitratextile.org/questionnaire.htm.

sludge, which require their recycling or disposal, after storing them for not more than 90 days. They end up being stored in the factory premises.

6.2.2 Current Abatement Technologies in India

Water pollution in textile processing sector has been addressed in India, mainly by treating the effluents, through the ETPs and CETPs. These plants involve physico-chemical treatment of the wastewater using lime and ferrous sulphate. Primarily, the effluents contain inorganic salts such as sodium sulphate and sodium chloride. In a typical ETP, some or all of the following processes are carried out[12]:

- Screening: This is done to filter out relatively larger solids to avoid abrasion of mechanical equipment and blocking in the hydraulic system.
- Equalisation: Given that effluent undergoes changing its concentration and pH, it is stored from 8 to 12 h in a tank, to mix it homogeneously and to neutralise it. This would ensure uniform feeding to the next process and prevent solids from settling down. Pre-heating may also be done at this stage, combined with evaporation to increase the concentration.
- Flash mixing: Coagulants like lime (800–1000 ppm, to bring the pH to 8–9), ferrous sulphate (200–300 ppm, to remove colour) and poly electrolyte (0.2 ppm, to settle the suspended matters) are added and mixed rapidly with the effluents.
- Flocculation: With the continuous circulation of water, the solid particles settle down as they crystallise or flocculate. They are then collected separately and dried as primary sludge.
- Aeration tank: By passing a thin film of water and effluent over a staircase-like arrangement, the oxygen that gets dissolved into it reduces the BOD value.
- Clarification: Once the water is found to be safe and within the limits prescribed by CPCB, it is released into the river or other sources.
- Sludge thickening: The liquid and solids are separated from the final effluent, by passing it through the centrifuge. Then, the water content is reduced to around 40%. From the reprocessed effluent, the secondary sludge is collected at the bottom.
- Drying: Primary and secondary sludge is dried on the drying beds, subjected to solar evaporation.
- Pre-treatment: In addition to the above processes, in a CETP that comprises industries other than textiles, usually the textile dyeing effluent is

[12]Summarised from the following sources: Kathuria (2007). http://www.industrialeffluenttreatment.com/textile-dyeing-industries.html, http://www.fibre2fashion.com/industry-article/3/215/textile-effluent-treatment-a-case-study-in-home-textile-zone1.asp.

non-biodegradable, while most others are not. So, before being mixed with other effluents, this needs to be chemically pre-treated to remove its non-biodegradable components.
- Sludge disposal: Sludge is mostly disposed within the factory premises. It is usually packed in polyethylene bags and covered with rainproof sheets. In very few industries, it is safely incinerated in landfills authorised by the government.

However, these are not widespread and the pollution-related parameters in the treated water are still not within the safe limits. There is a scope of improving the infrastructure and functioning of these plants. The issue of treated wastewater still exists, as this could either be mixed with rivers or other water resources, or conveyed to a suitable safer place using a system.

Another question pertains to the way one disposes the sludge that remains after treating the effluent. Usually, this is just accumulated in places that are permitted by the government or dumped in the factory premises or elsewhere. Even in the developed countries, such waste is enormous: for example, in the USA, over quarter billion tons of waste is disposed in on-site industrial facilities in textiles manufacturing alone, most of it being disposed in surface impoundments. Some safer options have been secure landfill sites and incineration systems. All these require cooperative action among the SSIs and SMEs, which are traditionally known to be more cooperative in states like Gujarat.

Despite all these systems that rarely exist, much of the sludge is openly dumped, leading to pollution of soil, surface and groundwater. For example, in Tiruppur, 200 tons of sludge is dumped from the textile ETPs daily and 55.76 tons from 13,925 kl of wastewater per day (Patel and Pandey 2008).

Waste minimisation is an effective way of pollution abatement, which is also economical, due to the savings in energy and raw material costs. Clusters under WMC programme were able to save power and fuel, reducing their operating costs considerably. For example, in Ludhiana, some cotton dyeing units opted for simultaneous scouring and bleaching, which reduced rinsing and acid treatment, resulting in a reduction in steam use of 50% and power use of 30%. In Surat, man-made textile industries reused the dye-bath and used direct-fired gas heating instead of thermic fluid heating resulting in savings in power and fuel of 95% and 50%, respectively.

In Tiruppur, a WMC programme has led to 15–16% reduction in the usage of chemicals such as acids and salts and also of water.[13] However, waste minimisation has to be coupled with proper abatement technologies in order to comply with the regulations. In such an effort, a textile processing and garment manufacturing unit named "Together Textiles" in Coimbatore has an efficient ETP, which produces such a clean treated water that is reused for watering a garden full of plants that supply vegetables for the canteen of the factory. At the same time, the unit also minimises waste during the processing stages as well.

[13]http://wmc.nic.in/case-studies1.asp#4.

6.2.3 Some Latest Abatement Technologies

Although there are many advances in ETP technologies, which are mostly physico-chemical, sludge disposal remains a practically unresolved issue in India. Conventional physico-chemical methods including coagulation, precipitation and flocculation discussed in the previous section are costly, less effective and inefficient. They have limited applicability due to the sludge formation as its disposal is a complex concern.

In the developed countries such as the USA, conventional biological processes such as anaerobic decomposition were being followed for the degradation of the sludge as well as the treatment of effluent for many decades (see Flood 1937; Gaffney 1976a, b). However, these methods are not very effective to treat the effluent itself, as they cannot decolourise it efficiently. Many recent studies suggest the use of living microbial organisms to decompose and degrade the colour and other chemical properties of the sludge. Some microbes enhance the wastewater treatment process, for example, in terms of improved flocculation caused by hydrophobic marine bacteria (Khemakhem et al. 2005). Even agricultural waste may be used to produce enzymes that can facilitate decolourisation of the effluent; for example, enzymes such as laccase and lignin peroxidase, produced from the solid-state fermentation of otherwise unusable agro by-products such as peanut straw, wheat bran and neem hull waste, can be used to decolourise textile reactive dyes (Sun et al. 2009; Verma and Madamwar 2002).

Other studies address the issue of sludge treatment in particular. For example, Dawkar et al. (2009) find that *Bacillus* sp. VUS, along with some inducers, causes decolourisation and biodegradation of a textile azo dye, reducing its toxicity. Dias et al. (2007) review the applications of fungal and plant systems in decolourising textile wastewater and related dyestuffs. Xu et al. (2007) show that *Shewanella decolorationis* S12 can cause biodegradation of the economical and effective but heavily toxic and carcinogenic azo dyes, under certain conditions. Some other studies in this stream of literature include Bakshi et al. (1999) and Moosvi et al. (2005) to treat reactive, sulphur and mix dyes, and Corso and Almeida (2009) to treat azo dyes. Many of these studies suggest that bio-remediation techniques may be used to treat the effluents and release them to water sources directly, leaving behind little or no sludge. These appear to be attractive cost-competitive options, especially for the small-scale industries in India. For example, Dias et al. (2007) mention as follows:

> "…Microbial treatments can be performed either in the presence (aerobic) or absence (anaerobic) of oxygen. Both processes have lower operational costs, when compared to chemical and/or physical treatments, which tend to concentrate pollutants rather than degrade them. More importantly, they pose less health and safety risks. However, the selection of the most adapted microorganisms to a particular operation is an arduous task…."

Another development that is said to be going beyond the limits of microbial bio-remediation is the use of constructed wetlands or phyto-remediation. This is a low-cost technique, with low maintenance needs (Schwitzguébel et al. 2002; Susarla et al. 2002). It can tolerate high fluctuations in flow, temperature and the composition and/or concentration of pollutants in wastewater (Winthrop et al. 2002).

Other techniques such as ozonation, adsorption, incineration and chemical transformation are effective but are rather costly. There are numerous ways of recycling the dye-bath, water and other resources (Senthilkumar and Muthukumar 2007). Polyelectrolyte membranes are found to remove the colour and COD from the textile effluents very efficiently (Aravind et al. 2010).

Researchers are also trying to identify ways in which the sludge may be reused for some constructive purposes, such as the following:

- for replacing up to 30% of cement for non-structural building materials such as flooring tiles, solid and pavement blocks and bricks (Balasubramanian et al. 2006);
- for replacing 30–70% of cement in building bricks up to a strength of 25 N/mm^2, corresponding to the "°C" to "K" classes of structural applications as defined by BIS, using solidification/stabilisation technologies (Patel and Pandey 2008);
- for reusing the treated wastewater for textile processing, resulting in zero discharge (Krishnaswamy et al. 2009);
- for recycling the nutrients useful for agriculture by vermicomposting with cow-dung, epigeic earthworm and agricultural residues (Kausik and Garg 2003, 2004).

6.3 Pollution Abatement Costs in Indian Textile Sector

6.3.1 Global Environmental Standards: Targets for Indian Textile Sector

The international standards exist for a whole gamut of processes in the textile industry. They exist for water quality in general and for textile effluents in particular. However, it is difficult to compare the standards across the countries as they are measured differently (Sargaonkar and Deshpande 2003). Standards are laid mostly by governmental and intergovernmental bodies. There are also labelling agencies and associations that set even more stringent standard and then issue labels and certifications to individual firms that meet these requirements.

For example, some of the standards mentioned in Oeko-Tex 1000 are discussed. These are both product and process standards. They conduct on-site evaluation and issue the certificate on a three-year basis, with grades that are based on the actual performance of the firm.

In Oeko-Tex 1000 Standard, the use of various chemicals is prohibited; some of them are azo dyes and pigments, carcinogenic dyes and pigments, allergenic dyes and pigments, dyes containing heavy metals such as lead and cadmium, acutely toxic (LD50 < 100 mg/kg)[14] dyes, environmentally risky dyes, chlorinated organic carriers, flame retardants containing arsenic, antimony, bromine, chloro-paraffines and fluorides; detergents, cleaning and degreasing agents without some chloro-hydrocarbons and phosphates; other chemicals such as asbestos, chloroform, cyanide, aromatic hydrocarbons such as solvents, ozone-layer-reducing substances, heavy benzene for printing, dichromate[15] to improve colour fastness, chlorinated organic solvents, etc. Wastewater treatment has to ensure reduction of phosphor content by 80%.

There are various other stringent requirements in this labelling, in terms of exhaust air, noise, workplace and social standards. Particularly, there are some conditions on packing. Packing for internal handling must be avoided as far as possible. Recycled or reusable materials should be used for packing systems. Quantity and whereabouts of the packing materials should be documented. Parikh et al. (1995) find most of the Indian exporters to European Union to be completely complying with the packing standards.

Table 6.6 summarises the permissible levels for various parameters in the effluent to be released into the waters or a public sewage treatment plant (or CETP) for different grading levels of certification. When compared with these standards, the Indian standards mentioned in Tables 6.1, 6.2 and 6.3 come under various grades of Oeko-Tex 1000 Standard. For the concentration of all minerals/chemicals except nickel, chlorine and chromium, CPCB standards are far lower. For others, however, Indian standards are much better. Further, CPCB has set various other standards that do not exist at international level, e.g. sodium absorption ratio, suspended solids and dissolved solids.

Table 6.7 shows some of the standards laid by the European Commission for surface water suitable for aquatic environment. CPCB standards are much lower for most of them. Particularly, while the European Commission has notified substances such as cadmium, chlorine-based compounds, lead, mercury, nickel and phenolic compounds as priority substances in the field of water policy in 2001.[16] Another Directive (2006/11/EC)[17] of the European Commission lists zinc, copper, chromium and cobalt as substances whose discharge into surface waters with aquatics is limited.

---

[14]This is the lethal dose of the material required to kill 50% of a test population in a specified time. This is measured in milligrams of the material required per kilogram of the body mass. The lesser it is, more toxic is the material.

[15]If some chemicals like this are used because there are no other alternatives, they should be removed completely from the effluent.

[16]Decision No 2455/2001/EC of the European Parliament and of the Council, available online at: http://eur-lex.europa.eu/LexUriServ/LexUriServ.do?uri=OJ:L:2001:331:0001:0005:EN:PDF.

[17]See http://eur-lex.europa.eu/LexUriServ/LexUriServ.do?uri=OJ:L:2006:064:0052:0059:EN:PDF.

Table 6.6 Oeko-Tex standard classification for effluents: comparison with CPCB

Parameter	Grade					CPCB value	CPCB grade
	−3	−2	−1	0	1		
pH (acidic/alkaline)	5.5–10.0	6.0–10.0	6.5–9.5	6.5–9.0	6.5–8.5	5.5–9	−3/−2
Maximum effluent temperature	50 °C	45 °C	40 °C	35 °C	30 °C	NA[a]	0/1
Colour/spectral adsorption coefficient at 436 nm	20/m	15/m	11/m	9/m	6/m	400 Hazen Units[b]	<−3
525 nm	15/m	12/m	9/m	7/m	4/m		
620 nm	10/m	8/m	6/m	4/m	3/m		
COD (mg/l)	400	300	250	180	120	250	−1
Total organic carbon (mg/l)	200	150	100	70	40	NA	NA
Phenolics as C_6H_5OH (mg/l)	0	0	0	0	0	1	<−3
Cadmium as Cd (mg/l)	0	0	0	0	0	0.2	<−3
Copper as Cu (mg/l)	2.0	1.5	1	0.4	0.1	2	−3
Manganese as Mn	0	0	0	0	0	2	<−3
Lead as Pb	0	0	0	0	0	0.1	<−3
Mercury as Hg	0	0	0	0	0	0.01	<−3
Nickel as Ni	2.0	1.5	1	0.4	0.1	2	−3
Zinc as Zn	0	0	0	0	0	5	<−3
Chromium as Cr hexavalent (mg/l)	0.7	0.4	0.2	0.1	0.02	0.1	0
Chromium total (mg/l)	2	1.5	1	0.4	0.1	2	−3
Cobalt as Co (mg/l)	2	1.5	1	0.4	0.1	NA	NA
AOX as Cl (mg/l) for antifelt finishing of wool (mg/l)	5 20	2 15	1 10	0.4 4	0.1 1	1	−1
Reduction of oxygen depleting substances (in TOC or COD) by recycling and cleaning	70.00%	75.00%	80%	85%	90%	NA	NA

Source Compiled from Oeko-Tex Standard 1000 (Edition 01/2011), published by International Association for the Assessment of Environmentally Friendly Textiles (http://www.oeko-tex.com/xdesk/ximages/470/15540_1000-DEF.pdf) and Indian standards set by CPCB (http://cpcb.nic.in)

[a]Though CPCB does not specify the temperature, it does say that the wastewater should be no warmer than 5 °C above the water temperature. This boils down to around 20–35 °C depending on the region and season

[b]Hongve and Akesson (1996) find that Hazen units are very close to spectral adsorption coefficient at 410–450 nm. So CPCB standards are well below Oeko-Tex standards, but CPCB recommends minimal practicable colour and odour in the effluent

Table 6.7 Water quality standards: a comparison of EU and India

Parameter	EC limit for surface waters	CPCB limits for surface waters
pH (acidic/alkaline)	6–9	5.5–9
Maximum temperature of the discharge above that of the water surface	1.5–3 °C	5 °C
Suspended solids, mg/l max.	25	100
BOD[a]	6	30
Total residual chlorine, mg/l max	0.005	1.0
Total organic carbon (mg/l)		NA
Phenolics as C_6H_5OH (mg/l)	0.001–0.002	1
Copper (mg/l)	0.04	2
Cadmium as Cd (mg/l)	0.00045–0.0015	0.2
Lead as Pb	0.0072	0.1
Mercury as Hg	0.00007	0.01
Nickel as Ni	0.002	2
Zinc as Zn	1	5
Chromium as Cr hexavalent (mg/l)	0.02	0.1
Chromium total (mg/l)	0.1	2
Cobalt as Co (mg/l)	0.1	NA
AOX as Cl (mg/l)	0.0012	1

Note The CPCB limits for surface water refer to surface water suitable for aquatic life and not drinking water

Source European Council Directives 2008/105/EC (http://eur-lex.europa.eu/LexUriServ/LexUriServ.do?uri=OJ:L:2008:348:0084:0097:EN:PDF) on environmental quality standards in the field of water policy and 2006/44/EC (http://eur-lex.europa.eu/LexUriServ/LexUriServ.do?uri=OJ:L:2006:264:0020:0031:EN:PDF) on the quality of fresh waters needing protection or improvement in order to support fish life

[a]This is measured by the EC for "five days at 20 ± 1 °C" and by CPCB for "3 days at 27 °C"

European Union has set up an Integrated Pollution Prevention and Control (IPPC) directive in 2008, to set standards for establishing industries with environmentally sound practices and technologies. IPPC directive is based on the concept of best available techniques (BAT), which is applicable merely for plants above a certain capacity. Under this directive, every plant that produces, processes or treats more than 10 tons of textile products per day should provide all information on emissions to the public.[18]

German Federal Environment Agency has prepared BAT reference documents for different industries, including textiles, developed by Schönberger and Schäfer (2003). This document addresses the best available techniques, selected from hundreds of currently practiced technologies across the globe, for the whole gamut of processes in the textile industry.

---

[18]See Regulation (EC) No: 166/2006 of the European Parliament and of the Council http://eur-lex.europa.eu/LexUriServ/LexUriServ.do?uri=OJ:L:2006:033:0001:0017:EN:PDF.

Starting from general best management practices, numerous advanced environmentally friendly techniques have been discussed in this report. It suggests the usage of eco-friendly chemicals to be used for various processing requirements, dyeing, etc. Recycling of the materials used in the processes has been recommended wherever possible. Technologies such as electrochemical and ultrasonic dyeing are recommended to reduce the usage of materials. Some techniques related to wastewater treatment include activated sludge treatment, recycling wastewater, anaerobic colour removal of dyestuff and printing paste, incineration of sludge and use of biopolymers for wastewater treatment.

Kahlenborn et al. (2009) discuss the extent to which the developing countries including India have been adopting these BATs. Wastewater treatment in India is mostly limited to primary and secondary processes (mechanical and biological wastewater treatment), which are not very effective in the removal of pollutants such as sulphides, colours and heavy metals. The level of environmental pollution caused by the textile industry in India is correspondingly high. The concentration of textile industry in clusters increases the environmental impact on geographically narrow areas. This impact is even more significant given the limited local water supply. Cluster concentration results in large volumes of wastewater being discharged to receiving media and causing great environmental pollution. Many Indian organisations do apply some of the technologies mentioned in the BAT reference document. A wide spectrum of activities is found that promote cleaner production.

6.3.2 Costs of Using Natural Dyes for Abatement

There are many studies on natural dyes, showing that they reduce pollution by a great deal (Bechtold 2003; Agarwal 2003; Rubeena et al. 2002; Patra et al. 2002; Teli et al. 2000). They also reduce the requirements of an ETP, as they are much less polluting and more biodegradable than other dyes. Effluent from using natural dyes is generally safe (Parham 1994). Many natural dyes exhibit good performance and dyeing properties, mostly matching that of synthetic dyes (Furry 1945; Bahl and Gupta 1988).

Historically, natural dyes were used to colour clothing or other textiles even until mid-nineteenth century (Kharbade and Agrawal 1988), when chemists began producing synthetic substitutes for them. By the early part of this century, only a small percentage of textile dyes were extracted from plants. Lately, there has been increasing interest in natural dyes, as the public becomes aware of ecological and environmental problems related to the use of synthetic dyes. Use of natural dyes cuts down significantly the amount of toxic effluent resulting from the synthetic dyeing process.

Narayanan (2007) considers a set of natural dyes derived from sources such as fenugreek seeds, golden dock seeds, secretions from some insects, some barks, some fruits, lac, madder roots and pomegranate rinds. Based on the literature, their suitability is figured out for the natural fibres—cotton, silk and wool sectors—and synthetic fibres—polyester and nylon sectors. The author verifies the claim that natural dyes reduce pollution in textile processing industries, using a multi-scenario analysis of adoption of natural dyes done under different paces in different sub-sectors in India till 2020.

Currently, natural dyes are mostly used in silk sector, due to the ban of azo dyes and lack of suitability of other dyes for silk. In future, natural dyes might be adopted by other sub-sectors as well. Considering these aspects, following scenarios were built by Narayanan (2007) for the years 2005–2020:

Business as usual (BAU): 100% of the dyes used for all the categories of materials are synthetic throughout the period of analysis, except for silk, in which 70% are natural dyes. As an evidence for the proposition that natural dyes reduce emissions, BAU shows maximum emissions in the study.

Scenario 1 (optimistic): The shares of natural dyes and synthetic dyes for different years start at 20% in 2005 and increase by 10% points every five years, except for silk for which 70% natural dyes are assumed for all periods. This scenario indeed causes least emissions, showing that natural dyes were "pollution-reducers".

Scenario 2 (realistic): For cotton, wool and silk, the same percentage of dyes are maintained as in scenario 1, while for synthetic fibres, the rates of 0% for 2005 and a rise of 10% points every five years are assumed. Hence, this scenario is realistic given the lower applicability of natural dyes on natural fibres. Scenario 2 gives second least level of emissions. This is yet another support for the proposition of pollution reduction by natural dyes, since this scenario has the second fastest adaptation rates for the synthetic fibres and fastest rates for the natural fibres.

Scenario 3 (pessimistic): In this scenario, the assumption is that the natural dyes are not adapted to synthetic fibres throughout the period of analysis and that they are adapted to natural fibres at a pace at which they were assumed to be adapted to synthetic fibres in the Scenario 2. Silk is assumed to use natural dyes at 70% throughout the period. This scenario is still more optimistic than BAU, given that other natural fibres sectors do adopt natural dyes albeit at a slower pace than other non-BAU scenarios. This results in second largest level of emissions.

Scenario 4 (no synthetic fibres with natural dyes): Natural dyes are adapted by the natural fibres sectors at a pace defined in scenario 1, while synthetic fibres do not at all adapt them. As the natural fibres adapt to natural dyes at higher pace in this scenario than in Scenario 3, this scenario causes less emissions than Scenario 3, i.e. third largest level of emissions.

The overall results confirm that natural dyes do cause significant reductions in the total dissolved solids (TDS) by 2020, even while assuming that 70% of the chemicals used in dyeing are retained in the natural dyeing effluent though merely 40% is retained for synthetic dyeing effluent. The emissions were calculated based on the dyeing recipes.

However, there are some concerns involved with widespread use of natural dyes, in terms of availability of land, over-intensification of agriculture (Glover 1995), possible toxicity in the effluent from certain natural dyes (Rubeena et al. 2002), lower eye appeal and colour value (Kirtikar 1947; Gulati 1949), fastness properties (Duff 1977a, b) and excessive use of supporting chemicals (Glover 1995).

To address the controversy about other concerns of the natural dyes, opinion was sought on the relative importance of these aspects from various experts such as the people working in the industries, academicians and researchers who are involved in textile processing. Using such opinions, Narayanan (2007) assigned weights for colour fastness, which reflects the dye quality, TDS emissions derived from the analysis and cost. Based on analytical hierarchical programming (AHP) analysis to rank dyes, natural dyes were found to be better than other dyes in many cases, though there were a few cases in which synthetic dyes were better.

Table 6.8 summarises the costs and fastness indices of various dyes and their applicability to different fibres, compiled by Narayanan (2007) from the commercial websites of various dye manufacturers. In most cases, natural dyes are poorer in colour fastness than synthetic dyes. But there are many new studies that come up with new natural dyes and dyeing processes that result in superior performance and fastness properties (e.g. Vankar et al. 2009).

While computing their average cost difference, it is more realistic to use the output weights of the processing sectors of the corresponding applicable fibres. Table 6.9 shows the simple average costs of synthetic and natural dyes for each of the applicable fibres. Then, using 2007–2008 production values of these fibre sectors, the weighted average costs of natural and synthetic dyes are computed and used in total. Assuming that the same amount of natural and synthetic dyes are used for dyeing any given amount of textile materials, the difference between these costs gives the approximate overall abatement cost by using natural dyes.

Table 6.8 Natural dyes versus synthetic dyes: cost, fastness and applicability

S. no.	Dye	Natural/synthetic	Cost (US$/lb)	Fastness index	Applicable fibres
1	Acid dye	Synthetic	25	5	Cotton, wool
2	Azo dye	Synthetic	20	5	Silk
3	Direct dye	Synthetic	20	5	Cotton
4	Disperse dye	Synthetic	26	5	Polyester, nylon
5	Reactive dye	Synthetic	30	5	Cotton
6	Sulphur dye	Synthetic	19	5	Cotton
7	Gallnut	Natural	43	4	Cotton
8	Kamala	Natural	8.25	3	Polyester
9	Gum Arabic	Natural	18	4	Wool, nylon
10	Fenugreek	Natural	43	4	Cotton
11	Dolu	Natural	27.5	4	Wool, nylon
12	Madder	Natural	25	4	Silk
13	Indigo	Natural	28	4	Polyester
14	Pomegranate	Natural	19	4	Silk
15	Shellac	Natural	14	4	Polyester, silk
16	Golden dock	Natural	14	3	Wool, nylon, cotton

Source Narayanan (2007)

Table 6.9 Sector-wise cost differences between natural and synthetic dyes

Sector	Average cost US$/lb		Difference in US$/lb: natural—synthetic	% price difference
	Natural dyes	Synthetic dyes		
Cotton	33.33	23.5	9.83	41.84
Wool	19.83	25	−5.17	−20.67
Silk	19.33	20	−0.67	−3.33
Polyester	16.75	26	−9.25	−35.57
Nylon	19.83	26	−6.17	−23.72
Overall	27.23	24.47	2.76	11.29

Source Own calculations based on Narayanan (2007) and ASI

Using the final price difference figure of 2.76 $/lb, the total abatement cost using natural dyes is calculated. For this, it is assumed that about 5 billion kilograms of yarn produced in India, which is about 90% of the total of 5.512 billion kg produced in 2008–2009, is dyed currently using synthetic dyes.[19] In order to dye this quantity of textile goods, an average amount of 100–200 million kg of dyes are required.[20] This translates into a total expenditure of 603.7 to 1207.41 million US$, which turns out to be around Rs. 2717 to 5434 crores, assuming an exchange rate of around 45 Rs/US$ in 2008–2009.

Considering the organised processing sector output as Rs. 12,068 Crores (from ASI), forming 59% (based on Table 1.1) of the total processing output in India, the total textile processing output is valued at Rs. 20,454 Crores. Thus, the total abatement cost of using natural dyes varies from 13.28 to 26.56%. This also turns out to be 5–10 Rs. per kg of textile goods dyed. This cost might appear very high, but there are numerous benefits in terms of savings in effluent treatment plants as discussed above. Further, if one considers this expenditure as a percentage of the textile industry output as a whole (not including apparel sector), it works out as 0.96–1.93%, which is the same as the percentage change in textile prices owing to adapting to natural dyes.

6.3.3 *Costs of Other Abatement Technologies*

There are various estimates in the literature for complying with regulation and standards. In one of the early studies, Pasurka (1984) finds one percentage increase in prices of textile commodities due to complying with the USEPA's standards in the late 1970s, based on some publicly estimates of abatement expenditures.

[19]Source: The website of Officer of Textile Commissioner of India www.txcindia.com.

[20]It is assumed that 18–36 g of dyestuff is required per kilogram of textile substrate as given by Schönberger and Schäfer (2003).

However, this is in the context of USA and 1970s, and hence, one is not sure to what extent this can reflect today's situation in India.

Parikh et al. (1995) estimate an increase of 3–5% of product cost with the compliance to environmental standards, based on a survey among Indian textile and garment exporters. Other studies estimate the adjustment costs for complying with the ban of azo dyes to be 8–10% for large-scale companies and 15–20% for small-scale companies in India in terms of total cost. However, these studies are applicable for older regulations in India, which have already been more or less fully complied with now. Therefore, the analysis relies on more recent studies here: Malik and Datta (2005) and Kathuria (2007).

Malik and Datta (2005) select five individual industries in West Bengal and assess the financial aspects of ETPs set up for them. Two among them are textile industries: Eastern Spinning Mills India Ltd (ESMIL), a large-scale industry (LSI), and Samson Processing Industry (SPI), an SSI involved in textile dyeing. Their environmental and financial aspects are summarised in Table 6.10.

Table 6.10 Environmental and financial aspects of ETPs

Parameter	ETP: West Bengal		CETP: Kundli				
	ESMIL (an LSI)	SPI (an SSI)	Cotton yarn dyeing	MMF yarn dyeing	Fabric dyeing	Fabric bleaching	Wool processing
COD	1750 (209)	1050 (247)	2035	2547	2305	6424	1040–6000
O&G	7.8 (4)	5.2 (3.8)	<5	<5	<5	<5	<5
pH	8.5 (7.6)	9.2 (8.1)	11.8	8.3	9.3–13	13	2.7–5
BOD	310 (120)	380 (82.5)	924	302	1159	946	170–469
TSS	234 (42)	203 (78)	465	144	140	1610	59–1200
Capital Rs. Mn	5.685	1.615	1.247–4.921				
Operation Rs. Mn	2.151	0.517	3.491–9.193				
Effluent volume	145	50	491				
Capital Rs./m^3	107	89	7–28				
Operation Rs./m^3	41	28	20–51				

Note Figures in parentheses are the target values for the parameters in the final discharge; effluent volume is in m^3/day; capital and operation costs are in 2008–2009 prices of millions of rupees
Source Own calculations based on Malik and Datta (2005) for ETPs and Kathuria (2007) for CETP

Kathuria (2007) found 17 textile dyeing units accounted for over 50% (i.e. 491 m^3/day) of the total industrial wastewater flow in the Kundli CETP. In this system, the firms shared 20% of the capital cost, which is about Rs. 1.163 million; 40% was financed as soft loans and 40% was a government subsidy. So one could consider the total capital cost required by the firms in total as Rs. 3.48 million, with the remaining Rs. 2.33 million being government subsidy.

There are two components of the costs borne by the firms: 70% COD load share and 30% volume share, based on the COD load and volume discharged, respectively. Their daily average wastewater discharge is in the range of 25–50 m^3. Their daily average COD load is in the range of 30–186 kg, which is calculated based on the average COD range of 1040–6424 mg/l and the total discharge of 491 m^3/day. Given these, the total one-time capital costs borne by the dyeing firms are estimated to range between Rs. 0.75 million and Rs. 2.96 million and the annual operational costs to range between Rs. 2.1 million and Rs. 5.53 million in 1997–1998 prices, which have been inflated to 2008–2009 prices in Table 6.10.

Per unit capital costs are the lowest for a CETP, owing to the fact that the firms share the costs. However, the operational costs depend on the extent to which the industries pollute. Therefore, one can construct a range for ETP costs using the figures calculated in Table 6.10. Schönberger and Schäfer (2003) suggest that a maximum of 618 l[21] of wastewater is discharged for processing per kg of textile materials (woven fabrics) in Germany, but given that the technologies adopted by Indian industry are more water intensive, this is assumed as the average effluent discharge. Using this ratio and the fact that 5.512 billion kgs (see Sect. 6.2.2) of yarn and cloth is dyed in Indian textile sector in 2008–2009, the total liquid required is calculated and taken as the volume of effluent.

Based on the calculations from the above figures, discharge of effluent per year by the Indian textile processing sector is estimated as 3406 billion litres, the total capital cost required for ETPs for all Indian textile industries is estimated to be in the range of Rs. 23.85–364.49 billion and annual operational costs are estimated to be in the range of Rs. 68.13–139.66 billion. Approximately, for the whole textile industry, the capital cost turns out to be 0.85–12.94%, while the operational costs turn out to be 2.42–4.96% of the total output. These numbers also cause identical percentage price changes for the total output. There are many ways to reduce ETP costs such as using natural dyes and using non-conventional methods like low-cost adsorbents for dye removal.

[21]If only textile dyeing is considered, this would be far lower.

6.3.4 Total Pollution Abatement Costs in Indian Textile Sector

Based on the discussion in Sects. 6.2.2 and 6.2.3, one can estimate the total pollution abatement costs in Indian textile sector. The data on the environmental compliance of Indian textile industries are rather scarce. It is seen from the literature that many of the clusters with register SSI units as well as large-scale industries have already been complying with the regulations since the late 1990s, especially in terms of establishing and operating ETPs and CETPs, despite various institutional issues therein (Malik and Datta 2005; Kathuria 2007).

However, it is perhaps reasonable to assume that India's unorganised and small-scale textile sector does not comply with any environmental standards, although the registered SSI sector does so. Close to 36% of the total textile output is produced by unorganised and unregistered SSI sectors. Revising calculations for abatement using ETPs merely for this sector, the capital costs are 0.3–4.7% and operational costs are 0.9–1.8%.

Using natural dyes likely reduces the operational costs of the ETPs that have already been established, because the pollution parameters of the effluent from natural dyeing are far lower and hence need far less intense treatment, which translates into reduction in the cost of abatement. In extreme cases, use of natural dyes might even mean that no ETP is required, as the effluent could be treated using far cheaper methods like adsorption using waste materials, which are more effective when the effluent has reasonably low COD.

Therefore, in a scenario of adoption of natural dyes, one could also envisage a fall in ETP operational costs for unorganised and unregistered SSI sectors, which produce relatively lower pollution load, meaning that the total abatement costs are almost zero in the aggregate textile sector. Indeed in a scenario where ETP capital operational costs can be saved even for the organised sector due to the adoption of natural dyes, the industry can indeed benefit by 1.4–3% of the total output, even if capital is considered as sunk cost. Of course, this is an extremely optimistic scenario. The following are taken as reasonable scenarios:

1. Gradual adoption to natural dyes: 50% cut in the adoption costs estimated in Sect. 6.3.2, which means about 0.5–1% cost of abatement due to the adoption of natural dyes.
2. Compliance enforced on unorganised sector: ETP operational and capital costs, estimated in Sect. 6.3.3, are deemed reasonable.

In this scenario, the overall cost of abatement is about 1.7–7.5%, including capital costs. In a scenario where all industries adopt natural dyes and ETPs are enforced on all firms, the total abatement cost is 2.2–8.5%.

6.3.5 Economy-Wide Impacts of Pollution Abatement on Trade

Economy-wide modelling encompasses analysing the impacts of policies and changes in one or more sectors in the economy across different sectors, using inter-sectoral linkages and on the economy as a whole. Particularly, a computable general equilibrium (CGE) model, using solvable mathematical equations based on standard economic theories, captures complex interactions among the markets. In this framework, demand for each good depends on the prices of all other goods and on income, which, in turn, depends on wages, profits and rents, which depend on technology, factor supplies and demand-driven production. Many of the variables are interdependent in this framework.

Hertel (1997) documents the GTAP model, which is a well-known multi-regional and multi-sectoral CGE model, used mainly for international trade policy analysis. The mathematical relationships assumed in the GTAP model are generally rather simple, with some of the most important relationships estimated econometrically, e.g. international trade elasticities and the agricultural factor supply and demand elasticities. The GTAP model is a comparative static linearised model, based on neoclassical theories, assuming perfect competition in all markets.

Demand and supply are balanced in all markets, which imply the price received by the producer the same as the producer's marginal cost. By imposing taxes and subsidies on commodities and primary factors, regional government can drive wedges between prices paid by purchasers and prices received by producers. These policy interventions are modelled as ad valorem taxes, tariffs and subsidies, or quantitative restrictions in the case of textile and apparel trade. International trade is linked through Armington substitution among goods differentiated by country of origin. Therefore, in markets for traded commodities, buyers differentiate between domestically produced products and imported products with the same name. Product differentiation between imports by region of origin allows for two-way trade across regions in each tradable product.

There are two types of inputs—intermediate inputs and primary factors used for production. In each region, each sector is assumed to mix the inputs to minimise total cost at a given output level. A three-level nested production technology constrains the sectors' inputs choice. At the first level, intermediate input bundles and primary factor bundles are used in fixed proportions according to a Leontief function. At the second level, intermediate input bundles are formed as combinations of imported bundles and domestic goods with the same input–output name, and primary factor bundles are obtained as combinations of labour, capital and land. In both cases, the aggregator function has a constant elasticity of substitution (CES) form. At the third level, imported bundles are formed as CES composites of imported goods with the same name from each region.

Each region in GTAP model has a single representative household that collects all the regional income. This representative household aggregate income is exhausted through constant share to private household consumption, government expenditures and national savings. The private household buys bundles of commodities to maximise utility subject to its expenditure constraint. The constrained optimising behaviour of the private household is represented by constant difference elasticity (CDE) demand system. The CDE function is not as general as the commonly used CES and linear expenditure system (LES) but is more flexible and easy to calibrate with different price and income elasticities of consumption by region. The bundles are CES combinations of domestic goods and import bundles, with the import bundles being CES aggregations of imports from each region.

The share of aggregate government expenditure in each region's income is held fixed. Government expenditure is allocated across commodities by a Cobb–Douglas distribution. The allocation of total expenditure on each good to domestically produced and imported versions is based on the same nesting scheme used to allocate total household expenditure on each good.

Investment in each region is financed from a global pool of savings. Each region contributes a fixed proportion of its income to the savings pool. Two alternative ways can be used to allocate the savings pool. The first way is where each region's share increases by the proportion in which aggregate pool increases. The second way is where the investment allocation is done according to the relative rates of return. Regions, which experience increases in their rate of return relative to the global average, will receive increased shares of the investment budget, whereas regions experiencing reductions in their rate of return relative to the global average will receive reduced shares.

In each region, there are five types of factors of production. First, the model recognises two types of labour (skilled and unskilled) and a single, homogenous capital good. Then, there is land and other natural resources that also form part of the set of the factors of production. In the typical closure of the model, total supplies of labour and land are fixed for each region, but capital can cross regional borders to equalise changes in rates of return. In other words, there is a clear distinction between those factors that are perfectly mobile and those that are sluggish to adjust. In the case of the mobile factors, they earn the same market return regardless of the use location. As for the sluggish factors, returns in equilibrium may be different across sectors.

The GTAP framework described above relies on the GTAP database, which comprises: input-output data for each region, and bilateral trade data derived from United Nations trade statistics (UN Statistical Division 2004). This is supplemented with individual countries global trade information and trade totals or aggregate bilateral trade statistics such as from the IMF, FAO and World Bank. Another important sub-component of the GTAP database is the protection data. The MacMap database (ITC 2006 and Boumellassa et al. 2009) contains bound, most favoured nation (MFN) and bilateral applied tariff rates (both specific and ad valorem) at the 6-digit harmonised systems (HS6) level, aggregated to GTAP concordance (57 sectors) using trade weights. Other components of GTAP database are from different sources: energy data (OECD and IEA 2003), domestic support (OECD 2008) and input–output tables from individual country contributors.

The GTAP 7.1 database documented in Narayanan and Walmsley (2008) is used for this study. While these data come with 113 regions and 57 sectors, for the purpose of analysis here an aggregated version of it is used, with 10 regions and 10 sectors. Following are the aggregated regions considered for this study:

1. India
2. China
3. South East Asia
4. Rest of South Asia
5. USA and Canada
6. Latin America
7. European Union (27 Countries)
8. Other Developed Countries (Australia, New Zealand, Japan, Korea, etc.)
9. Middle East and Africa
10. Former Soviet Union members and Eastern Europe.

Following are the aggregated sectors covered in this study:

1. Crops
2. Meat and Livestock
3. Extraction Industries
4. Food Processing
5. Textiles
6. Apparel
7. Light Manufacturing
8. Heavy Manufacturing
9. Utility and Construction
10. Services.

GTAP 7.1 database has a base year of 2004, and hence, the GDP and population are updated to 2009 levels, using growth rates from Shane (2009). While doing this, care was taken to ensure that India's trade in textiles and apparel is adjusted to 2009 levels, using figures from the website of Government of India.[22] Using the abatement costs computed in Sect. 6.3, the Global Trade Analysis Project (GTAP) computable general equilibrium (CGE) modelling framework was employed to evaluate the economy-wide impacts on trade and welfare of complying with environmental standards by Indian textile sector.

While it is clear that there are costs associated with pollution abatement, it is also found from the literature that there are benefits[23] associated with the consumers' premium for "eco-labelled" products. These benefits translate into price premia, which are estimated as, for example: 10–17%[24] for Danish consumers of detergents and paper towels and 5% for apparel that has low environmental impact and 30%

[22]See www.dgft.delhi.nic.in.

[23]See http://www.un.org/documents/ecosoc/cn17/1996/background/ecn171996-bp8.htm.

[24]See http://www.colby.edu/personal/t/thtieten/Russell.htm.

for those made of organic naturally coloured fibres (Nimon and Beghin 1999), for US textile and apparel consumers. Therefore, the analysis considers a broad range of 5–30% for the willingness to pay (WTP) by the importers in USA, Canada and the EU, who are the major overseas consumers of Indian textiles.

Assuming that the costs of 1.7–8.5% to abate pollution can be applied as import tariff equivalents for India and all of its competitors (China, South Asia and South East Asia), two scenarios are considered. First scenario, which is optimistic (OPTI) for the textile sector in India and her competitors, is one in which the abatement costs are the lowest in the range (1.7%) and WTP is the highest in the range (30%), meaning that textile goods there are produced at the lowest possible abatement cost and are offered highest possible price by the major global buyers. Second scenario is pessimistic (PESS), with highest abatement costs (8.5%) and lowest WTP in the range considered (5%). This means that Indian textile sector would abate pollution most expensively with no guarantee that its biggest importers would offer higher prices for "greener" textiles.

Both these scenarios are two extreme possibilities and less realistic, but this ensures that the reality lies between them and hence in real world, losses/gains must lie within the ranges arrived at herein. In all CGE simulations, the closure is crucial —it determines which of the variables are exogenous and endogenous. In the simulations done for this study, a closure is assumed which allows for unemployment in the developing countries, meaning that labour market is imperfect, while all other markets clear perfectly. Given the focus of this study, the focus is restricted to impacts on India and her textile and apparel exports of these two scenarios.

In the most optimistic scenario, India's textile output increases by 22.5% owing to growth in exports to USA, Canada and EU as shown in Table 6.11. Though there is an increase in costs due to abatement, causing a loss of about 1 billion US$ in terms of production, high WTP offered by the major importers triggers the expansion of textile trade from India, though similar incentives are offered to her competitors. Despite a decline in exports to the regions that do not offer higher WTP, the exports to USA, Canada and EU have been so high that the total textile exports rise by 56.5%. This is because textile export prices rise by merely about 3.4%, while the WTP is assumed to rise by 30%, due to which the export value gain has been about 4 billion US$ in total and change in exports has been tremendous at 9.1 billion US$. However, this is a utopian scenario and likely to overestimate the gains.

In the most pessimistic scenario, India's textile output falls by 8.3%, with a secular decline in exports to all regions as shown in Table 6.11, stemming from about 10% rise in export prices. The sector also loses about 5.3 billion US$ in terms of increased cost of abatement, despite gaining 459.3 million $ from the WTPs offered by major importers. A trade loss of 3.7 billion US$ is expected in this scenario. Even in terms of cost-benefit ratio, optimistic scenario yields about 1:4, while pessimistic scenario leads to 10:1.

One could expect the reality to be between these two sets of results, implying that the net result of abatement may end up being slightly positive. But it should be

Table 6.11 Impact of pollution abatement on Indian textile sector

Importing regions	% Growth in textile exports		% Growth in textile export prices		Change in exports US$ million		Gain due to WTP in US$ million	
	OPTI	PESS	OPTI	PESS	OPTI	PESS	OPTI	PESS
China	−8.3	−22.3	3.4	9.8	−28.6	−77.5	0	0
SE Asia	−4.2	−15.5	3.4	9.8	−19.9	−73.1	0	0
S Asia	−2.7	−11.3	3.3	9.7	−19.1	−81.3	0	0
Latin America	−23.4	−40.2	3.4	9.8	−93.5	−160.3	0	0
US/Canada	79.6	−18.8	3.4	9.8	3222.3	−759.9	1607.5	200
EU 27	126.9	−23.0	3.4	9.9	6909.9	−1255	2451.2	259.3
Other developed C's	−14.9	−19.1	3.4	9.8	−209.9	−267.5	0	0
Middle East and Africa	−19.8	−30.9	3.4	9.8	−585.9	−914.9	0	0
Soviet and E. Europe	−24.9	−39.2	3.4	9.8	−47.1	−74.1	0	0
WORLD	56.5	−22.9	3.4	9.8	9128.1	−3663	4058.7	459.3
Abatement cost loss	1120	5311	(million US$)					
WTP benefits	4059	459.3	(million US$)					
Output growth (%)	22.5	−8.3						

noted that environmental externalities are not considered in this study. If one takes them into account, the net benefits are bound to be very high. One can safely conclude from this simulation analysis that the higher the WTP by the major importers, the higher are the benefits of abating pollution in Indian textile sector, in terms of international trade.

6.4 Conclusions

Indian government has been developing a range of regulations to curb pollution over the years. Textile industry primarily generates water pollution at the stage of textile wet processing. Although the Indian environmental standards are quite comparable to the global ones, including Oeko-Tex and EC, their implementation is not stringent enough, particularly for the smaller firms and unorganised sector, which are the major part of textile sector in India. There are numerous technologies developed across the world, even in India, to mitigate pollution in the textile sector.

Effluent treatment plants, which operate based on the physico-chemical methods, comprise the main pollution mitigation technology all over the world. New techniques such as bio-remediation, recycling of sludge and dye-bath, and electrochemical processes are also available, but more at the research stage than at commercial implementation stage. Natural dyes are also commercially available, but cannot fully replace synthetic dyes and also cannot fully eliminate the need of ETPs.

Based on the literature review on the cost of abatement using ETPs and natural dyes, coupled with calculations from various government sources on textile production, a range of percentage costs of abatement is estimated as 1.7–8.5%. Similarly, based on the literature, it is estimated that the customers in EU, USA and Canada might be willing to pay a price premium of 5–30% for products that are certified to be produced using eco-friendly technologies. Using these values, optimistic and pessimistic scenarios are constructed in an economy-wide framework, resulting in a range of figures as impact of pollution abatement.

Optimistically speaking, there could be net export gains to the Indian textile exports of up to 9 billion US$, if EU and North American consumers pay a price premium of 30% for pollution-abated textile products, with a low pollution abatement cost of 1.7%. In the most pessimistic scenario, when the consumers pay merely 5% price premium and pollution abatement costs 8.5%, net export losses amount to 3.6 billion US$. Considering these extreme cases, both of which are almost unrealistic, one can anticipate the real export gains to be positive and at least a few millions of US$. If the environmental benefits in terms of say better water quality in rivers are also considered, the social benefits could be much higher than these figures.

Following are some policy implications of this analysis:

- Unorganised sector and small textile firms should be encouraged to mitigate pollution, by establishing CETPs and/or by adopting natural dyes and other eco-friendly processing agents, because the bigger firms have already implemented most of the standards. Government could consider subsidising some of the abatement costs for them. This would not only minimise pollution, but also expand the export markets for the smaller firms.
- New technologies that minimise pollution abatement costs should be commercialised and adopted. From the literature reviewed, it is assessed that there is an enormous amount of indigenous research happening in India in this regard. By identifying and promoting commercially viable and effective technologies, the cost burden of the firms to implement global standards is likely to come down, and hence, they are more likely to abate pollution. Cleaner production and waste recycling techniques such as recycling the dye-bath, sludge or wastewater are particularly useful in saving costs.
- The government and exporters' associations should be aggressive in promoting "Brand India" eco-friendly textiles. Such efforts would ensure that the importers are willing to pay higher prices for pollution-free textile products. With lower costs of abatement and higher WTPs of the importers, gains are more likely to be close to those in the optimistic scenario.
- Given that other competitors have similar levels of standards and implementation, some diplomatic pressure can be created over them, akin to how the developed countries pressurise the emerging economies, to cut pollution. Mutual agreements and common goals to reduce pollution can help India reduce pollution and still not face too much trade diversion owing to higher costs than the more pollution-intensive competitors.

Chapter 7
Conclusions

K.S. Kavi Kumar

7.1 Introduction

The previous chapters discussed the structure of textile industry in India, its comparative advantage, local and global environmental issues, non-tariff barriers and the linkages between pollution abatement and trade. This final chapter first summarizes the main features of Indian textile industry through a SWOT (strengths, weaknesses, opportunities, threats) analysis. The main findings of the study are then summarized. This is followed by a discussion on strategies for enhancing export prospects for Indian textiles and the emerging environmental challenges facing the textile sector in India.

7.2 SWOT Analysis of Indian Textile Industry

Strengths	Opportunities
• Low labor cost • Strong presence across the entire value chain—from fiber to garments • Abundant availability of various raw materials • Government's initiatives for export promotion and technology upgradation • Unique strength in traditional handlooms and handicrafts	• Increasing young population with rising incomes • Emergence of retail industry and development of various malls—providing opportunities for apparel segment • Scope for diversification—technical textiles • Increasing working female population—having 1.3 times more propensity to spend compared to home-makers • Replacement of MFA and integration of textile industry—giving huge opportunities for exports

(continued)

K.S. Kavi Kumar (✉)
Madras School of Economics, Chennai, India
e-mail: kavikumar@gmail.com

K.S.K. Kumar (ed.), *A Study of India's Textile Exports and Environmental Regulations*, https://doi.org/10.1007/978-981-10-6295-7_7

(continued)

Weaknesses	Threats
• High dependence on USA and EU for exports • Low yield of cotton • Highly fragmented industry with large presence of small-scale firms and technologically outdated firms • Structural weaknesses in weaving and processing—2% of shuttle-less looms as percentage of total looms as against world average of 16% • Infrastructural bottlenecks in terms of power, utility, road transport, etc. • Low labor productivity • The rigid labor laws—proving a bottleneck particularly to the garment sector. • Except spinning, all other segments are predominantly in decentralized sector	• Increased cost-based competition from other countries—Bangladesh, Sri Lanka, etc. • Pricing pressures due to removal of USA and EU quotas on imports from China • Fluctuations in the export demand • Rising input costs • Increasing environmental and social awareness is resulting in increased pressure on the industry to follow international labor and environmental laws • Regional alliances will continue to have a significant impact

7.3 Summary of the Study Findings

The textile industry has an overwhelming presence in India through its contribution to income, industrial output, employment generation and foreign export earnings. It is one of the leading industrial segments in India contributing about 14% to industrial production, 4% to the GDP and 17% to the country's export earnings. Given the significance of the textile industry, it is imperative to study the aspects that affect its competitiveness in the global arena. An important concern in the global textile trade is with regard to eco-friendly production and products.

The environmental concerns of the textile industry are centered around the textile processing which generates water pollution (in the form of effluents) during the process—mainly, dyeing. Some ways in which textiles affect the environment uniquely are as follows: wet treatments like desizing and scouring using oxygen-depleting substances reduce the cleanliness of the water; adsorbable organic halides (AOX) emissions, which are caused by less-biodegradable, organic, halogenated compounds result from bleaching processes; high chemical oxygen demand (COD) arising from cotton desizing; strong alkaline effluent from mercerization; dyeing process produces effluent with high COD, metals, toxic substances, salts, etc., originating from the dyes and dispersing agents. Such effluent is released to water sources such as river, resulting in pollution. Though textile industry produces both air and water pollution, it pollutes water more significantly than air.

The present study focussed on the following aspects: (a) the supply chain of the textile industry in India and in the world; (b) India's comparative advantage in the export of textile and apparel products; (c) domestic and global environmental issues concerning textile processing; (d) role of non-tariff measures and barriers in the textile sector and perception of the stakeholders on incidence and impact of non-tariff barriers; and (e) linkages between pollution abatement in the textile sector and the associated implications for India's trade prospects. The main findings of the study include:

1. Analysis of the trade data to assess the revealed comparative advantage in export of textile and clothing products has shown that: (a) in case of textile yarn/fabrics/articles, India is an efficient exporter of several products; (b) revealed comparative advantage is estimated to be stronger for curtains, carpets, cotton yarn, woven unbound cotton fabrics, woven silk fabrics, woven jute fabrics, woven cotton fabrics, woven synthetic blends, man-made textile articles and hand-woven rugs; (c) of total 59 commodities associated with the SITC four-digit classification, 28 commodities are found to have relative comparative advantage; (d) in case of clothing sector, out of 38 total items, comparative advantage is found with respect to 23 items; (e) the analysis also indicated that relative comparative advantage is declining for most of the products during recent years.
2. From different estimates on pollution abatement cost in textile sector, the total capital cost required for the effluent treatment plants for all Indian textile units is estimated to be in the range of Rs. 23.8–364.5 Billion and annual operational costs are estimated to be in the range of Rs. 68.0–139.6 Billion. These are, respectively, 0.85–12.9 and 2.4–4.9% of the total sector output.
3. To assess the economy-wide impact of pollution abatement on trade, the total output, exports and profits under two extreme scenarios are estimated using a CGE model.[1] Assuming that the costs of 1.7–8.5% to abate pollution can be applied as import tariff equivalents for India and all of its competitors (China, South Asia and Southeast Asia), the study considered two scenarios. In the optimistic scenario, there could be net export gains to the Indian textile exports of up to 9 billion US$, if EU and North American consumers pay a price premium of 30% for pollution-abated textile products, with a low-pollution abatement cost of 1.7%. In the most pessimistic scenario, when the consumers pay merely 5% price premium and pollution abatement costs 8.5%, net export losses amount to 3.6 billion US$. Considering these extreme cases, both of which are almost unrealistic, the study anticipates the real export gains to be positive and at least a few millions of US$. If the environmental benefits in terms of better water quality in rivers, etc., are also considered the overall benefits of pollution abatement are likely to be much higher than these figures.
4. Field-level analysis of various stakeholders of the textile exports suggests that the impacts of non-tariff measures/barriers in the form of stricter environmental standards imposed by the importing countries could be mixed. While meeting the stricter environmental standards would increase the costs for the exporters, it would also make them more competitive and the buyers are often agreeable to higher price associated with greener products.

The policy implications of the study include the following:

[1]Using GTAP framework that uses GTAP 7.1 Data Base.

1. Unorganized sector and small textile firms should be encouraged to mitigate pollution, by establishing CETPs and/or by adopting natural dyes and other eco-friendly processing agents, etc., because the bigger firms have already implemented most of the standards. Government could consider subsidizing some of the abatement costs for them. This would not only minimize pollution, but also expand the export markets for the smaller firms.
2. New technologies that minimize pollution abatement costs should be commercialized and adopted. From the literature reviewed, we find that there is enormous amount of indigenous research happening in India in this regard. By identifying and promoting commercially viable and effective technologies, the cost burden of the firms to implement global standards is likely to come down and hence they are more likely to abate pollution. Cleaner production and waste recycling techniques such as recycling the dyebath, sludge or waste water are particularly useful in saving costs.
3. The government and exporters' associations should be aggressive in promoting "Brand India" eco-friendly textiles. Such efforts would ensure that the importers are willing to pay higher prices for our pollution-free textile products. With lower costs of abatement and higher WTPs of the importers, gains are more likely to be close to those in the optimistic scenario presented in this study. The field-level findings also corroborate this point.
4. Given that other competitors have similar levels of standards and implementation, some diplomatic pressure over them, akin to how the developed countries pressurize the emerging economies, would reduce overall pollution.
5. Given that most exporters are willing to comply with the stricter environmental standards demanded by the importing countries, the government could facilitate their compliance by setting up a denser network of testing facilities and working toward enhancing their capacity.
6. Given growing environmental awareness across the world, eco-labeling has emerged as one of the key requirements for global competitiveness of textile and clothing industry. Indian textile and clothing industry, a fragmented industry having a lot of small-scale units in the value chain, requires support/assistance from the government and industry associations in achieving widespread adoption of eco-labeling.

7.4 Strategies for Enhancing Exports

While the present study focussed on trade and environment linkages in the Indian textile sector, there are several other important factors that have similar, if not greater, influence on India's export prospects. Often these strategies are mutually complementary in nature, necessitating simultaneous policy attention. This section provides a brief discussion on various opportunities and strategies that could boost the country's exports.

1. Even though India is enhancing its capacity in the textile sector, compared to China, the capacity expansion is minimal. India, therefore, needs to enhance further its capacity to be competitive as a global player.
2. The textile and clothing industry in India is highly fragmented with large number of players, which hampers its ability to emerge as a world-class supplier. Also very few players have integrated their operations. One of the reasons for China's supreme position in global textile and clothing industry is its integrated production and consolidated supply chain facilities. The global buyers prefer to buy from a few large vendors at competitive cost. The disintegrated nature of textile and clothing value chain in India hampers the chances of securing such large orders as also achieving the economies of scale. There are also challenges associated with productivity, nonavailability of adequate resources to invest in high technology. All these issues need urgent policy attention.
3. The fiber mix of textile industry in India is skewed toward cotton—with about 75% of yarn production in India being cotton based. The global fiber mix, on the other hand, is skewed toward man-made fibers—with about 60% of fiber being man-made. Jute also constitutes an important component of India's fiber mix. In the recent past, the jute production showed declining trend—even though India continues to be global leader in this subsector. To continue its comparative advantage, India should maintain this distinction from the global scenario.
4. To comply with global labor standards, the government must encourage the textile firms to get to be a part of global initiatives such as SA8000 system developed by Social Accountability International.
5. The rising household incomes and increasing disposal incomes in urban India are increasing the demand for high-value apparel products.
6. Abundant supply of cost-competitive skilled labor makes India an important global hub of activities.
7. One of the major advantages of Indian textile industry is widespread the presence of companies engaged in the textile-value chain, starting from field to shelf. This sharpens India's competitive edge vis-à-vis Sri Lanka and Bangladesh who focus more on apparel production.
8. At present, the Indian textile industry is having technological obsolescence and subscale operations. Indian textile industry should turn into hi-tech mode to reap the benefits of scale operations and quality. The technology upgradation fund scheme (TUFS) has a major role in strengthening the technology upgradation of the Indian textile and garment industry.
9. Very few players in India are integrated with garment business. However, integration of operations from weaving to garment making would ensure quality and facilitate undertaking of bulk orders at low cost. Such integrating would also bring down turn-around time and thus help the firms to stick to the delivery schedules. Thus, more and more Indian players need to be focusing on integration in order to reduce lead time, cut down the cost and improve the quality.

10. India needs to augment its infrastructure, especially the export-related infrastructure, including the modernization of ports. Further, efforts should be on for strengthening infrastructure to create brand equity, enhance supply chain management, and augmenting educational facilities.
11. An area that has potential for innovation is technical textiles. This segment is different from the conventional fiber to fashion value chain. Inventions and product development in the technical textiles would help India capture niche position and relieve it from the competition with countries like Vietnam and Bangladesh.

7.5 Emerging Environmental Challenges

Carbon neutrality is emerging as a very important concept for a sustainable development. Carbon neutrality means achieving zero carbon emissions by compensating carbon dioxide released into the atmosphere from burning fossil fuels, with renewable energy that creates a similar amount of useful energy. In other words, it refers to having a net zero carbon footprint. The amount of carbon dioxide released can be offsetted by funding carbon projects that will prevent future greenhouse gas emissions. The projects can be (a) renewable energy projects, (b) resource conservation project, (c) waste reduction projects, or (d) forestry projects.

Various subsectors of textile affect the environment to a great extent by releasing carbon dioxide in the atmosphere. The weaving and spinning sector contributes a lot to emission in carbon dioxide. Besides adoption of energy efficient technologies (such as, installation of automatic power factor correction system with capacitors, conversion of V-belt drives to flat-belt drives, replacement of conventional rapid jet dyeing machine with low-liquor ratio jet dyeing machine, etc.) in the spinning unit, weaving unit and wet processing units, the textile and clothing sector can opt for new and innovative inputs for reduce its carbon footprint. For instance, Du Pont, the USA-based chemicals major has developed Sorona—a man-made fiber made with agricultural feedstock instead of petrochemicals and that has high content of renewable ingredients. It is claimed that fabrics made from Sorona reduce carbon dioxide emissions by 30%. Similarly, widespread adoption of genetically modified crops such as BT-Cotton could reduce dependence on pesticides and fertilizers (and thus the carbon foot print) and could facilitate progress toward greener ecology and environment in the country.

While the present study has not paid specific attention to the carbon neutrality issues, the dynamics of environment and trade interlinkages could get significantly affected in the context of this emerging environmental challenge and hence may need fresh assessment.

7.6 Limitations

The study could be further improved by considering the following aspects in potential future exercises:

(a) On the modeling front, the study could further improve the analysis by reconsidering some of the assumptions: (i) the scope for adoption of natural dyes may not be higher than 5–10%; (ii) abatement costs will be significantly higher than those assumed especially if TDS removal is strictly followed; (iii) the willingness to pay for greener textile products could be lower than assumed and should be assessed through primary survey of the overseas buyers.
(b) Since the clean technology options at affordable prices are almost non-existent for the small-scale units, the future studies could explore the welfare implications of unilateral movement of polluting industries to developing countries (pollution haven hypothesis) and the closure of numerous textile units that do not meet the environmental standards.
(c) Similar to research work done in the context of horticulture products, future works in Indian textile industry could explore the institutional aspects including creation of third-party certification across the value chain to minimize the rejection rate and enhance export prospects.
(d) India's comparative advantage in new products such as "technical textiles" should be explored as the country presently imports these high-value products. In this context, the real threat to Indian exports may not be from China, but from countries like Bangladesh and Vietnam which have specialized in the new products.

Annexure I
Textile Wet Processing and Environmental Concerns

Increasing environment consciousness, newer legislations to preserve environment and human rights, scarcity of water and energy has driven efforts in search of safe substitutes of the dyes and auxiliaries, and in this customer-driven market, specific needs of customers such as flame retardancy, antibacterial property, stain repellency have further increased challenges to the textile manufacturers.

These above-mentioned factors are responsible for the present day change in scenario of the wet processing of textiles. Good quality at competitive prices is becoming important with global trade. Hence, the wet processing sequence is accordingly being modified, keeping in mind the objective of obtaining high-quality goods at the most competitive rates.

For international quality fabric, one needs to have the best of spinning and weaving technologies employed, before subjecting the fabric to various operations of wet processing. However, for a textile wet processor, it becomes a challenging task to get the shades right first time and also at competitive cost with the best quality. The high-performance standards expected by the present day consumer are to be met with, in addition to the adherence to the norms of eco-friendly processing, which is the need of the day. All these characteristics navigate the direction of research in textile wet processing and the various operations actually carried out in the processing industry. Many a times, it has been observed that there is a large difference in the process sequence to be ideally followed vis-a-vis the one actually followed at the shop floor.

Broadly, wet processing can be divided into pretreatment, bleaching, dyeing, printing and finishing. Irrespective of the various stages of operations falling under this classification, every single method followed finds its basis and objective of:

- Maintenance of high quality
- Cost-effectiveness
- Improved functionality
- Lower generation of waste
- Minimum use or reuse of water and chemicals
- Overall environment friendliness
- Application of appropriate machinery and technology

This annexure has been compiled by Dr. Zareena Begum.

K.S.K. Kumar (ed.), *A Study of India's Textile Exports and Environmental Regulations*, https://doi.org/10.1007/978-981-10-6295-7

Pretreatment

Desizing

Nowadays enzyme desizing is the widely used technique for the removal of size from the textile material. For cotton desizing, amylase-based enzymes are widely used; generally, these enzymes works at different pH range mostly 5–7 and the temperature range of 40–70 °C. Advantage of such enzyme is that cotton waxes get partially emulsified due to the alkalinity, and the desizing is attained almost instantly due to the high temperature maintained. Enzymes such as lipases and proteases are used in wool processing, which impart antifelting property and also improved dye uptake.

Scouring

Incorporation of persulphate in scouring eliminates the separate desizing stage. Simultaneous desizing and scouring can be carried out by padding fabric with potassium persulphate (2–3 gL^{-1}) and NaOH (40–50 gL^{-1}) and subsequently steaming in J-box. Desizing can be achieved in 1–3 min and scouring takes 90–120 min, in J-box or 2–10 min in vapour locks machines. Many companies have introduced novel enzyme product which are used for scouring, generally these enzymes are mixture of enzymes such as pectinase, lipase. The pectinase enzyme is used to hydrolyse the pectins and remove the same from cotton causing lossening of hydrophobic waxes which are easier to get rid off in subsequent washing. The action of lipase subsequently brings about hydrolysis of such hydrophobic waxes.

Solvent-assisted scouring makes use of 5% solvent, which is emulsified and also can be coupled with bleaching and desizing. In this case, the hydrogen peroxide not only acts as bleaching agent, but also as an oxidative desizing agent in processing of cotton goods. However, complete recovery of solvent brings limitations on its use. The continuous bleaching ranges are becoming popular as scales of operations have increased although capital investment is high. The small processor makes use of modern jiggers for scouring, bleaching and dyeing in which the goods weighing up to about 1400 kg can be processed.

Bleaching

Hydrogen peroxide bleaching is carried out at around pH 10.5–10.7 and temperature 85–90 °C so scouring and beaching can be combined together. Bleaching recipe consists of 4–10 gL^{-1} of 35% H_2O_2, 2–3 gL^{-1} stabiliser and about 1–3 gL^{-1} NaOH (100%), and a liquor ratio 8:1 is maintained on Jigger. In case of continuous bleaching on J-box, the recipe indicates 20 ml/L of H_2O_2 (35%), 4 gL^{-1} NaOH (100%), and 6 ml/L of sodium silicate at 90–95 °C for 15–30 min.

From the environmental point of view and also from the point of view of permanent whiteness, chlorine-based bleaching agents are objectionable. The goods for exports are thus required to be peroxide-based which is relatively an expensive process. The general trend is to carry out initial bleaching with hypochlorite, and instead of giving antichlor treatment, the subsequent process is hydrogen peroxide bleaching of relatively lower concentration. In this case, not only the final whiteness is ensured to be permanent but objectionable chlorine-based bleaching agent can be avoided with better economy. From the point of view of exports, hydrogen peroxide has no substitute as far as bleaching is concerned. However, it is to be noted that the peroxide remains on the fabric even after thorough washing which poses specific problems in getting consistent dyeing with the dyes sensitive to oxidation such as reactive dyes. And hence, many a times the peroxide bleached goods necessitate initial rinsing of the fabric with the reducing agents more known as peroxide killers. The peroxide bleaching is also sensitive to metal ions, which initiates the accelerated decomposition of H_2O_2 causing uneven bleaching which will reflect in patchy dyeing in the subsequent dyeing process. Nowadays, zeolite and bentonites which are clay materials are also used as stabilisers although they are not much in use. Bleaching with peracetic acid has been reported as eco-friendly process in which case it is produced using hydrogen peroxide and glacial acetic acid.

However, it is to be carried out at 50–80 °C at 6–7 pH for about 20–60 min, and many a time, it is used as substitute for hypochlorite bleaching. From the environment point of view, bleaching with ozone is recommended. Ozone–oxygen mixture is highly unstable liberating hydroxy radicals giving good degree of whiteness in a short time at room temperature, the absence of harmful chemicals and use of low quantity of water are promising factor from environment point of view.

Ozone bleaching operation could be made continuous too. Potassium permanganate is also used as powerful oxidising bleaching agent and said to be economic and non-polluting. One of the reported methods makes use of electrolysis of sodium chloride solution in which chlorine is liberated at the cathode which is used for bleaching. One-step scouring and bleaching process makes use of grey fabric or desized fabric to be treated with caustic soda/soda ash, stabiliser and hydrogen peroxide at 80 °C for 4–6 h. This incurs high chemical cost due to higher concentration of H_2O_2.

Mercerisation

Mercerisation improves lustre, enhances dyeability and improves the strength and also soft feel. For cotton fabrics 50–54 Tw (22.5%), sodium hydroxide solution is used at room temperature for 45–60 s in which case caustic pick up varies from 25 to 40%. Normally, 10% of the caustic is consumed in the operation on the weight of the fabric and 75% of the caustic is recovered. Wet-on-wet mercerisation and hot mercerisation are the additional two processes. In the latter, 60 °C temperature is used causing the even effect on the skin and core of the fabric, and the better dyeability can thus be obtained. Hot mercerisation can make use of shorter machine. The efficiency of such mercerisation operation can reflect in barium activity number or deconvolution count; the former method is however more preferred.

Dyeing

Once the fabric undergoes controlled pretreatment and brought in a ready-to-dye stage, the dyeing becomes the next challenge to get uniform and consistent shades right at first attempt. The proper selection of dyes and machine depends upon number of factors. The first and the topmost is the nature of the fibre, the variety and the quality of fabric being processed as well as quality standards required. Number of challenges faced by the dyer includes shade matching, production of solid and defect-free dyeing. The advancement in reactive and disperse dye classes is apparent in the market. Developments in reactive dyes are aimed at improving their exhaustion and fixation by improving the reactivity and decreasing their sensitivity to temperature and pH variations. Dyes showing high exhaustion are thus recommended for dyeing of knit goods, which is carried on winches where a lot of variation in temperature and pH occur. The reactive dyes which make use of low salt and some based on fluorine are increasingly recommended. In India, the dyes which are extensively used are as follows.

The newly developed TULAREVS XL range, a state-of-the-art reactive system, manufactured using innovative membrane technology, to meet stringent fastness requirements (like that of M&S fastness) and deliver high reproducibility from laboratory to bulk (RFT) and also from Bulk to Bulk (RET). These dyes are recommended for exhaust dyeing of cotton yarn, knits and woven goods.

CIBA has introduced new reactive dyes ranges such as CIBACRON FN, CIBACRON LS, CIBACRON H, CIBACRON W for dyeing and CIBACRON P for printing. Cibacron FN range has been created for warm exhaust application on cellulose and its blends, especially with wool, polyamide and acrylics in jets. These dyes have excellent washing-off performance, offer high fixation and thus lead to less hydrolysed dye in effluent. Further they possess excellent dye-fibre bond stability that is highly resistant to oxidants, acid and alkaline condition. CIBACRON W complements the CIBACRON C and CIBACRON FN ranges.

Cibacron LS is special range designed for hot exhaust application on cellulose and its blends. These dyes are virtually insensitive to changes in dye liquor ratio, thus ensure right-first-time production. Reactive dyeing with these dyes requires less than a quarter of the salt, a major environmental benefit, especially in the regions that are short of water. **Sumufix HF** dyes by Sumitono of Japan contain novel reactive group connected to dye chromophore based on modified vinyl sulphone. These dyes are characterised by higher level of fixation and exhaustion as compare to conventional reactive dyes and also require less salt for dyeing.

Unlike conventional vinyl sulphone dyes, these novel products are applied at (60–80) °C. As dyes exhibit an equivalent substantivity for both cotton and regenerated cellulose, solid, on tone shades, can be attained on blended substrate. These dyes also offer easy wash-off and excellent fastness properties. **Kayacelon React Dyes** introduced by Nippon Kayaku which is also first range of bis-nicotinic quaternary ammonium reactive dyes. They are particularly suited to neutral, high temperature exhaust dyeing, although they are often used with a small amount of alkali. These dyes are characterised by easy application and better reproducibility. Also ensures smooth exhaustion and fixation corresponding to rise in temperature, resulting in good levelling properties. These dyes are suitable for one bath, one-step polyester/cotton blended textiles. Though expensive, one-step dyeing of the same allows savings in utilities and labour expenses.

Procion XL+ reactive dyes were developed by BASF and are now marketed worldwide by DyStar is based on monochlotriazine reactive groups attached to carefully designed chromophores. The reactivity of chlorotriazine unit towards cellulose has intentionally been tuned to the desired 90 °C application profile by selection of appropriate di- and tri-amine linking units. Unexpected strength enhancement is derived from engineered chromophore-chromophore interactions within the multi-chromophore dyes. These may, for example, result in excitonic coupling between the chromophores. The beauty of the Procion XL+ system with its higher dyeing temperature is that it allows a shorter, simpler and most reliable application profile.

Of particular note is the ability to combine scouring and dyeing process in a single stage. The net effect of this is a load-to-unload time of only 3 hours, less than half of a conventional reactive dyeing process. Levafix CA reactive dyes marketed by Dystar are suitable for all dyeing processes and have a wide range of favourable dyeing properties. These dyes are characterised by high fixation yield and excellent wash-off properties. These dyes are also free of AOX (Absorbable Organic Halogen), thus minimise effluent pollution and reduce the cost of treating waste water.

In continuous dyeing with reactive dyes, the commercial and environmental benefit of a shorter process and elimination of large amount of urea of which is often required as humectants for heat fixation, the Econtrol process seems to have been well accepted to provide a very simple Pad-Dry process without the need of large amount of chemicals. Utilising the high reactivity of dichlorotriazine dyes (e.g. Procion MX) ,only mild alkali sodium bicarbonate is required and no urea, no sodium silicate, any common salt or glauber salt or other chemicals are necessary. In this process, the fabric is padded and dried in Monforts Thermax hot flue at (120–130) °C with controlled humidity, which ensure dye fixation within (2–3) min. For homobifunctional and heterofunctional dyes, as those are less reactive, they do not react as easily in the mild process; however, in this case, stronger alkali and higher level of RH% are required for better results: The vat dyes are the costliest class of dyes, although they offer best of performance properties and many a times in polyester/cotton blends, disperse-reactive and disperse-vat are recommended. In such blends, selection of disperse dyes is also equally important as needs to be stable to alkali. Alkali stable disperse dyes are available in the market which are suitable for polyester cotton blends where the cotton component requires alkalinity for application of reactive, vat or sulphur dyes. While dyeing with disperse-vat, once the polyester component is dyed, the vat pigment which is mechanically deposited is reduced in alkaline blank vat solution and gets fixed on the cotton component. The additional reduction clearing treatment is totally eliminated in this case. A new range of microdisperse Vat dyes-Novatic MD, a full range covering entire shade gamut exclusively suited for dyeing of Cotton & blends in woven fabric form on continuous dyeing range giving perfect solidity with minimal staining on polyester.

The present trend is to modify the cotton by cationisation and apply reactive dyes in acidic conditions so that the protonated or cationised cotton adsorbs the reactive dye anions at the enhanced rate and subsequent fixation in alkali medium gives very high shade build up. Cationisation can be done by using quaternary ammonium compound or cationising agents, and in many cases, this can lead to low salt or no salt dyeing and impart antimicrobial properties to the fabric. This also reduces the TDS of the effluent along with the drastic reduction of unfixed dye in drain or in effluent. Sarex has claimed grey dyeing of cotton yarn and cotton knits for dark shades without peroxide bleaching using Saralan Jet LF/Celldet R + Saraquest W in pretreatment followed by dyeing in the same bath with addition of Sarakol RDL.

A newly developed method recommends the simultaneous dispersion—acid dyeing and finishing of polyester/cotton blend. Initially, the method was developed for one bath acid dyeing—resin finishing of cotton/cellulosic material. The selection of acid dye however is quite critical, and it should have abstractable -H in its amino group substituent. Finishing agents like DMDHEU gets attracted to cotton to one end while anchoring or holding acid dye molecules on the other end. Dyeing was quite fast and so-called non-substantive acid dyes can be applied on cotton simultaneously resulting in improvement in crease recovery angles. When the same system is extended to polyester/cotton blend for disperse—acid—dyeing—cum resin finishing from single bath by pad—thermosol technique, it was found that polyester and cotton component can be dyed with respective dyes and heat—setting as well as finishing takes place almost simultaneously.

Washing-off problem of reactive dye can be solved by using enzyme wash/biorinsing by Bylase RP/Assist RP from Sarex, the enzyme which decolourises selectively the hydrolysed dyestuff from fabric and also the unfixed reactive dyestuff in unexhausted bath provides a great promise. This reduces the consumption of water, energy and time as it is claimed to be quite efficient washing-off process. Cationic dye fixing agent treatment can be given to the reactive dyed material because the hydrolysed dye acting as a direct dye and being held on the fabric by hydrogen bonding, complexes with cationic dye fixing agent and brings about fixation of dye, improving its wet rubbing fastness at least by half a grade.

In case of garment dyeing, mainly at the post-finishing stage, reactive dyes can used provided the garments so finished are subjected during finishing with certain nitrogen containing additives. These additives used during finishing render the dyeability to the finished garment and upto about 85% dyeability can be regained even after finishing the garment at intermediate level, which otherwise is known for displaying only 15–20% dyeability. This phenomenon of additives improving the finished goods dyeability works similar to process of cationisation and requires almost similar conditions as used in dyeing of cationised cotton.

From the environmental point of view, the general trend is to make use of non-dusting powders of the dye, and thus, granules are preferred to dusting powders. As Automation has increased in dyeing machinery such as colour kitchen and auto dispensing systems, liquid dyes have become an important and essential formulation. The procian T dyes are acid fixable liquid reactive dyes based on phosphoric acid condensation product and they also carry the potential of making the fabric flame retardant while being the integral part of the fabric.

The problem of thermomigration, which is common on finished polyester, becomes more severe in case of microdenier variety and rubbing fastness, wet fastness and light fastness are deteriorated in this variety. Such garments when washed with garments made of nylon give cross-staining distinctly visible to human eye. This problem initiated dyestuff manufacturers to come up with the wet fast disperse dyes. There is also need of very high light fast disperse dyes may be of order of "8" specifically in case of upholstery used in automotive industry, and many dyestuff manufacturers have come up ranges with light fast dyes.

One more technology which is still on the pilot scale is dyeing of polyester with super critical CO_2. In this case under very high pressure, CO_2 is liquefied in which disperse dye dissolves and is used for dyeing of synthetic fibre. The liquid CO_2 has the advantage of very high diffusibility, and it has low viscosity than any normal liquid.

Most of the dyes based on objectionable banned amines are already out from the market, and hence, the use of eco-friendly dyes becomes obvious expectation of every one. In this regard, the use of Natural dyes is also becoming increasingly popular. The new area in natural dyes can be colours from micro-organisms. The microbial dyes studied in our laboratory showed dyeability towards polyester similar to disperse dye. Dyeings obtained were uniform without dispersing agent requiring no addition of dispersing or levelling agents during dyeing. Carrier dyeing proved to be the best method for dyeing of polyester with microbial dye. Light fastness of microbial dyed fabric was poor, although excellent wash fastness and sublimation fastness were observed. The dyed fabrics showed a cidal effect on the micro-organisms under study, increasing the value of the fabric for commercial use. Since the dye can be produced on a large scale by culturing microbes in laboratory and production being independent of seasons, controllable and with a predictable yield. This natural dye and others obtained by this method have potential to change the way of thinking as well as dyeing with natural dyes.

The Environmental Cataclysm

Though the dyeing industry delayed implementation of zero discharge system for a long time, the unveiling present scenario is definitely not in favour of this industry, forcing it to immediately adopt cleaner production technologies within a very short time. The public opinion is divided on this issue. While it is beneficial to provide logistical support for the smooth running of the dyeing and bleaching units to fuel our growing economy and to feed many lakh people employed in this industry, the environmental damage caused by this industry is immense and is irreversible. Due to the pollution by textile wet processing effluent, groundwater system has been totally affected, soil fertility is partially or totally lost, surface water ways and ponds are totally polluted, agricultural production in the downstream areas are severely affected, and the extent of health hazards caused to the public due to groundwater contamination and through the food webs certainly unknown. The restoration of the environment to the earlier state is totally unachievable due to non-biodegradability of the dyestuff in the environment. Further, the salt in the effluent has also affected soil fertility and the ability of the biota to grow and enrich the soil. Thus, the benefits accruing from this industry such as foreign exchange earnings and employment opportunities can no longer be held as a protective shield against the implementation of the zero discharge system due to financial constraints in undertaking such a large expansion scheme. Thus, there is an immediate need for this industry to adopt cleaner production technologies through waste minimisation, adoption of newer technologies, and carefully planning resource utilisation in processing units.

Components of Zero Discharge System

Zero discharge system is meant to treat all the incoming effluent and leave nothing behind. However, practically this is not feasible since some waste is always generated in the treatment process. Therefore, the main aim is to recover usable materials such as water and salt from the effluent, and minimise the generation of waste so that it can be safely stored on-site minimise without the need for discharge into the environment.

As far as textile dyeing/bleaching operations are concerned, the following "critical components" form the basis for the zero discharge system.

Machinery	Function/purpose
Reverse osmosis (R.O) system	Recovery of pure water from the effluent for reuse in textile wet processing operations (dyeing and bleaching)
Nanofiltration (N.F) system	Recovery of salt from the effluent; R.O reject management
Multiple effect evaporator (MEE)	Recovery of reusable water from reject generated by reverse osmosis and nanofiltration units

(continued)

(continued)

Machinery	Function/purpose
Solar pond	Evaporation of waste water (mother liquor) from multiple effect evaporator
Additional components for the maintenance of zero discharge system	
Windmill/biomass gasification plant	Electric power generation to meet the demands of R.O and N.F systems
Wood	To meet the demands of the boiler used with the Multiple Effect Evaporator; To meet the needs of biomass gasification plant

Resource Utilisation and Requirement for Zero Discharge System

The energy demand of the zero discharge system is very high. An approximate estimation for the requirement of energy resources is listed below:

Natural resource	Demand/day	Cost (in INR)
Water	80 million litres (~72 million litres could be recovered by R.O/N.F and MEE)	5,760,000 (cost of recovered water)
Electricity	12,67,200 kWh/day	5,068,800
Wood	400–500 tonnes/day	8,00,000–1,000,000

By recovering water, an estimated amount of around Rs. 58 Lakhs/day is saved —which is otherwise spent by the industry for purchasing water. However, the electricity requirements of the zero discharge system cost around Rs. 51 Lakhs/day, spending on purchase of wood requires another Rs. 8–10 Lakhs/day. Thus, there is a deficit of around Rs. 3 Lakhs/day, which has to be borne by the industry. By providing support for the establishment of windmill and biomass gasification plant, the electricity bill could be drastically reduced. This saving could result in the lowering of textile wet processing charges, and potentially improve our international competitiveness. In addition to this, the loss of around Rs. 14 Lakhs/day (Loss of Ecology) due to environmental degradation is averted, and water pollution is prevented, whereby the water storage could be used for irrigation to promote agricultural production. Noting that Tamil Nadu stands in the second place, next to Rajasthan, with regard to water scarcity, implementing zero discharge system is very essential which could avert groundwater depletion in the surrounding areas of Tirupur viz., Avinashi, Annur, Palladam, etc where majority of the dyeing industry is located.

Reject Management: Need for Research and Development

Reject management is a critical issue while considering the implementation of zero discharge system using reverse osmosis and nanofiltration units. It is very important that at this stage itself the government takes necessary steps towards finding the right solutions for reject management. Since the reject from the reverse osmosis and nanofiltration units are highly concentrated with a total dissolved solids of around 50,000–70,000 mg/, it would greatly affect the environment. Thus, the government should initiate necessary research and developmental activities for finding the right kind of treatment for the reject. Otherwise, whatever resources and efforts that have been put up towards implementation of the zero discharge system will become unproductive.

Environmental Benefits of Implementing Zero Discharge System

(1) Groundwater pollution as well as groundwater depletion in the surrounding areas is greatly minimised.
(2) The loss of ecology (agricultural production, fisheries loss & detrimental effects on water supply schemes) due to pollution by the industries (in Tirupur alone) is estimated at Rs. 51.34 crores annually. By the implementation of zero discharge system, further loss to the ecology is averted.
(3) Pollution of rivers and dams located near the dyeing industry could be prevented.
(5) Production of hazardous waste (sludge) is averted by the elimination of conventional treatment system, and upgradation to the zero discharge system with salt recovery and reuse.

Economic Benefits of Implementing Zero Discharge System

(1) Reuse of water and salt through the implementation of the zero discharge system would greatly reduce the processing expenses. Thus, the dyeing and bleaching units can potentially compete with other nations.
(2) Generation of necessary power through windmill, biomass gasification plant and co-generation units would significantly reduce the operating cost of the zero discharge system. Thus, the savings in electricity bill could be invested somewhere for the promotion of business.
(3) Water cost, and fuel cost for its transportation, requires around Rs. 300 crores per annum for the dyeing and bleaching units. This expenditure is exclusive of road damage by tanker lorries, power requirement for pumping water to the

lorries, and other associated expenditures. By reusing the water, around Rs. 300 crores could be saved every year, which will greatly benefit the dyeing and bleaching units. Also, groundwater depletion in the surrounding areas could be averted, leading to enhanced agricultural production and better rural livelihood.

(4) The present foreign exchange of US$800 million earned by the textiles industries can be further increased without imparting any damage to the local environment and ecological loss.

(5) Due to stricter environmental compliance, and adoption of cleaner production technologies, the dyeing and bleaching units will get more export orders from foreign countries in the open market economy.

(6) Zero discharge imposes no boundaries on the amount of effluent that dyeing and bleaching units can generate, since it discharges nothing into the water media. Thus, the dyeing and bleaching units can augment their productivity in the coming years without self-imposing its output capacity due to the concerns on discharge limits.

The above factors, combined together, will significantly promote the economy of the country through higher productivity. The overall result is a significant progress towards the target set for textile exports and better livelihood for the people.

Printing

Printing is a complex process and involves proper selection of thickening paste and its method of preparation, selection of dyes, its fixation, after treatment and drying (Adivarekar and Kanoongo 2008). The choice of thickener is as important as that of selection of method and style of printing and depends on colour, brilliance of shade, penetration, levelness of print, ease of preparation of stock thickening etc.

From ecology point of view, pentachlorophenol that is used as preservative for thickener is being objected to and substitutes like sodium silico fluoride though expensive is recommended. Some of the companies have also come out with natural preservatives. The substitution of sodium silicate and sodium alginate in reactive printing, kerosene–water emulsion with synthetic thickener in pigment printing are the challenges still to be fully met with in the field of printing. Transfer printing received the limited response earlier. However, this technology is very much in vogue as far as garment printing is concerned.

Thermotropic colours (temperature sensitive), solvatochroic colours (moisture sensitive) and the pressure sensitive colours will also have increased demand for creating fancy designs and will receive more impetus from fashion industry.

Though printing machine manufacturing technology particularly rotary printing is at its peak for rapid bulk production, human tendency for exclusivity will lead developments in machine manufacturing suitable for smaller batch sizes and such flexibility is possible with inkjet printing which is getting popular. The development in suitable inks at affordable price is indeed needed by the industry.

Finishing

Nowadays, multifunctional finishes are becoming increasingly important for high-value fabrics. Some of the finishes which are increasingly being used include:

- Wrinkle free/Durable press/Easy care finish.
- Stone wash or enzyme wash/Biofinishing.
- Softeners giving better resiliency bouncy effect and sometimes hydrophilicity.
- Water proof/stain repellent but breathable finishes.
- Antimicrobial/Deodorant finishes.
- Flame retardant finishes.
- Perfumed Textiles.
- Super absorbent polymer finish.
- Mosquito Repellent Finish.

Wet processing of textiles constitutes innumerable steps leading to finished product, each having a number of complex variables and every lot is like a new lot and much depends on the well-trained manpower rather than modern machines and technology. However, developments are taking place at a rapid pace to satisfy the customer with quality product and competitive price. Though underlying principle for developments is satisfying customer needs, much emphasis is being paid for conserving water and energy and simultaneously being environment friendly. This in turn will impart cost competitiveness. Developments need to focus on minimising water pollution and air pollution and possibly through on use of biodegradable chemicals preferably from renewable sources. More and more emphasis of developments is on conservation of energy, heat and electricity by following shorter processes or modified processes, eg, continuous pretreatment and dyeing of cotton knits and terry towels, instead of batch operations, pigment printing instead of reactive printing etc. More and more functional finishes are also being developed. However, trend is to use more mechanical finishes than chemical finishes. All said and done the key to success in textile wet processing technology will be the indication of highly trained manpower at lucrative wages in structured manner.

Annexure II

Questionnaire for Textile Exporters

Company name ____
Address____
____
Contact person____
Designation____
Contact phone no_______________________________________
Contact E-mail____

(Tick the relevant boxes, wherever applicable)

SECTION A- GENERAL INFORMATION

1-Year of establishment__________

2-Please indicate the ownership status of your factory

Proprietorship	Partnership	Private Ltd	Joint venture	others

i) If others, please specify____
____
____

3. Source of raw materials?
Have your own spinning and weaving establishment __________________________
Have regular suppliers______________________________

4-Specify if you have feeder units other than own manufacturing_________________
____
____
____

5-What kind of garments are manufactured by your company? __________________
____
____

5 a. How many employees are there ? a) Manufacturing__________
(b)Administrative____________ c) Trade __________ d) others______________

6- Is your company /you member of any Industry Association (specify)
____

7-Is your company certified under (ISO 9001; ISO 14001; ECO MARK)? YES/NO
If yes,

Certification	Year

K.S.K. Kumar (ed.), *A Study of India's Textile Exports and Environmental Regulations*, https://doi.org/10.1007/978-981-10-6295-7

8. Who certifies - Local or foreign certification agencies. Is local certification accepted?

____

____

9- Is there market(s) where you don't export for lack of adequate certification bodies? Which market____

____

Details regarding the problem ______________________________

____

SECTION B- Importing country or buyers Requirements regarding product standard

1- Please specify the restricted substance of the countries and testing details

S.NO.	Restricted substance	Countries requiring substance	Testing		
			Place	Cost percent	No of test in a year
1.	Cadmium (Cd)				
2.	Lead (Pb)				
3.	Chromium (Cr+6) - hexavalent				
4.	Chromium				
5.	**Chemical Name/Color Index Name**				
6.	Mercury				
7.	Arsenic				
8.	Copper				
9.	**AZO Dyes**				
10.	Others specify				

2- Are you aware of all the requirements that your product(s) must comply on the foreign markets where you export?

3-Do your buyers insist laboratories where product should be tested? YES NO

4-If yes mention the name of laboratories______________________________

____

____

____

5-In case buyers insist conducting the test abroad, who bears the cost?

a) Are the costs affordable? YES NO

---

b) Is there market(s) where you don't export for lack of financial resources to cover the costs? YES NO

6- Do you have adequate laboratories of specified nature available in your locality for testing samples? YES/NO

7-If not, do you need to increase such facility? Please specify____________________

____

____

SECTION C- Complying with Domestic Environmental Regulation

1-Specify the treatment plant you depend on:

IETP		CETP	
Year of establishment		Year of establishment	
Investment Cost		Initial deposit	
Operating cost		Monthly / yearly payment	
Capacity		Capacity	

SECTION D- Importing country's or buyers Requirements Regarding Domestic Regulation

1-Does any importing country/buyer specify that your company should conform to national environmental regulation with regard to (tick whichever is applicable)

S.no	Countries	Buyers	Liquid waste disposal	Solid waste disposal	Gaseous Emissions Abatement	Occupational Safety and health
1	USA					
2	European countries					
3	UK					
4	Japan					
5	Australia					
6	Hong Kong					
7	South Africa					
8	others					

2-Is there market(s) where you don't export for lack of information regarding the Requirements or did you have any problem regarding requirements because of lack of information? YES NO

3-- If the answer is "Yes", could you briefly explain what kind of problem did you have?

____
____
____
____
____
____

SECTION E-Competition

1-Does compliance to new regulation provide better quality product? YES/NO
2- Does adherence to regulation (domestic & external) affect the price of final product?
YES/NO
If yes, what is the percentage increase___________________________________
3-Do buyers mind paying higher price for environment friendly product? YES/NO
4- Does adherence to regulations adversely affect the competitiveness? YES/NO

5-If yes, specific Instances
____
____

SECTION F- Industry's suggestions for Improving Competitiveness

1- what kind of measures you expect of the government to help you become export-compliant in all respects?

1	Setting up more laboratories for testing	
2	Assisting you by forewarning about changes	
3	Contesting changes that are not scientifically tenable	
4	Making available cost –effective technology/processes	
5	Keep the cost of imported inputs for meeting environmental requirement low by keeping the import duty nil or very low	
6	Publicizing those conforming to requirements in global markets	
7	Enhancing awareness of the industry about the changes and avenues available for meeting such changes	

2- Any other suggestions____
____
____
____
____
____
____
____

SECTION G- Production and Export

1-Are you frequent or regular exporter? YES/NO

2-What percentage of your production do you export?

3-For how many years has your company been involved in exporting?

Value (Rs. Crore)	2006-07	2007-08
	Production	Export
< 5		
5-10		
10-15		
15-20		
20-25		
25-50		
Above 50		

4-Export Destinations:

Product	Country	Percentage

SECTION H-Administrative and Transaction cost

1-What is the export formalities involved for the Textile products?
(Documentation and clearance from various governmental agencies)

____

2- In all, how many forms, clearance are required before the consignment is ready for export?____

3-Transportation cost is borne by you (or) importers? How much is the cost per unit

____

4- Which agency is doing final checking of your product before exporting it?____

5- Testing and certification charges (please specify)______________________

____

7-Occupational health and safety audit charges if any____________________

____

8-Costs of others audits.(please specify)____

____

Please comment on any aspect not covered by this questionnaire and provide additional information that you consider useful to ascertain the effects of the safeguard measures on imports originating in the country concerned on your business.

References

Agarwal, K.K. 2003. Problems and Prospects of Using Natural Dyes in an Industrial Enterprise. *Colourage* 50 (6): 37–40.

Aravind, U.K., B. George, M.S. Baburaj, S. Thomas, A.P. Thomas, and C.T. Aravindakumar. 2010. Treatment of Industrial Effluents using Polyelectrolyte Membranes. *Desalination* 252 (1): 27–32. doi:10.1016/j.desal.2009.11.006.

Bahl, Deepti, and K.C. Gupta. 1988. Development of Dyeing Process of Silk with Natural Dye-cutch. *Colourage* 35 (22): 22–24.

Bakshi, D.K., K.G. Gupta, and P. Sharma. 1999. Enhanced Biodecolorization of Synthetic Textile Dye Effluent by Phanerochaete Chrysosporium under Improved Culture Conditions. *World Journal of Microbiology and Biotechnology* 15: 507–509.

Balassa, Bela. 1965. Trade Liberalization and "Revealed" Comparative Advantage. *Manchester School of Economic and Social Studies* 33: 99–123.

Balasubramanian, J., P.C. Sabumon, J.U. Lazar, and R. Ilangovan. 2006. Reuse of Textile Effluent Treatment Plant Sludge in Building Material. *Waste Management* 26: 22–28.

Balasubramanyam, V.N., and Yingqi Wei. 2005. Textile and Clothing Exports from India and China: A Comparative Analysis. *Journal of Chinese Economic and Business Studies* 3 (1): 23–37.

Baldwin, R. 1970. *Non-Tariff Distortions in International Trade*. Washington, D.C.: Brookings Institutions.

Bechtold, T., A. Turcanu, E. Ganglberger, and S. Geissler. 2003. Natural Dyes in Modern Textile Dyehouses—How to Combine Experiences of Two Centuries to Meet the Demands of the Future? *Journal of Cleaner Production* 11: 499–509.

Bedi, Jatinder S., R. Verma, S. Kumar, Rajkumar, P. Biswas, M. Kapoor, and R. Gupta. 2009. *Assessing the Prospects for India's Textile and Clothing Sector*, National Council for Applied Economic Research, New Delhi, July.

Boumellassa, Houssein, Laborde, David, and Mitaritonna, Cristina. 2009. A picture of tariff protection across the World in 2004: MAcMap-HS6. *Version 2. IFPRI Discussion Paper 903*. International Food Policy Research Institute (IFPRI), Washington, D.C. Available online at http://www.ifpri.org/sites/default/files/publications/ifpridp00903.pdf.

Cattaneo, O., G. Gereffi, and C. Staritz. 2010. *Global Value Chains in a Post-crisis World: A Development Perspective*. Washington, D.C.: World Bank.

Central Pollution Control Board. 2009a. *Guidelines for Development of Location Specific Stringent Standards*, Programme Objective Series PROBES/127/2008-09, Ministry of Environment and Forests, New Delhi, February.

Central Pollution Control Board. 2009b. *Comprehensive Environmental Assessment of Industrial Clusters*, Ecological Impact Assessment Series EIAS/5/2009-2010, Ministry of Environment and Forests, New Delhi, December.

K.S.K. Kumar (ed.), *A Study of India's Textile Exports and Environmental Regulations*, https://doi.org/10.1007/978-981-10-6295-7

Central Pollution Control Board. 2009c. *Criteria for Comprehensive Environmental Assessment of Industrial Clusters*, Ecological Impact Assessment Series EIAS/4/2009-2010, Ministry of Environment and Forests, New Delhi, December.

Chakraborty, P. 2011. Environmental Standards and Trade: Evidence from Indian Textile and Leather Industry. Working Paper No. 374, FREIT. www.freit.org/WorkingPapers/Papers/FirmLevelTrade/FREIT374.pdf.

Chandra, P. 2007. The textile and apparel industry in Indian. In *The Oxford Companion to Economics in India*, ed. Kaushik Basu, 525–529. Oxford: Oxford University Press.

Corso, C.R., and A.C.M. de Almeida. 2009. Bioremediation of Dyes in Textile Effluents by *Aspergillus oryzae*. *Microbial Ecology* 57: 384–390.

Dalum, B., K. Laursen, and G. Villumsen. 1998. Structural Change in OECD Exports Specialization Patterns: De-Specialization and Stickiness. *International Review of Applied Economics* 12: 447–467.

Das, B.L. 2004. *The WTO and the Multilateral Trading System: Past, Present and Future*. London: Zed Books.

Dawkar, Vishal V., Umesh U. Jadhav, Gajanan S. Ghodake, and Sanjay P. Govindwar. 2009. Effect of Inducers on the Decolorization and Biodegradation of Textile Azo Dye Navy Blue 2GL by *Bacillus* sp. VUS. *Biodegradation* 20: 777–787.

Dias, A.A., A. Sampaio, and R.M. Bezerra. 2007. Environmental Applications of Fungal and Plant Systems: Decolourisation of Textile Wastewater and Related Dyestuffs. In *Environmental Bioremediation Technologies*, ed. S.N. Singh and R.D. Tripathi, 445–463.

Dias, Albino A., Sampaio, Ana and Bezerra, Rui M. 2007. Environmental Applications of Fungal and Plant Systems: Decolourisation of Textile Wastewater and Related Dyestuffs. In *Environmental Bioremediation Technologies*, ed. S.N. Singh and R.D. Tripathi, 445–463.

Duff, David G., Roy S. Sinclair, and David Stirling. 1977. The Fastness to Washing of Some Natural Dyestuffs on Wool. *Studies in Conservation* 22 (4): 170–176.

Duff, David G., S. Roy, and David Stirling. 1977. Light-induced Color Changes of Natural Dyes. *Studies in Conservation* 22 (4): 161–169.

Flood, Frank L. 1937. Sewage Treatment Plant at North Adams. *Sewage Works Journal*, 9 (4): 590–598 (July).

Furry, Margaret S. 1945. Some Natural Dyes Give Long Life to Cotton Fabric. *Rayon Textile Monthly* 26: 603–605.

Gaffney, Peter E. 1976a. Carpet and Rug Industry Case Study I: Water and Wastewater Treatment Plant Operation. *Journal* (*Water Pollution Control Federation*) 48 (11): 2590–2598 (November).

Gaffney, Peter E. 1976b. Carpet and Rug Industry Case Study II: Biological Effects. *Journal (Water Pollution Control Federation)*, 48(12): 2731–2737 (December).

Glover, Brian. 1995. Are Natural Colorants Good for Your Health? Are Synthetic Ones Better? *Textile Chemist and Colorist* 27 (4): 17–20.

Government of India. 2008. *Economic Survey,* Ministry of Finance, Government of India.

Green Textiles and Apparel. 2008. *Environmental Impact and Strategies for Improvement*, Textiles Intelligence, February.

Gstohl, S., and R. Kaiser. 2004. Mechanisms of Global Trade Governance: The 'Double Standard' on Standards in WTO. In *New Rules for Global Markets*, ed. A.A. Schirm. New York: Palgrave-MacMillan Publishers.

Gulati, A.N. 1949. Natural Indian Dyes and the Art of their Application. *Indian Textile Journal* 60: 223–229.

Hertel, T.W. 1997. *Global Trade Analysis, Modeling and Applications*. Cambridge: Cambridge University Press.

Hessel, C., C. Allegre, M. Maisseu, F. Charbit, and P. Moulin. 2007. Guidelines and Legislation for Dye House Effluents. *Journal of Environmental Management* 83: 41–50.

Hongve, D., and G. Akesson. 1996. Spectrophotometric Determination of Water Color in Hazen Units. *Water Resource* 30: 2771–2775.

ICICI. 1996. *Beyond MFA: Strategies for the Indian Apparel Industry*. Mumbai: Industrial Credit and Investment Corporation of India.

International Trade Center. 2006. User Guide—Market Access Map: Making Tariffs and Market Access Barriers Transparent. Market Analysis Section, Division of Product and Market Development, International Trade Center, Geneva, December. Available online at http://www.macmap.org/User%20Guides/MAcMap-userguide-EN.pdf.

Kahlenborn, Walter, Sawhney, Puja, and Zwagerman, Nanne. 2009. *Internationalising BAT Promotion of Best Available Techniques (BAT) in the Textile and Leather Industry in Developing Countries and Emerging Market Economies*. Environmental Research of the Federal Ministry of the Environment, Nature Conservation and Nuclear Safety Research Report No. (UBA-FB) 001315/E. Federal Environment Agency, Germany.

Kathuria, V. 2007. Managing Pollution from SSIs—Designing for a Sustainable Institution. *Environment, Development and Sustainability* 9 (2): 107–130.

Kaushik, P., and V.K. Garg. 2003. Vermicomposting of Mixed Solid Textile Mill Sludge and Cow Dung with the Epigeic Earthworm Eisenia Fetida. *Bioresources Technology* 90: 311–316.

Kaushik, P., and V.K. Garg. 2004. Dynamics of Biological and Chemical Parameters during Vermicomposting of Solid Textile Mill Sludge Mixed with Cow Dung and Agricultural Residues. *Bioresources Technology* 94: 203–209.

Kharbade, B.V., and O.P. Agrawal. 1988. Analysis of Natural Dyes in Indian Historic Textiles. *Studies in Conservation* 33 (1): 1–8.

Khemakhem, W., E. Ammar, and A. Bakhrouf. 2005. Effect of Environmental Conditions on Hydrophobicity of Marine Bacteria Adapted to Textile Effluent Treatment. *World Journal of Microbiology and Biotechnology* 21: 1623–1631.

Kirtikar, D.B. 1947. Indigenous Indian Dyes. *Indian Textile Journal* 58: 159–160.

Koprulu, A., and Albayrakoglu, M. 2007. *Supply Chain Management in the Textile Industry: A Supplier Selection Model with the Analytical Hierarchical Process*. http://www.isahp.org/2007Proceedings/Papers/Working%20Sessions/Suppliers%20Selection/Supply%20Chain%20Management%20In%20The%20Textile%20Industry.pdf.

Krishnaswamy, R., S. Kaliannan, T. Kannadasan, and P.K. Duraisamy. 2009. Study on Treatment and Re-use of Wash Water Effluent From Textile Processing by Membrane Techniques. *Modern Applied Science* 3 (10): 2–8.

Laursen, Keld. 1998. Revealed Comparative Advantage and the Alternatives as Measures of International Specialization. *Druid Working Paper No. 98-30,* Danish Research Unit for Industrial Dynamics, Aalborg University.

Malik, P.K., and S. Datta. 2005. Financial Sustainability of Environmental Investment Under an Empirical Pollution Abatement Policy Instrument in India: The Case of Wastewater Treatment. *Environmental Science and Policy* 8 (1): 67–74.

Moosvi, S., H. Keharia, and M. Datta. 2005. Decolourization of Textile Dye Reactive Violet 5 by a Newly Isolated Bacterial Consortium RVM 11.1. *World Journal of Microbiology and Biotechnology* 21: 667–672.

Narayanan, G. Badri, and Terrie L. Walmsley (eds.). 2008. *Global Trade, Assistance, and Production: The GTAP 7 Data Base*, Center for Global Trade Analysis, Purdue University. Available online at: http://www.gtap.agecon.purdue.edu/databases/v7/v7_doco.asp.

Narayanan, G. Badri. 2007. Pollution Control by the Natural Dyes. In *Economic Studies of Indigenous Traditional* ed. Nirmal Sengupta, 251–282. Knowledge Academic Foundation in association with Indian Economic Association Trust for Research Development, New Delhi.

Narayanaswamy, V., and J.A. Scott. 2001. Lessons from Cleaner Production Experiences in Indian Hosiery Clusters. *Journal of Cleaner Production* 9 (4): 325–340.

National Environmental Policy. 2006. National Environmental Policy—2006. MoEF, GoI, New Delhi. Available at https://envfor.nic.in/nep/nep2006e.pdf.

NCAER. 2009. *Assessing the Prospects for India's Textile and Clothing Sector*. New Delhi: National Council for Applied Economic Research.

Neelavannan, M.G., M. Revathi, and C. Ahmed Basha. 2007. Photocatalytic and Electrochemical Combined Treatment of Textile Wash Water. *Journal of Hazardous Materials* 149 (2): 371–378.

Nieminen, E., M. Linke, M. Tobler, and B. V. Beke. 2007. EU COST Action 628: Life Cycle Assessment (LCA) of Textile Products, Eco-efficiency and Definition of Best Available Technology (BAT) of Textile Processing. *Journal of Cleaner Production*, 15 (13–14): 1259–1270.

Nimon, Wesley, and John Beghin. 1999. Ecolabels and International Trade in the Textile and Apparel Market. *American Journal of Agricultural Economics* 81 (5): 1078–1083.

Organisation for Economic Cooperation and Development. 2008. *Agricultural Policies in OECD Countries, Monitoring and Evaluation*. Paris, France: OECD.

Organisation for Economic Cooperation and Development and International Energy Agency. 2003. *IEA Online Database Services*. Paris, France: OECD/IEA.

Parham, Rita J. 1994. Elimination of Production and Environmental Problems in Cellulose Dyeing: Neutral Dyeing Reactives, Bifunctional Reactives, and Natural Dyes. In *Book of Papers - International Conference & Exhibition, AATCC*, 398–403.

Parikh, Jyoti, V. K. Sharma, Ghosh, Upal and Manoj Panda. 1995. *Trade and Environment Linkages: A Case Study of India*, UNCTAD, April.

Pasurka, C. 1984. The Short-Run Impact of Environmental Protection Costs on U.S. Product Prices. *Journal of Environmental Economics and Management* 11: 380–390.

Patel, H., and S. Pandey. 2008. Physico-chemical Characterisation of Textile Chemical Sludge Generated from various CETPs in India. *Journal of Environmental Resources and Development* 2: 329–339.

Patra, A.K., Aditi Sareen, and Deepti Vohra. 2002. Performance Studies of Some Natural Dyes on Cotton. *Man-Made Textiles in India* 45 (8): 319–323.

Priyadarshini, K., and O.K. Gupta. 2003. Compliance to Environmental Regulations: The Indian Context. *International Journal of Business and Economics* 2 (1): 9–26.

Rodrik, D. 1997. *Has Globalisation Gone Too Far?* Institute for International Economics, Washington, D.C.

Rubeena, Sheikh, R.C. Sharma, and G.P. Pandey. 2002. Biochemical Analysis of Natural Dyes: An Empirical Study. *Research Journal of Chemistry and Environment* 6 (4): 67–72.

Saini, G.K. 2009a. Non-Tariff Measures and Indian Textiles and Clothing Exports. Working Paper No. WP-2009-002, Indira Gandhi Institute of Development Research, Mumbai.

Saini, G.K. 2009b. Non-Tariff Measures Affecting India's Textiles and Clothing Exports: Findings from the Survey of Exporters. Working Paper No. WP-2009-008, Indira Gandhi Institute of Development Research, Mumbai.

Sargaonkar, A., and V. Deshpande. 2003. Development of an Overall Index of Pollution for Surfacewater Based on a General Classification Scheme in Indian Context. *Environmental Monitoring and Assessment* 89: 43–67.

Schönberger, Harald and Schäfer, Thomas. 2003. *Best Available Techniques in Textile Industry.* Environmental Research of the Federal Ministry of the Environment, Nature Conservation and Nuclear Safety Research Report UBA-FB 000325/e. Federal Environmental Agency, Germany.

Schwitzguébel, J.P., S. Aubert, W. Grosse, and F. Laturnus. 2002. Sulphonated Aromatic Pollutants—Limits of Microbial Degradability and Potential of Phytoremediation. *Environmental Science and Pollution Research* 9: 62–72.

Senthilkumar, M., and M. Muthukumar. 2007. Studies on the Possibility of Recycling Reactive Dye Bath Effluent After Decolouration Using Ozone. *Dyes and Pigments* 72 (2): 251–255.

Shane, M. 2009. *Real Historical Gross Domestic Product and Growth Rates 1969-2009*.United States Department of Agriculture, Washington, D.C. Available online at www.ers.usda.gov/data/macroeconomics.

Srinivasan, T.N. 1996. International Trade and Labour Standards from an Economic Perspective. In *Challenges to the New World Trade Organisation*, ed. Pitou van Dijck, and Gerrit Faber, 219–243. Klewer Law International: The Netherlands.

Sun, Q.Y., Y.Z. Hong, Y.Z. Xiao, W. Fang, and J. Fang. 2009. Decolorization of Textile Reactive Dyes by the Crude Laccase Produced from Solid-state Fermentation of Agro-byproducts. *World Journal of Microbiology and Biotechnology* 25: 1153–1160.

Susarla, S., V.F. Medina, and S.C. McCutcheon. 2002. Phytoremediation: An Ecological Solution to Organic Chemical Contamination. *Ecological Engineering* 18: 647–658.

Teli, M.D., Roshan Paul, and P.D. Pardeshi. 2000. Natural Dyes: Classification, Chemistry and Extraction Methods Part-I: Chemical Classes, Extraction Methods and Future Prospects. *Colourage* 47 (12): 43–48.

Tewari, M. 2008. Deepening Intraregional Trade and Investment in South Asia the Case of the Textiles and Clothing Industry. Working Paper No. 213, ICRIER, New Delhi.

Uchikawa, Shuji. 1999. Economic Reforms and Foreign Trade Policies: Case Study of Apparel and Machine Tools Industries. *Economic and Political Weekly* 34 (48): M138–M148.

Uimonen, P., and J. Whalley. 1997. *Environmental Issues in the New World Trading System*. London: Macmillan Publishers.

United Nations. 1997. *Trade Effects of Eco-Labelling*. New York: United Nations Organization.

United Nations Statistics Division. 2004. *UN COMTRADE. International Merchandise Trade Statistics*, United Nations Statistics Division, New York, USA. Available online at http://comtrade.un.org/.

Vankar, P.S., R. Shanker, S. Dixit, D. Mahanta, and S.C. Tiwari. 2009. Chemical Characterisation of Extract Derived from *Daphne Papyraceae* and Sonicator Dyeing of Cotton, Silk and Wool with the Extract. *Pigment and Resin Technology* 38 (3): 181–187.

Verma, P., and D. Madamwar. 2002. Decolorization of Synthetic Textile Dyes by Lignin Peroxidase of *Phanerochaete chrysosporium*. *Folia Microbiologica* 47 (3): 283–280.

Verma, Samar. 2002. Export Competitiveness of Indian Textile and Garment Industry. *Working Paper No. 94,* Indian Council for Research on International Economic Relations, New Delhi, November.

Winthrop, C.A., P.B. Hook, J.A. Biederman, and O.R. Stein. 2002. Temperature and Wetland Plant Species Effects on Wastewater Treatment and Root Zone Oxidation. *Journal of Environmental Quality* 31: 1010–1016.

World Bank. 1999. *India Cotton and Textile Industries Reforming to Compete,* Volume II, Report No. 18857-IN, World Bank, Washington, D.C.

WTO. 2011. *Trade Policy Review India, Document WT/TPR/S/249*. Geneva: World Trade Organisation.

Xu, Meiying, J. Guo, and G. Sun. 2007. Biodegradation of Textile Azo Dye by Shewanella Decolorationis S12 under Microaerophilic Conditions. *Applied Microbiology and Biotechnology* 76 (3): 719–726.

MIX
Papier aus verantwortungsvollen Quellen
Paper from responsible sources
FSC® C105338

If you have any concerns about our products,
you can contact us on
ProductSafety@springernature.com

In case Publisher is established outside the EU,
the EU authorized representative is:
Springer Nature Customer Service Center GmbH
Europaplatz 3, 69115 Heidelberg, Germany

Printed by Libri Plureos GmbH
in Hamburg, Germany